AMAZING
BOAT
Journeys

60 unforgettable trips over water and how to experience them

AN ABRA JOURNEY IN
DUBAI: p30

THE SUN SETS ON A TURKISH GULET: p222

Contents

NIAGARA FALLS: p62

ON THE BANGKOK CHAO PHRAYA RIVER: p158

DUBROVNIK ON THE DALMATIAN COAST: p176

Foreword

● JESSICA WATSON

Travel becomes an adventure aboard a boat, just as the business of getting from A to B becomes something far more when you venture out on to a lake, sea, ocean or river. Stepping onto a ship, whatever its size, means letting go of certainties, precise timetables and the status quo, and embracing a little bit of uncertainty.

Being on the water means that you are at the mercy of mother nature, and if you step aboard a boat I'd encourage you to surrender to this. Deciding where you want to go and exactly what sort of day you want to have are no longer decisions you alone can make. You'll have to work with the conditions and let the weather offer up the unexpected.

In fact, it's sometimes adverse weather conditions that provide the most memorable moments. For example, a total lack of wind – a situation very frustrating to a sailor who can go nowhere without it – provided me with perhaps the most beautiful experience I've had on the water. On this particular night, in the middle of the southern Indian Ocean, the ocean became so still that the stars reflected perfectly in it. I couldn't tell where the sky stopped and the water began – there were stars in every direction.

Travelling by water is also an excellent way to slow down and disconnect from the fast-paced world. It gives you an appreciation for the simple things, the big open sky, empty horizons, sunrises and sunsets. There's nothing like a sea breeze to give you a healthy appetite and heightened appreciation for your food.

Another of these simple things is the water itself. During the 210 days I spent alone at sea during my 2010 sail around the world, I gained a special appreciation for the beauty of the ocean. I never bored of watching the waves, sometimes for hours on end, noticing the unique detail and shape of each; the way they form and reform, and hurry along on windy days with tumbling white tops and spray flying high into the air.

Take a moment to stop and watch, and you'll see that the water below, whether it be a river, lake or the ocean, is a moving mosaic, speaking to you about the weather that shapes it. Watching it is mesmerising and incredibly calming.

Perhaps it's also this simplicity of life on board, and the deprivation of the things we take for granted on land, that gives a renewed sense of wonder for your destination when you reach it. On returning to land after having not seen it for many months, I was overwhelmed by the smells of earth and vegetation, the vivid colours and, of course, a hot shower. Life's little luxuries are cherished again. Even a shorter time on board can provide a reset and a new perspective, and the constant motion of life on the water can be a surprising comfort. I love nothing more than being rocked to sleep by the gentle movement of a boat. Whether you take one of the journeys in this book or set out on your own, fair winds!

VOLGA VALLEY: p190

COLOURS OF THE CARIBBEAN: p82

ANTARCTICA BECKONS: p288

About this Book

NORA RAWN SENIOR EDITOR, LONELY PLANET

Whether salt breezes or river safaris are more your speed, Lonely Planet writers have turned over every hull to collect these inspiring journeys by water. There's something about stepping onto a boat that immediately gives a feeling of adventure, of stepping outside the common routine. It's why writer Jack London set off on a cruise across the Pacific ocean in *The Cruise of the Snark*, and for centuries before his lark, ships took humanity across the oceans in every imaginable direction, from the seafaring Polynesians to the Chinese Age of Discovery. Travel by water shaped the world as we know it.

That same spirit of exploration compelled Lonely Planet writers to travel by cargo freighter and fishing vessel to the world's most remote islands; to hop onto mailboats in the Bahamas; and to experience life on a historic sail-powered windjammer. It's not just the charm of the craft, either: a water journey is a chance to ply rivers long used as centres of transport, hubs of world culture and biodiversity such as the Volga and the Amazon. It's also the best way to visit some of the world's most intoxicating places from the Greek Islands to the teeming Galapagos.

The vessels in this book date from every period of history: traditional dugout canoes called *mokoro* in Botswana's Unesco World Heritage Okavango Delta; *felucca* in Egypt, with their elegant lateen-rigged sails; classic *gulet* yachts in Turkey; and nostalgia-inducing narrowboats in the UK and France, relics of a time when most transportation happened by canal. As much as cruise ships and ferries now come with the latest and greatest conveniences, travel on board a ship is a chance to travel back in time and experience the pace of life as it used to be. These are journeys that will take you from roughing it without an onboard bathroom and sleeping on deck under the stars with fellow passengers to journeying around the world in a suite attended by its own butler.

Options are eclectic and wide-ranging, from the nostalgia of a glass-bottomed boat ride through Florida springs to the ease of a thatch-roofed *kettuvallam* exploring Kerala's famed backwaters. Old-fashioned paddlesteamers ply the length of the Mississippi in the style of the 1800s, cruise ships on the Yangtze feature enthusiastic karaoke in Mandarin, and you can string up a hammock on the slow boat down the Amazon. Interested in a more traditional cruise but want to explore off-the-beaten path? Try a trip to Antarctica or Papua New Guinea. Want to live like a local? Stretch out on the seats of the Hurtigruten ferry along Norway's fjord-strewn coast, or share space with indigenous Fuegians on the ferry through Patagonia.

On the opposite end of the spectrum from a weeks-long journey over open seas is the charm of seeing a city from the water. From crossing Victoria Harbour via Hong Kong's classic Star Ferry, viewing the banks of London from the Thames, or traversing Bangkok on the Chao Phraya River, every trip can benefit from getting on the water. Lonely Planet writers celebrate their 60 favourites in this collection, and we hope you find inspiration follows in their wake.

CLOCKWISE FROM TOP: © LUXERENDERING / SHUTTERSTOCK; © PETER SITTERLI / 500PX; ©PETE SEAWARD / LONELY PLANET

KEY TO ICONS

 Cruise Ship

 Sail Boat

 Local Boat

 Ferry Boat

 Walk or hike

 View

 Aquatic adventure

 Detour

 Activity

 Food and drink

 Budget: ticket <US$50

 Mid-range: ticket US$50–$750

 Top end: ticket >US$750

AFRICA &
THE MIDDLE EAST

AMAZING BOAT JOURNEYS

Chobe River Safari

START **KASANE, BOTSWANA**		⊕
END **SAME**		
DISTANCE **31 MILES (50KM)**	DURATION	**3 HOURS**

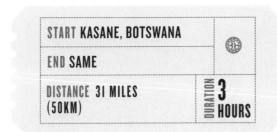 *The Chobe River blows everything else out of the water with what is, arguably, one of the greatest wildlife spectacles on earth. Flowing through the northern reaches of Chobe National Park and demarcating the watery frontier between Botswana and Namibia, this quietly majestic river bordered by lush floodplains is renowned for its elephants, backed by a supporting cast of practically every other animal in the African food chain. Watching them congregate by the riverside as you float* smoothly past, avoiding the bumps and bruises of the uncomfortable road, is beyond extraordinary.

❶ RIDING THE WAVES

The Chobe River arises in Angola before flowing east through the Caprivi Strip to join the mighty Zambezi River at 'Four Corners', the point where the countries of Botswana, Namibia, Zambia and Zimbabwe meet.

Kasane is the centre of operations for boat cruises, a small Botswanan town with an edge-of-the-bush flavour that abuts the Chobe 5 miles (8km) west of its confluence with the Zambezi. Numerous safari companies and lodges line Kasane's well-ordered waterfront, and all offer a litany of river cruises from deluxe to discount. Luckily for budget travellers, big bucks don't necessarily mean bigger fauna sightings.

Shunting quietly west out of Kasane, the Chobe appears wide and serene as you leave town, the latent dangers of hippos and crocodiles momentarily

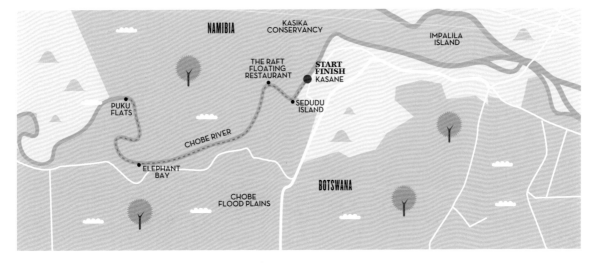

forgotten. Expensive safari lodges sit directly on the river's south bank, their gabled, thatched roofs poking temptingly through the trees. Many lodges have their own docks, little wooden jetties where private watercraft await expectant guests.

As you motor slowly upriver, the excitement mounts. Animal-spotting charts are passed around on deck, salutations are exchanged with other boats, and cameras with tripods and long zoom lenses are adjusted and polished. In the wildlife stakes, the Chobe River doesn't take long to deliver. A couple of miles out of Kasane and you're in a different world – a savage natural food chain patrolled by lions and leopards but dominated physically by the largest and most majestic land mammals on the planet: African elephants.

Depending on the time of year, you may or may not notice reedy Sedudu Island as you head west. In the dry season, water buffalo, elephants and red lechwe cross the river to feed on Sedudu's soft green grass, but at the height of the rainy season, the island is practically submerged. The flooding doesn't deter hippos that sit, eyes and noses poking above the water like periscopes, in huddled pods. Anchored on the north side of Sedudu Island, close to the Namibian shore, is The Raft Floating Restaurant – a magnet for safari groups – where it's possible to enjoy a barbecued lunch buffet without taking your eyes off the unfolding wildlife show.

Estimates of Chobe's elephant population vary wildly. Most counts agree there are more than 50,000; some claim the park hosts as many as five elephants per square kilometre (about 250 acres). Whatever the true figure, Elephant Bay is an iconic place to watch them, a sandy slope on the riverbank where great herds come down to the water to drink, play and swim. The size of these magnificent beasts is astounding in close-up (and the boats can get very

SEDUDU ISLAND

Sedudu Island was the subject of a fractious border dispute between Namibia and Botswana in the 1990s, with the matter finally being resolved by the International Court of Justice, which ceded the island to Botswana in 1999. In the spirit of international cooperation, wildlife-watching boats from both countries are still allowed to cruise freely on both sides of the island.

close), as they move with surprising grace through the bush or – even better – take to the water to swim.

They're not the only distraction. Crocodiles are common in these waters, and playful baboons often patrol the shoreline. Then there are the giraffes, zebras, water buffaloes and wildebeests that emerge from the denuded riparian forest to feed on the river's verdant shoreline. Predators like lions, leopards and cheetahs are harder to spot but can occasionally be seen licking their chops at sunset. As the boat meanders around the grassy Puku Flats, it's possible to see pukus, a rare type of African antelope distinguished by its notched, inward-curving horns and its small, stocky build.

The return trip to Kasane offers a chance to focus on the Chobe's less obvious, but no less spectacular, avian population. The birdlife along the riverfront is extraordinarily varied, with over 450 species listed. The loudest contributors are the screaming fish eagles,

 Spy luxury riverside lodges through the trees as you head west out of Kasane.

 Sail carefully around a pod of hippos near the shores of Sedudu Island.

 Watch herds of elephants bathing, drinking, playing and swimming at Elephant Bay.

whose distinctive call as they dive for fish evokes the powerful spirit of sub-Saharan Africa. It's a sound that will ring in your ears long after your boat has reclaimed its berth in Kasane.

❷ LIFE ON BOARD

For day trips, watercraft are relatively simple, with hard seats and canvas roofing to provide shade. Small boats carry roughly 10 passengers; larger vessels with upper and lower decks can transport up to 40. More expensive boats have bars serving drinks.

❸ LUXURY ALTERNATIVE

Several luxury houseboats ply the Chobe River. The *Zambezi Queen* is equipped with 14 upscale suites with air-conditioning, big windows and private balconies, meaning you can effectively wildlife-watch from your bed. It offers two- or three-night river excursions. See https://zqcollection.com for details.

❹ MAKE IT HAPPEN

Boats depart from the small town of Kasane in Botswana or from various private lodges that line the river nearby. There are multiple morning and afternoon departures, plus options for day trips or even two- to three-day voyages. Most operators allow you to book in advance via their websites. Be sure to book early in the dry season, as demand is high. If you're staying in a riverside lodge, ask about cruises when making your reservation. For the best wildlife viewing, go in the dry season. **BS**

FROM TOP: Zebra crossing; on the Chobe River; a male lion in Chobe National Park. **PREVIOUS PAGE:** An elusive leopard in repose.

 Keep your eyes peeled for rare puku antelopes on the grassy Puku Flats.

 Look out for lions on the banks, or their prey, wildebeest.

 Once you've returned from your day's river safari, ponder going back out for a sunset cruise.

Felucca Nile Journey

EGYPT

START **ASWAN**	
END **EDFU**	
DISTANCE **74 MILES (119KM)**	DURATION **3 DAYS**

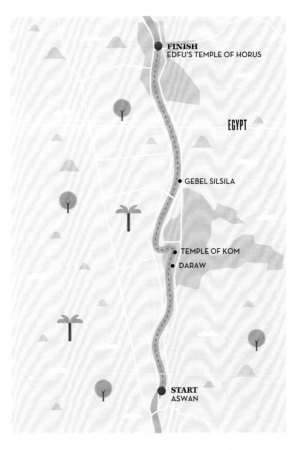

FINISH
EDFU'S TEMPLE OF HORUS

EGYPT

• GEBEL SILSILA

• TEMPLE OF KOM
• DARAW

START
ASWAN

You wake up to the gentle swell of the river rocking the boat. A pair of egrets swoop over the deck and glide onto the palm-tree-lined bank as you poke your head out of the sleeping bag. Later the lateen sail will be unfurled to flap rhythmically in the breeze, and the anchor is raised for another day on one of the world's greatest rivers. Watching the fertile rural heartbeat of Egypt pass by, you laze on the cushion-strewn deck and chat with the Nubian crew. A journey down the Nile is a winding tour through ancient history.

⊕ RIDING THE WAVES

During the Pharaonic era, Aswan acted as a gateway between the civilisations of ancient Egypt downriver and Nubia to the south. Today this town is still dominated by its strategic position upon the Nile, which slithers through the centre. Fittingly, this is the starting point for a *felucca* (traditional Egyptian sailboat) trip down the Nile.

Life aboard is simplicity at its best and an opportunity to log out from the world for a couple of days. Most trips include stops (with three days you'll definitely want to visit the grand temples of Kom Ombo and Edfu), but the itinerary is completely up to you and the captain, and is really decided by the

whims of the wind in the sail. Cast off from Aswan where the Nile is wide and languid, speckled with islands and huge boulder outcrops, and head north towards Luxor. Sitting on deck leaves you only a hand's length above the Nile's surface, allowing for an unfettered, close-up experience of river life.

If you time your trip right, on day one you can moor up at Daraw and dive into the fly-blown chaos of its market. Here hundreds of camels, brought up

> *"The most strenuous a felucca trip gets is diving off the boat to cool off."*

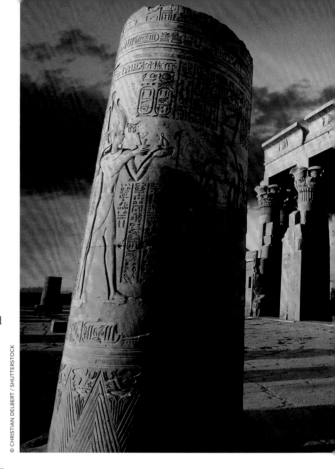

© CHRISTIAN DELBERT / SHUTTERSTOCK

from Sudan, are bought and sold. With the yells of the camel sellers still ringing in your ears and your skin encrusted with dust, reboard the felucca to get back to the real point of a Nile journey: a to-do list of nothing. The scenery slides past at a hazy, sun-dappled pace – strips of lush crop fields, date palms lining the river, a farmer riding a donkey along the bank. The only soundtrack is the slap of water against the boat and the wind beating the sail. Egypt's Nile valley will seduce you to sink into its languorous pace. When the breeze fails to blow, it's time for dark, strong tea to be brewed and for a swim. The most strenuous a *felucca* trip gets is diving off the boat to cool off.

© LISA S. / SHUTTERSTOCK

GEBEL SILSILA

If your historical interest stretches beyond the big temples, arrange for your *felucca* trip to include a stop at Gebel Silsila, between Kom Ombo and Edfu. The ancient sandstone quarry here, used in the construction of some of Luxor's grandest monuments, is littered with stelae, shrines and rock inscriptions.

 At Aswan, leave wi-fi and modernity behind to simply sit back and soak up tranquil Nile views.

 Cool off at Daraw with a refreshing dip in one of the world's great rivers.

 Stretch your legs while marvelling at the Temple of Kom Ombo's reliefs and columns.

CLOCKWISE FROM LEFT: Kom Ombo temple; a traditional spread; the Temple of Edfu. **PREVIOUS PAGE:** Jumping overboard a *felucca*.

Day two's big anticipated site is the Temple of Kom Ombo, with its columned facade looming dramatically over the Nile's bank. It's a chance to stretch your river legs out amid the vast hypostyle halls and goggle at the sanctuaries where Sobek, the local crocodile god, was once worshipped. With a third day, the Nile journey ends near the town of Edfu, with a visit to the Temple of Horus after you disembark. Its golden-hued stone walls, covered in massive reliefs, and gateway guarded by statues of Horus in his falcon form are a grand goodbye to your Nile sojourn.

These temples of ancient Egypt were probably what pulled you onto this trip, but they won't be your lasting memory. Instead you'll remember pulling onto the bank to moor for the night as the sun dips below the palm trees. Eating dinner by the flicker of candles as the crew light a campfire on the bank and bring out the *darbuka* (goblet drum) to supply the beat to their

traditional Nubian songs. Then unfurling your sleeping bag on deck to drift off to sleep to the gentle rocking of the boat under a star-studded sky.

❷ LIFE ON BOARD

A *felucca* is an open-topped wooden sailing boat, usually taking between six and eight passengers and carrying a crew of two to three. Besides sailing the boat, the crew cook meals, provide copious cups of tea and often treat you to traditional drumming when you've moored for the evening.

Sleeping happens en plein air on deck, and there is no toilet on board. During the day the captain can stop on the riverbank for you to disembark on a toilet break; during the evening, when the *felucca* is moored, organised crews will dig a hole and erect a tarpaulin around it to create a toilet tent. Food and tea are

 Stargaze, unhindered by light pollution, after watching sunset streak the sky orange near Gebel Silsila.

 Visit Edfu's Temple of Horus, one of Egypt's best-preserved ancient monuments.

 Finish up the trip with your last night sleeping under the stars.

included in the cost of the trip, but alcohol and soft drinks aren't. The crew will supply an icebox for any cold drinks you want to bring aboard.

❸ OTHER ROUTES

For a shorter *felucca* itinerary, disembark at Kom Ombo (two days, one night); for a longer route, finish up at Esna (four days, three nights). If a few days aboard a *felucca* sounds a bit rustic, you can still sample a slice of Nile sailing by hiring one to sightsee around Aswan's islands for a day or half-day.

❹ LUXURY ALTERNATIVE

Plenty of bigger cruise ships ply the Aswan to Luxor route, offering the chance for Nile sightseeing with the comfort of your own cabin and an onboard swimming pool. Due to the speed at which these floating hotels travel, a typical three-night trip only spends one actual day travelling along the Nile. The historic MS *Sudan*, used in the film *Death on the Nile*, and Oberoi Hotels' MS *Philae* both offer itineraries with more time devoted to being on the river.

For the cabin comforts of a cruiser but the slower pace of a felucca, a larger, double-lateen-sailed dahabeeyah is the premium choice. The *Orient* and the *Meroe* are two of the best plying the river.

❺ MAKE IT HAPPEN

Multi-day *felucca* journeys begin in Aswan. April, May, October and November are the best months to set sail. There are no set departure dates; trips are normally booked on the ground in Aswan. Solo travellers and couples may need to wait around in Aswan for a day or two while the captain rounds up more passengers. Approach captains directly on Aswan's Nile Corniche and get recommendations from your hotel. For pre-booking, two reputable local operators are Captain Jamaica and Aswan Individual. Captains need to register passengers with the police, requiring a registration fee (between 5LE and 10LE) the day before departure. **JL**

21

Okavango Delta Mokoro

BOTSWANA

START	**MAUN**
END	**SAME**
DISTANCE	**1 MILE (1.6KM) TO 20 MILES**
DURATION	**2 HOURS TO A WEEK**

In the heart of southern Africa, the Okavango River meets its end. Spectacularly, in the red sands of the mighty Kalahari Desert in Botswana, its thick channel splinters into countless streams and spreads like delicate tentacles to form an almost 7,722 sq mile (20,000sq km) inland delta. With these waning annual waters comes an incredible profusion of life, both of flora and iconic African fauna. It is one mighty desert flower. This is arguably Africa's most pristine wilderness, and there is no better way to explore it than by gliding through its myriad reed-lined channels in a narrow mokoro, *a traditional dugout canoe.*

❶ RIDING THE WAVES

A *mokoro* journey is as much about letting go as it is about holding on. It may not be long into your experience before – to your surprise – your overwhelming desire for the next Big Five safari sighting romantically dissipates, as you are caught in an enthralling embrace with the natural wonders and beauty of the Okavango Delta itself.

From your seated position on the floor of the *mokoro*, there is majesty and awe in the simplest of acts, whether you're reaching a hand out to gently brush the passing reeds or lying back to watch flocks of lesser flamingos painting the African sky with strokes of bright pink and black. Without the rumbling clatter of an open-topped wildlife drive vehicle, there is a newfound splendour in both nature's silence and sounds. Ears soon pick up the subtlest of noises, such as the water's caress of the *mokoro* or palm leaves dancing in a light breeze, and when birds sing or animals call, the notes are elevated to chorus-like proportions.

Eyes join in on the parade too. No longer intently focussed on the search for the outline of a massive rhino or prowling lion, they relax into a curious, childlike gaze, finding joy in the minutest details of the immediate surroundings: minuscule frogs clinging to the reeds or the supple ripples in the water migrating away from the *mokoro*.

Perhaps it's the contrast to the bumpy and rattling tracks driven down in the preceding days, but the stillness of the *mokoro* softly cradled in the delta's

waters feels serene beyond measure. Yet before the love affair with the *mokoro* starts, most visitors' trips begin with the same five words: 'Am I getting in that?'

Likely the most rudimentary vessel you've ever seen, let alone stepped into, a *mokoro* is water transport at its most basic. Crooked and warped, with its sides floating less than a foot above the waterline, this traditional craft is just wide enough to sit in. The idea of potentially coming across an elephant in something so fragile and seemingly unstable may take you a few minutes to get over, even with the knowledge that the poler – who stands at the back – uses experience, know-how and a raised vantage point to avoid such encounters. But once the poler has pushed off from the bank and expertly navigated you through the first channel or two, nerves quickly settle: it's the first instance of just letting go.

Soon you're relishing the fact that you're actually sitting below the water's surface. You feel part of the environment, and with your eyes so close to the waterline, the scale of everything is amplified to no end. From here on in, it's simply a matter of relaxing and enjoying what the Okavango decides to show you – colourful flocks of rare birds, herds of distant buffalo or simply the mesmerising maze of scenic, reed-lined channels.

You may be moving at a snail's pace, yet excitement in a *mokoro* isn't registered in miles per hour but rather in moments per hour.

❷ LIFE ON BOARD

Traditional *mekoro* (plural for *mokoro*) were rudimentary to the core. Carved from logs, they offered no amenities other than perhaps a cushion on the floor for sitting. Modern varieties are much the same – neither looking nor feeling any different – but they are made from fibreglass to avoid

DELIGHTFUL DRY SEASON FLOODS

In an oddity of the natural world, the Okavango Delta is at its wonderful wettest during the climax of its dry weather season. This is because the waters that swell the delta to epic proportions are born from rains that fell months earlier in the distant highlands of Angola. As these waters swell the Okavango, they create an oasis amidst the surrounding Kalahari Desert.

 Find yourself face-to-face with your first *mokoro* at Boro poling station after a 4WD transfer from Maun.

 Savor the moment the majesty of the Okavango Delta comes to the fore.

 Embark on a late afternoon guided wildlife walk from camp; elephant sightings are not uncommon.

LEFT & BELOW: A traditional *mokoro*; a lilac-breasted roller bird defends its nest. **PREVIOUS PAGE:** Aerial view of the Okavango Delta.

needless deforestation. Each *mokoro* holds up to two passengers, sitting one in front of the other, in a semi-reclined position. Behind the pair stands the poler, who slowly and skilfully propels the vessel through the delta's shallow waters.

❸ MAKE IT HAPPEN

There are no scheduled *mokoro* journeys, though it's possible to organise independent trips in the eastern sections of the delta via the Okavango Kopano Mokoro Community Trust (OKMCT; www.okmct.org.bw). Based out of the delta's safari hub town of Maun, these return trips range from single-day options to multi-day voyages. Overnight trips can be catered or self-catered, depending on your budget, though you'll still need to arrange your own cooking equipment and such. You'll also need to bring your own tent. The best time for these journeys is when water levels are high and the skies are blue, from July through October. In season most lodges in the delta also offer short *mokoro* trips, typically late-afternoon undertakings ending with sunset drinks at a quintessentially scenic location. **MP**

 Try your hand at poling the *mokoro* after a morning exploring the delta.

 Feel yourself starting to dread the end of your *mokoro* foray although you're only halfway through day four of five.

 Sight your last wildlife of the trip and promise to come back for more.

Tsiribihina Descent

MADAGASCAR

START	MIANDRIVAZO	
END	BELO-SUR-TSIRIBIHINA	
DISTANCE	105 MILES (169 KM)	DURATION **3** DAYS

Drifting down the Tsiribihina River has become a popular trip in Madagascar, and with good reason: the three-day descent between Miandrivazo and Belo-sur-Tsiribihina allows you to see a part of the country that is ruled by the river, not the roads. It's slow travel at its best, a rare moment of utter relaxation where admiring the landscape, watching the world go by (literally), reading a book and chatting with the crew or your fellow passengers are your only occupations.

❶ RIDING THE WAVES

As your flat-bottomed *chaland* sets off in the late morning, the river starts out broad, crossing vast agricultural plains and paddy fields. It's not the most beautiful part of the journey, but the people-watching is captivating: men fishing or trying to cross the river in their overloaded zebu carts, women washing their laundry on the riverside and kids frolicking on shore. In a land that has seen occasional security incidents, it's a joy to experience the quiet rhythms of life as

they unfold away from the occasional headlines. For the intrepid, this is a wonderful chance to experience Madagascar's day-to-day.

By early afternoon the landscape changes dramatically: the river narrows, bends become tighter and the banks of the river turn from fields to steep red cliffs. The Tsiribihina Gorges are the most scenic part of the river, with plenty of wildlife, including birds,

crocodiles, bats and lemurs. The skipper will usually slow down or even head back upriver to get another view of whatever animal is spotted.

The other highlight of the afternoon is a stop at local waterfalls (your shower for the day), followed by a walk to a local village. Wherever you go, you'll have a trail of delighted children in your wake.

As evening approaches, camp is set on a large

MOZAMBIQUE CHANEL

MADAGASCAR

START
MIANDRIVAZO

FINISH
BELO-SUR-TSIRIBIHINA

MANIA RIVER

THE MIGHTY BAOBAB

Six of the nine baobab species are native to Madagascar, and some specimens are as old as two thousand years. The Malagasy have nicknamed baobabs 'roots of the sky' after their root-like, scraggly branches. Legend has it that God made the baobab the most beautiful tree on earth. So jealous was the Devil that he decided to plant them upside down so that he could see them from hell!

sandbank, with tents pitched around a campfire. Dinner is served on board, before everyone settles around the fire. The crew will often join in with chatting and singing; local musicians and dancers are sometimes invited as well.

The next morning, after a hearty breakfast, the boat sets off for another day of riparian landscapes. You will make a couple of stops, including Begidro, once the home of extensive tobacco farms. The crop is still cultivated here, but not as extensively. You'll cross small gorges towards the middle of the day before entering a landscape of deciduous forests. The tall kapoks, also known as silk-cotton trees, and iconic baobabs look especially striking in their winter guises. Your guide will take you for a walk through the forest and tell you about different plant species and their uses. Camp is then set for another night of campfire jolliness and prime views of the Milky Way.

On the third day, the boat enters the delta of the Tsiribihina River. The landscape widens, interspersed with increasingly frequent baobabs. Lunch is served on board for the last time, before everyone disembarks at Belo-sur-Tsiribihina's pier. From there, travellers either head off south to the city of Morondava, with its famed Avenue of the Baobabs, or north to the Tsingy de Bemaraha National Park, named for its jagged, limestone pinnacles.

 Enjoy a front-row seat as you watch the daily life of rural Madagascar.

 Settle on the top deck to make the best of the beautiful Tsiribihina Gorges.

 Splash about and refresh yourself at gorgeous waterfalls.

❷ LIFE ON BOARD

Although trips start in Miandrivazo, the actual boarding point is about 19 miles (30km) south in a village called Masiakampy. Transfer is by 4WD and takes around 90 minutes, during which time you'll get to meet your fellow passengers. The boats, called *chalands*, take between six and 12 people, depending on their size. They're motorised and in a previous life were used to transport tobacco. The *chaland* sets off in the late morning. The bottom deck is fitted with two bench seats on either side of a long table, where meals are served. The top deck has sun loungers to take in the splendid views, with an awning to offer shade. The biggest downside of the otherwise relatively comfortable *chaland* is the noise of the engine. There are no toilets on board, either; all business is done outdoors when the boat stops. The crew set up camp every night on the river's sandbanks, covering the

basics – two-person tents, camping mats, sheets and blankets. Meals are usually excellent.

❸ BUDGET ALTERNATIVE

For a cheaper – and some will say more authentic – experience, eschew the *chaland* for a wooden *pirogue*, the traditional dugout canoe. It's slower, quieter and less conspicuous than the *chaland*. On the other hand it's harder work (all that paddling!) and less comfortable than the motorised boats, with no space to move and no shade. It's usually one or two people per canoe, plus the *piroguier* (the canoe skipper). You can book through the same operators that run the *chaland* trips or find operators locally in Miandrivazo.

❹ MAKE IT HAPPEN

The security situation can be variable here, so check with trusted local sources before departing. If conditions allow, you'll find boat trips down the Tsiribihina throughout the dry season (April to November), with increased frequency during the high season (July to September). It's an all-inclusive package, given how remote the area is; alcoholic drinks cost extra. The two main operators are Mad Caméléon and Espace Mada; single travellers may be able to book at the last minute, but groups are advised to book well ahead, especially if working with set dates. If you also intend to go to the Tsingy, a package is well worth considering but it's not compulsory. **EF**

 Take a guided walk through some of Madagascar's iconic baobab trees.

 Enjoy campfire camaraderie and spectacular stargazing on the banks of the river.

 After the end of your trip, make your way to the Tsingy de Bemaraha National Park.

Dubai Creek Abra

UAE

START **OLD SOUQ**	
END **AL SABKHA**	
DISTANCE **500YDS** **(450M) TO 9 MILES**	DURATION **5 MINUTES TO SEVERAL HOURS**

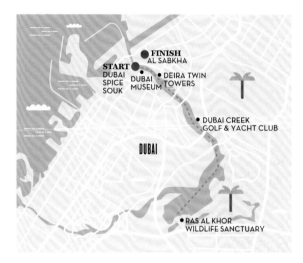

 *As maritime journeys go, taking an abra along Dubai's creek is pretty short. In fact it could be as short as five minutes. But it only takes a few moments in one of the traditional wooden vessels for your whole view of Dubai to be turned on its head. Abras have been used hereabouts for centuries, and the simple boats almost double as a time machine. It is here, as you pass the old markets and narrow lanes, that you get a fleeting insight into the Dubai of yore; the Dubai that existed before record-breaking skyscrapers, weather-defying ski resorts and city-sized shopping malls, each with its own climate.*

❶ RIDING THE WAVES

Perhaps best described as the offspring of a raft and a boat, *abras* are used by pretty much everyone in the space-age city of Dubai – locals on midday shopping trips, businesspeople hopping across the creek for a quick meeting and tourists searching for the soul of the city beneath all the glitz and constant construction. The standard routes simply ferry passengers across the creek in a journey lasting no more than 10 minutes, though visitors have been known to stay on board for multiple crossings, trying to soak up some sense of bygone Dubai as they sail

from the old souqs to downtown Dubai and back.

For those who want a longer journey, there is the chance to hire one of the 150 *abras* for a private excursion to explore further into the 9-mile-long (14km-long) creek. The creek is more than just a tourist attraction; it is the very lifeblood of the city, launching Dubai as a trading hub for the region back in the 19th century. Indeed the creek has been described by Dubai's ruler, Sheikh Mohammed bin Rashid Al Maktoum, as the emirate's raison d'être.

Setting off from the Old Souq in Deira, vessels chug along the creek in an aquatic journey through Dubai's history. As they leave the old town behind, the skyline leaps forward a few decades, and glass towers begin to line the banks of the creek. But as *dhows* and *abras* vie for space with larger vessels, you can still imagine what the creek might have been like in its heyday as a place to trade in pearls and the catch of the day.

Soon you pass under Al Maktoum Bridge, the first bridge to be built in the city. It's not much to look at,

FROM LEFT: Flamingos feed at Ras Al Khor reserve; a captain piloting his *abra*.
PREVIOUS PAGE: Travelling up Dubai Creek, where the city has changed little.

but in 1963 it created a welcome way to quickly cross the creek. Here the water traffic thins out, and it's time to sit back and take in some of the city's remarkable landscaping, with the Dubai Creek Park on the western bank mirroring the perfect lawns of the Dubai Creek Golf & Yacht Club to the east.

Dubai is a master of mystery, surprising visitors just as they think they have the city figured out. As your journey nears its end, you're stunned with the sight of hundreds of flamingos roosting with storks, sandpipers, plovers and other wetland birds. A bird sanctuary is perhaps the last thing you expect to find tucked away behind mega malls and upmarket hotels, but in Dubai you learn that the unexpected is practically the norm. Viewing the Ras Al Khor Wildlife Sanctuary from the seat of an old wooden *abra* provides a fitting finale to the short trip that takes you behind the scenes of downtown Dubai.

❷ LIFE ON BOARD

The *abra* is a bare-bones vessel seating 20 people on wooden benches in the centre of the deck. Whether you're opting for a swift hop across the creek or a two-hour journey to explore further, the vessels are the same: simple, wooden boats with a single class of travel.

❸ MAKE IT HAPPEN

Scheduled *abras* leave every five minutes. The Deira Old Souq to Bur Dubai route operates from 5am to midnight, while the slightly longer ride from Al Sabkha to Dubai Old Souq operates 24/7. For these short hops there is no need to book in advance, but if you want to hire a private *abra*, a minimum of 24 hours' notice is required. Book through the Roads & Transport Authority (RTA): www.rta.ae. The most scenic time to take an *abra* is at sunset. **LC**

DUBAI WATER CANAL

In 2016 the Dubai Water Canal was officially opened, essentially turning central Dubai into an island. The canal carries on where the creek leaves off, cutting a 2-mile (3km) channel through Business Bay and connecting the creek with the Persian Gulf. The canal comes with the usual Dubai trimmings: hotels, a mall, countless restaurants and plenty of pathways to appreciate the engineering feat up close.

 Wander the narrow alleys of the Dubai Spice Souq before you set off.

 Whip your camera out for a shot of the Deira Twin Towers.

 Watch out for stray balls as you pass the Dubai Creek Golf & Yacht Club.

 Marvel at the migratory birds nesting at Ras Al Khor Wildlife Sanctuary.

 Admire the traditional wooden *dhows* crossing the *abra*'s path on Dubai Creek.

 Visit the Dubai Museum, based in the old Al Fahidi Fort, on your return to the quay.

Cape Town Fishing Vessel

SOUTH AFRICA

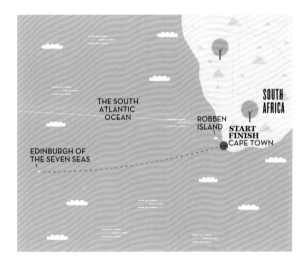

START	CAPE TOWN
END	TRISTAN DA CUNHA
DISTANCE	1740 MILES (2801KM)

DURATION **7 DAYS**

In a world where we Instagram every moment of our travels, where satellite navigation ensures we don't get lost, where ride-share services get us to where we need to go and Airbnb guarantees us a place to lay our heads when we get there, a trip to Tristan da Cunha is a trip back in time. If you've ever longed for the sort of journey you generally only read about in pre-internet-era travelogues, you can make your dream reality with the week-long voyage from Cape Town, South Africa, west to one of the world's most remote inhabited islands (Tristan de Cunha vies with Pitcairn Island for the title). This is a back-to-basics adventure, a bring-your-own-entertainment crossing in a working fishing vessel, where departure and arrival times have less to do with published schedules and more to do with the weather forecast.

❶ RIDING THE WAVES

From the moment Cape Town's Table Mountain slips out of view, the sense of solitude begins. First to go is the cell phone signal. Then suddenly you're surrounded by nothing but the vast expanse of the Atlantic Ocean stretching seemingly endlessly in every direction. The hours on board are spent in simple ways; you read in your bunk, seasickness permitting.

You emerge on the deck every so often, grabbing a deckchair and watching the waves as you slowly chug along. At mealtimes you join your fellow passengers – a mix of Tristanian islanders heading back home and the occasional traveller looking for an intrepid break – in the mess, where simple meals are served by the crew. If you're lucky enough to share the voyage with a chatty islander, these meals are a highlight of the trip, giving you some insight into life on an island that sits some 1500 miles (2415km) from the nearest settlement.

If seasickness does set in – and even seasoned sailors find their stomachs lurching when they skirt the notorious roaring forties (strong westerly winds in part of the southern hemisphere) – the week-long voyage can seem a little like purgatory. If only we could pull over for the night, you think, just a few hours without rolling in the waves. Then, just as you begin to wonder if you'll ever arrive, the looming shape of volcanic Tristan da Cunha emerges in the distance.

Of course the journey isn't over quite yet – there is

CLOCKWISE FROM LEFT: Isolated Tristan de Cunha; Table Mountain; a squid leaps on the journey. **PREVIOUS PAGE:** A Cape Town fishing boat.

© JOHN WARBURTON-LEE PHOTOGRAPHY / ALAMY STOCK PHOTO

© ANTHONY PIERCE / ALAMY STOCK PHOTO

still the often exhilarating matter of disembarking to be dealt with. Tristan's harbour cannot accommodate large ships, so getting ashore often involves anchoring in open waters and completing the last leg in a small fishing boat or an inflatable. How you change crafts depends a lot on the landing conditions. You could be hoisted from the ship in a metal box dangling from a crane, or you might find yourself inching down a rope ladder attached to the ship's hull. Beneath you a boat bobs in the waves, and you can only hope that you'll choose to step down in a moment of calm, rather than when a nerve-racking swatch of icy ocean suddenly appears at your feet.

When at last you set foot on the island – and you could wait several days for a suitable moment to disembark – you'll find many of Tristan's 254 inhabitants at the harbour to greet you. Much like the journey to get there, being on Tristan is a lot like stepping back in time. Old-fashioned hospitality over tea and cake takes the place of people ignoring each

 Glimpse Robben Island, home to the prison that once held Nelson Mandela.

 View nothing but vast, choppy ocean in every direction for five full days.

 Watch albatross searching for fish in the ship's wake as you begin to near Tristan.

ON THE ISLAND

Visitors usually get around a week to explore the island, where simple pleasures await: hiking the vertiginous volcano, sipping a can of beer in the island pub or playing a rugged round of golf with cows and chickens for company. Birders can take a trip to nearby Nightingale Island, inhabited by roughly a million birds, including several endemic species, but no people.

© ALEXCPT / GETTY IMAGES

"Much like the journey to get there, being on Tristan is a lot like stepping back in time."

other in person while chatting to absent friends on WhatsApp. Although the journey to get here can be a little arduous, a few days of motion sickness seems a small price to pay for the chance to travel through time.

❷ LIFE ON BOARD

The majority of the ships making the journey to Tristan are working fishing vessels. Hearty meals are served in the ship's mess, with full board included in the rate. There is nowhere to buy anything on board, so bring snacks, drinks and your chosen seasickness remedies along. Cabins are simple – bunk beds, a small table and a locker, with a bathroom shared among the dozen or

so passengers. The exception to this is the SA *Agulhas*, which travels once a year in September, carrying up to 100 passengers. Facilities on board this research vessel include a gym, library and restaurant.

❸ MAKE IT HAPPEN

Ten ships per year make the journey, and all journeys must be booked through the island council (www.tristandc.com). There are only a few beds on most ships, so it's best to book several months ahead. There are no stop-offs along the way. Summer (November–January) is the best time to visit. Tristan is a British territory, so check in advance to see if a visa is required. Permission to visit must be granted in advance by the island council.

You need to have flexible travel dates since weather and sea conditions can hold up the ships for days at a time. Also, if an islander needs medical evacuation, you might have to give up your spot. **LC**

 Make out the outline of Queen Mary's Peak after days without sighting land.

 Smile as the entire island turns up to greet your boat as it arrives at Edinburgh of the Seven Seas.

 Bring your binoculars on a visit to Nightingale Island to spot some of its many feathered residents.

AMERICAS

AMAZING BOAT JOURNEYS

Mississippi Paddle Steamer

USA

START ST LOUIS, MISSOURI	
END ST PAUL, MINNESOTA	
DISTANCE 588 MILES (947KM)	DURATION 9 DAYS

 Few rivers provoke such a rush of feeling as the Mississippi, the very lifeblood of the country, which Jack Kerouac neatly summed up as smelling "like the raw body of America itself" in his Beat novel On the Road. *At times appearing as wide as the open sea, at others as narrow as a canal, America's second-longest river wends 2350 miles (3784km) from Lake Itasca in Minnesota to the Gulf of Mexico, ticking off 10 states en route. Yes siree, this is one mighty big river. And there's no finer way to see it than aboard an old-school paddle steamer like the* American Queen.

❶ RIDING THE WAVES

There's a sense of occasion stepping aboard the *American Queen*, redolent of a more graceful era of river travel. The largest paddle steamer ever built befits its regal name, with shady decks decorated in lacy filigree and a glamorous bifurcated staircase for swishing down in evening attire. Crew with an old-school air of politeness mill around the stately dining room, keep the wood-panelled library polished to a sheen, and tend to the staterooms and suites, done out in flocked wallpaper and antiques. There's entertainment – including nightly bands in the Engine Room playing jazz and country – but many guests are

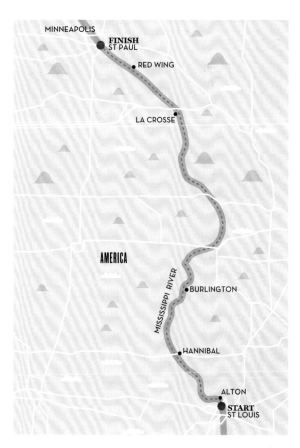

content to kick back in a rocking chair or lounge by the top-deck plunge pool and watch the river roll on by.

Then there's the Mississippi itself. While you can explore its quaint one-diner towns and rolling fields from the road, seeing them from the river reveals them in a completely new light. Paddle steamer itineraries vary, but one along the river's upper stretch, from St Louis to St Paul, aims right for the heart of Mark Twain country, taking in the sleepy little towns

and fertile farmland that inspired such tales as the *Adventures of Huckleberry Finn*, tales that are a vital part of the fabric of America.

Before the colonists and pioneers in the form of farmers, fur trappers and lumberjacks settled along the river in the 1700s and 1800s, the Upper Mississippi had long been home to Native Americans, a fact still evident in place-name remnants. It was French fur trappers who founded St Louis in Missouri in 1764, now a formidable city sitting on a bend in the river. Its most visible icon is the colossal Gateway Arch, built in the 1960s as a shimmering symbol of the westward expansion of the US in the 19th century.

The urban buzz quickly gives way to the open expanse of the river, as the paddle steamer chugs on. Days unfold languidly on deck, with herons and bald eagles occasionally gliding into view, and the calliope bursting into steam-whistle song whenever the paddle steamer passes through a lock.

A DIFFERENT LITERARY HERITAGE

In a 1930 letter to Pulitzer Prize–winning journalist Marquis W Child, the poet and playwright TS Eliot, born in St Louis, eulogised his childhood beside the big river, claiming that the Mississippi had 'made a deeper impression' on him than anywhere else in the world. Robert Crawford's biography *Young Eliot: From St Louis to The Waste Land* is an evocative portrayal of his early life.

 Bid farewell to St Louis and its monumental Gateway Arch as the paddle steamer sets sail.

 Bring binoculars to spot bald eagles, herons, cranes, pelicans and other birds from the deck

 Hang out in Mark Twain's old stomping ground, Hannibal, which inspired many of his books.

CLOCKWISE FROM LEFT: Jackson Square in New Orleans at the end of the Mississippi; the St Louis Gateway Arch; St Paul's sky line. **PREVIOUS PAGE:** A paddle steamer on the Mississippi near New Orleans. **NEXT PAGE:** The *American Dutchess* arriving at Prairie du Chien.

With galleries and antiques stores lining its Main Street, Hannibal is quietly unassuming at first glance. But this Missouri town has its place in literary legend as the boyhood home of Samuel Langhorne Clemens, better known as Mark Twain. In the local museum, which straddles eight buildings, visitors can become acquainted with the real-life characters from his early life that later inspired his novels, among them Tom Blankenship (from *Adventures of Huckleberry Finn*) and Laura Hawkins (Becky Thatcher in *The Adventures of Tom Sawyer*). Described by Twain as a 'white town drowsing in the sunshine of a summer's morning' in *Life on the Mississippi* (1883), a memoir of his time as a steamboat pilot, the town has a pace of life that seems almost as slow and timeless as the boats that drift along the muddy Mississippi.

On then to La Crosse in Wisconsin, so named by explorer Zebulon Pike in 1805, after the ball game being played there. In Red Wing, Minnesota, hiring one of the free bikes available on board is worthwhile for a spin along a stretch of the 20-mile (32km) Cannon Valley Trail, following a tributary of the Mississippi deep into broadleaf woods and prairie.

Not only Twain found romance in the river he called 'as reposeful as a dreamland' in *Life on the Mississippi*. The great F Scott Fitzgerald was born on the river, too – in St Paul. And as a ripe peach of a sunset gives way to a star-spangled night sky, and the paddle steamer cruises on to its final port of call, you can see why such writers found poetry in this river – a river that is wholly American through and through.

 Stroll through Riverside Park and the adjacent Friendship Gardens in La Crosse.

 Hop on a bike to pedal along the wildlife-rich Cannon Valley Trail in Red Wing.

 Explore the historic streets of St Paul, birthplace of F Scott Fitzgerald.

"Best of all, the vessels are true steamboats that actually use their paddlewheels."

❷ LIFE ON BOARD

You'll be travelling in high style in this old-timer of a paddle steamer; it evokes an elegant era of travel with its lattice metalwork, wood-panelled, antique-filled library, Grand Saloon presenting Broadway-style shows, and observation decks where the calliope plays. All accommodation – from deluxe outside staterooms with private verandas to plush suites – come with plenty of space and period details. Best of all, the vessels are true steamboats that actually use their paddlewheels.

❸ OTHER ROUTES

Three paddle steamers (the *American Queen*, the *American Duchess* and the *American Empress*), all operated by the American Queen Steamboat Company, ply a wide range of routes, including St Louis–Chicago along the Illinois River, New Orleans–Memphis along the Lower Mississippi, and a two-week Red Wing–New Orleans journey along the full course of the Mississippi River.

❹ MAKE IT HAPPEN

Paddle steamers make approximately four to five journeys a month. The average length of a sailing is nine days, though cruises taking in the entire length of the Mississippi are 23 days. Tickets can be booked online or by calling ahead. It's worth booking well in advance, particularly for the popular summer months. Most cruises are one-way, with frequent ports of call and a number of shore excursions included in the price; the majority of cruises are from spring to fall. Rates also include a pre-voyage hotel stay, transfers, all on-board meals, 24-hour room service, complimentary soft drinks, and beer and wine with dinner. **KW**

Maine Windjammer

USA ●

START **CAMDEN OR ROCKLAND**

END **SAME**

DISTANCE **50–125 MILES (93–222KM)**

DURATION **3,4,6 NIGHTS**

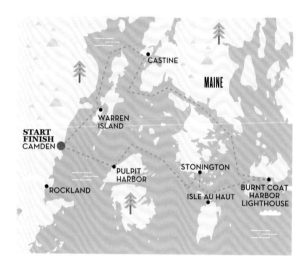

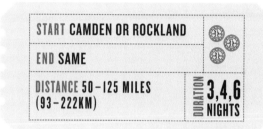

Sailing on a historic windjammer with no set schedule and no distractions from modern life: this is New England romanticism at its best. Days on a windjammer are spent flitting between lighthouses, colonial-era coastal Maine villages and hundreds of semi-secluded islands with pine forests and granite outcroppings. Before they carried travellers, these tall-masted schooners carried merchant sailors, fishers and oyster dredgers; two of the current passenger windjammers date back to 1871. Windjammer sails are more living history than cruise, complete with activities like hoisting sails and singing sea shanties – that is, when you're not too busy relaxing, hiking or feasting on fresh New England farm-to-table dishes.

❶ RIDING THE WAVES

With all the nautical terminology you'll learn on your first Maine windjammer sail – port and starboard, jibs and jibbing – it's a shame there's not a sailing term equivalent to 'amble'. Because nothing would describe a windjammer sail as well as a 'nautical amble' up and down the coast of Maine.

Sometimes travel energises you with physical or cultural challenges. Other times, it energises you by allowing you to relax fully and completely. Maine windjammers are decidedly in the latter category, with enough activities – when and if you want them – to still be an adventure. While you are free and even encouraged to rest and enjoy the scenery as much as possible, you're also invited to pitch in, making this an ideal trip for someone who has always wanted to learn the ropes of sailing. You'll help flake the chain (laying the anchor chain flat after it has been pulled aboard, so it drops smoothly), hoist sails, and you can even learn to tack.

After all that work you'll have earned a hearty repast. Lemon chive biscuits, seafood chowders, Maine wild blueberry pancakes drizzled with locally tapped maple syrup: windjammers are known for their fresh, delectable fare. Co-captain Annie Mahle of the *J & E Riggin* has even published three cookbooks from the meals she makes on her 1927 oyster dredger's cast iron stove.

In fact, this sail feels as if a 19th-century guesthouse

for convivial boarders has been combined with a floating national park campground. Within a day or two on board, most modern devices are forgotten in cabins in exchange for chatting with new friends on deck (about half of them return passengers in love with windjamming), sketching lighthouses or playing cribbage in between island hikes. Instead of a casino, shuffleboard or discos, the entertainment is skipping stones, watching shooting stars or learning about the history and culture of coastal Maine.

"Wherever you go on your windjammer, you can rest assured you'll see lighthouses."

One of the highlights is traversing Penobscot Bay's hundreds of islands and small villages. Maybe you'll dock in Pulpit Harbor on North Haven Island and hike over to a pond or rocky promontory overlooking the scenic bay. Or you might end up in the charming villages of Stonington or Castine, checking out the Georgian and Federal architecture, or hiking up Isle au Haut on the outpost trails of famed Acadia National Park. And wherever you go on your windjammer, you can rest assured you'll see lighthouses.

Because this is Maine, every single windjammer sail comes with a final-night lobster bake, with the crew picking up a few dozen lobsters from the day's catch and steaming them in foraged seaweed on a starlit island's beach. It's a wicked good end to a truly distinctive experience.

❷ LIFE ON BOARD

If you're all about adventure and history instead of luxury, this is your trip. Heads (toilets and showers)

are almost always shared. Cabins are cozy and tightly quartered; bring earplugs! A few windjammers have slightly less rustic accommodation, but the charm lies in the authenticity.

❸ OTHER ROUTES

The Caribbean is the only other location with historic sailing windjammers (Windstar Cruises may look like windjammers but are fuel-powered cruise ships). If the Maine fleet is a little rough, the Caribbean's fleet is more upscale. Cabins on windjammers in the Caribbean are a bit roomier, and many include private toilets or even showers.

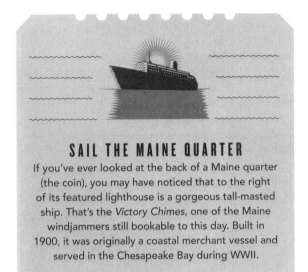

SAIL THE MAINE QUARTER

If you've ever looked at the back of a Maine quarter (the coin), you may have noticed that to the right of its featured lighthouse is a gorgeous tall-masted ship. That's the *Victory Chimes*, one of the Maine windjammers still bookable to this day. Built in 1900, it was originally a coastal merchant vessel and served in the Chesapeake Bay during WWII.

 Board your windjammer in the bustling port towns of Camden or Rockland after a day of shopping, sightseeing and eating a farm-to-table lunch.

 Gaze at more stars than you knew existed while docked at Pulpit Harbor on North Haven Island.

 Hike to get a bird's-eye view from Acadia National Park's picturesque Isle au Haut in the middle of Penobscot Bay.

❹ MAKE IT HAPPEN

Wednesday or Saturday is the most popular departure date, but three-, four- or six-night sails leave almost daily from late May to early Oct (including a few two-, nine- and 11-nighters). Eight windjammers have partnered through sailmainecoast.com, and three at www.mainewindjammercruises.com; there's also the *J & E Riggin* (www.mainewindjammer.com). A few of the more popular theme sails (leaf peeping, food and wine) reliably sell out months in advance. Each sail departs from either Camden or Rockland, Maine. The itineraries are decided day by day but will include a hike, most likely a historic village and most definitely a final-night lobster bake on the beach. Shoulder season (May and June, September and October) can be chilly, but sails are often less expensive. July and August are busy but have the best weather. **AL**

 Wander past stately 19th-century Georgian and Federal homes in Castine or Stonington.

 Stroll up to the Burnt Coat Harbor Light Station, one of a half-dozen historic lighthouses you'll typically see on a windjammer cruise.

 Indulge in a traditional Maine lobster bake, usually in a cove on a secluded island.

Florida Glass-Bottom Boats

USA

START **WAKULLA, SILVER & RAINBOW SPRINGS**

END **SAME**

DISTANCE **A FEW MILES**

DURATION **30 MINUTES TO A HALF DAY**

 *The first Europeans to see the inland springs of Florida thought that they were enchanted, and it's no wonder. The state's 700-odd natural springs bubble up from the earth in jewel-like shades – sapphire, turquoise, aquamarine – appearing like mirages amid the humid subtropical forest. Long before Mickey was even a glimmer in Walt Disney's eye, 19th-century tourists flocked to these springs via the newly built railroads. Today some of the springs are the sites of state parks, others are privately owned roadside attractions, and still others are simply used by locals as swimming holes. A handful of the larger springs offer glass-bottom boat tours, one of the best ways to explore these enchanting pools.*

❶ RIDING THE WAVES

When you think of Florida, you probably think about beaches, Miami and, of course, The Mouse. Beyond the state's fringe of golden beaches and tropical cities, though, lies a weirder, wilder Florida. This is the Florida of dusty roadside orange stands, of swamps overhung with Spanish moss, of alligators blinking silently in the mosquito-shrouded dusk, of remote oyster shacks playing tinny jukebox music late into the night. Here, down the rural routes and through

the citrus groves, you'll find some of the state's most magical offerings: natural springs glowing an otherworldly blue, teeming with fish, manatees and the occasional more mysterious creature. Board a vintage glass-bottom boat and glide into the magic.

At Wakulla Springs State Park, just south of the state capital, Tallahassee, tourists have been touring the 3-mile (5km) stretch of deep, green water since the 1870s. Back then it was said you could see more than 150ft (46m) into the abyss, watching turtles and gators far below. Today the visibility has decreased due to tannins flowing in from nearby tributaries, and the glass-bottom boats only go out on clear weekends. But the trip is still marvelous, as you drift along through the mossy cypress forest where parts of the 1930s Tarzan movies were filmed. Afterwards, take a cooling dip in the 69°F (21°C) water and then retire to your room in the Spanish-style Lodge at Wakulla Springs – don't miss a visit to Old Joe, the 11ft (3m) taxidermic gator in the lobby.

© MARK J. BARRETT / ALAMY STOCK PHOTO

THE MASTODON OF WAKULLA SPRINGS

In 1850, 20-year-old Sarah H Smith spotted something unusual in the depths of Wakulla Springs: what looked like enormous bones and tusks. Smith correctly identified these as a mastodon skeleton, which had lain preserved in the clear waters for more than 10,000 years. The skeleton was eventually retrieved in 1930, and today it stands, reconstructed, in Tallahassee's Museum of Florida History.

Near the quaint inland city of Ocala ('Horse Capital of the World') is Silver Springs State Park, the original Florida tourist attraction. Glass-bottom boats were first used here in 1878, ferrying tourists who had travelled down the Silver River on steamboats. Today you can cruise over eelgrass and craggy underwater rock formations, passing atop Mammoth Spring, the world's largest artesian limestone spring, which feeds the river. Though the albino alligator enclosures, carousel and beer garden have long since closed, the park retains a delightfully vintage vibe, with picnic areas, rocking chairs and an ice cream stand. Keep your eyes peeled for rhesus monkeys – in the 1930s, a tour boat operator released some here to add atmosphere to his Jungle Cruise. The simians can still be spotted swinging in the trees today.

Visiting Rainbow Springs in rural north-central Florida gives you a rare opportunity to captain a glass-bottom boat yourself. Rent one of the small vessels

and putter along the 5.7-mile (9.2km) Rainbow River, watching for bass, otters and turtles in the shallow aqua waters below. Afterwards, take a hike to a silvery waterfall, grab your binoculars to spy wading birds, or hop into the river for a snorkel. It's hard to imagine now, but this whole area was a major tourist attraction until the opening of Walt Disney World in the early 1970s siphoned off the crowds. Today it's blessedly laid-back – all the better for you and the wildlife.

❷ LIFE ON BOARD

Most glass-bottom boat tours are quick: a half hour or an hour. Expect slow speeds and colourful guide commentary. Allow at least a few hours for a self-

 Spot a manatee wintering in the placid waters of Wakulla Springs.

 Sleep in grand retro fashion in the 1930s Spanish-style Lodge at Wakulla Springs.

 Pass over Mammoth Spring, the artesian limestone spring that feeds Silver Springs.

© SCOTT PORTELLI / GETTY IMAGES

© NATIONAL GEOGRAPHIC IMAGE COLLECTION / ALAMY STOCK PHOTO

rental. The springs can get busy on weekends and holidays, so go early to avoid crowds.

❸ MAKE IT HAPPEN

Boat departures depend on season, day of the week and weather – check websites or call ahead of time. There's usually no reason to book tickets ahead of time for tours, and self-rentals can be arranged via operator websites. While summer is the nicest season for swimming in the springs, winter brings the highest chance of spotting manatees. If you pack a picnic, bring an absolute minimum of disposable containers, lest a plastic bag flutter into the water. **EM**

CLOCKWISE FROM LEFT: A glass-bottom boat at Silver Springs; a manatee in the springs; Silver Glen Spring. **PREVIOUS PAGE:** Spanish moss in Wakulla Springs State Park.

 Spy a rogue rhesus monkey climbing through the trees at Silver Springs.

 Pilot your own glass-bottom boat rental at Rainbow Springs along the 5.7-mile long Rainbow River.

 Hop out of the boat to snorkel around the shallows of the Rainbow River.

Lake Powell Houseboat

START **LAKE POWELL MARINAS**

END **SAME**

DISTANCE **YOU DECIDE**

DURATION **3-7 DAYS**

 Cut from the sandstone moonscapes of southern Utah, Lake Powell has a singular power that will connect you with the raw energy of the vast wilderness of the American Southwest. As you travel through the flooded canyon labyrinth along the 250 sq miles (647sq km) of this massive man-made lake, you'll have the chance to explore lost coves, hike up forgotten canyons to visit archaeological sites left behind by the Ancestral Puebloans, waterski across perfectly clear water or just sit back on the rooftop

of your 50ft (15m) houseboat. It's the perfect spot to enjoy the silence and serenity of one of America's largest man-made lakes.

❶ RIDING THE WAVES

Before the Glen Canyon Dam was built in the 1960s at the confluence of the San Juan and Colorado Rivers, Glen Canyon was home to a vast maze of canyons capped by gorgeous red Navajo Sandstone, an amazingly diverse array of native flora and fauna, and over 2000 archaeological sites. In the creation of Lake Powell out of this environment, one of America's most picturesque lakes was born, where over two million people come every year to play in the water, boat to forgotten coves and revel in the beauty, power and grandeur that mark one of history's greatest compromises between the avarice of humans and the generosity of nature. Along the 1960 miles (3156km) of shoreline, 96 major side canyons allow visitors access

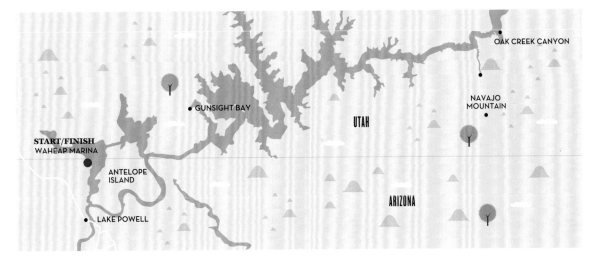

REQUIRED READING

Edward Abbey's books about the American Southwest are must-reads. In his 1975 novel *The Monkey Wrench Gang*, Abbey introduces readers to anti-establishment environmentalists working to destroy the Glen Canyon Dam. For a more bucolic read, try *Desert Solitaire*. This beautiful piece of environmental and naturalist writing includes an elegantly written chapter about exploring Glen Canyon before it was flooded.

to an incredible waterscape surrounded by sandstone on all sides. Here, where rock meets water and sky, you'll find the true glory of this lake.

The best part about Lake Powell is that you can explore most of the lake on your own. Most people choose to do this by houseboat, while others take to kayaks, speedboats, guided tours or other watercraft to explore the incredible canyons and wide-open channels that extend across the border from Utah to Arizona. Houseboating is a unique experience in itself. It's like RVing, but you get a waterslide and unlimited splash time in the surprisingly clear waters.

Your journey will start at the major marinas of Wahweap, Bullfrog, Halls Crossing, Hite, or Dangling Rope. Nearly anybody can master the steering of a houseboat without too much effort. From the marina, armed with a map, compass and full cooler, you can head out to explore the lake at your own speed. Many

people simply cruise out to a favourite cove and tie the boat up for the entirety of their trip. Others cruise from inlet to inlet, exploring the different side canyons. If you're a waterskier or wakeboarder, this place is only one step from heaven, and it's definitely worthwhile renting a speedboat along with the houseboat. This means you can camp out in one spot and take easy day trips to other parts of the lake with less gas usage.

The daily rhythm of the lake will determine your days. Wake at dawn to enjoy the sunrise over the red cliffs. Take a swim across your private inlet to that cool little island you wanted to check out. Lunch on the rooftop (with some card games thrown in for good measure). Take a group trip to a nearby cove (and maybe a cliff jump). Spend the afternoon taking a nap or in a reading session on deck. After dining al fresco on the houseboat, snuggle up for the night and revel in the simple delights of hunting for shooting stars.

 Get your houseboat and kick off your visit at the Wahweap Marina.

 Find a perfect white-sand beach in Gunsight Canyon.

 Hike the Navajo Stairs that are carved into the sandstone mound at the end of Oak Creek Canyon.

LEFT: Reflection Canyon at dusk. **PREVIOUS PAGE:** Cruising Lake Powell.

© JOHNNY ADOLPHSON / SHUTTERSTOCK

TVs and granite countertops. You can also just rent a speedboat or canoe and camp out, or take away all the DIY elements by going with a guided tour. The real luxury add-on is including a speedboat rental. This means easy exploration of far-off canyons, great wakeboarding and tubing, and fun for the whole family. Some marinas even offer chef-on-board packages for catered meals.

❹ MAKE IT HAPPEN

Houseboats are available year-round, but you'll need to plan your trip six months in advance to get the best deals. Guided trips are also available year-round. Book houseboats and guided trips at www.lakepowell.com, www.lakepowellhouseboating.com and www.houseboating.org. These DIY adventures last anywhere from three to seven days; consider a motorboat for shorter trips. Summer is high season but is hot as Hades. September is amazing, with cooler weather and smaller crowds. In early spring, winter and late fall, you might get cold days. Water levels have been an issue here, and may warrant checking, especially in drought years.

Most boats have group size limits, typically a maximum of 12. You need to be over 18 with a valid driver's license to captain the boat. Instructions are given at the marina, and captains can be hired if you don't feel comfortable driving the boat.

Bring more sunscreen and bug spray than you'd ever imagine. The fishing is excellent here, so it's advisable to bring a rod, tackle and reel, and get a fishing license. Bring your floatie toys too. **GB**

❷ LIFE ON BOARD

Plenty of operators offer guided tours of the lake, but renting your own houseboat is part of the charm. At the marina they'll give you a basic low-down on how to pilot the boat, how to anchor and how to avoid crashing. From there it just takes a little practice. You'll need to plan ahead to bring all the drinks, food, water toys, games and other entertainment you'll need for the entire trip. The marinas have small stores and fuelling stations, but these lack variety and are generally very expensive.

❸ BUDGET/LUXURY ALTERNATIVES

There are plenty of options for houseboat rentals, from super cheap 46-footers (boats 14m long) with few frills to two-storey, 75ft (23m) luxury cruisers with flat-screen

 Take your speedboat up Forbidden Canyon to the breathtaking Rainbow Bridge, one of the world's largest natural sandstone bridges.

 Hike to a lost waterfall at the end of Anasazi Canyon.

 Tromp your way to the canyon's rim at Hole in the Rock for amazing views across this raw wilderness.

Staten Island Ferry

USA

START **WHITEHALL FERRY TERM.**

END **ST GEORGE FERRY TERM.**

DISTANCE **ABOUT 5 MILES (8KM)**

FREE

DURATION **20 MINUTES**

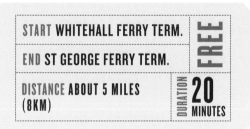

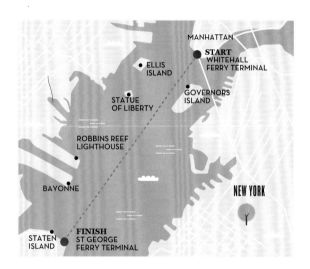

When wandering Manhattan's concrete canyons, it's easy to forget that you're on an island. But the sight of seagulls and the briny smell of water are always only a handful of blocks away. There's no better way to appreciate this, and take in iconic views, than hopping aboard the Staten Island Ferry, the city's only free public transportation. Nearly 23 million people a year ride the ferry and take in the harbour views on the trip from the Battery to Staten Island, the city's oft-overlooked fifth borough.

● RIDING THE WAVES

An orange lunchbox. The subway on the water. A poor man's cruise ship. The Staten Island Ferry in all its gritty glory is a window on the city. Cheesy poster-sized ads pitch for class-action lawyers, political campaigns and local electricians. The *Daily News*, the newspaper of choice, sits in dozing commuters' laps. Young finance types in slim-fitting pinstriped suits, old-timers studying the racing forms, club kids, would-be poets jotting in notebooks, stoners, nail clippers, scavenging recyclers pushing shopping carts filled with bottles, first-date couples: all mix with wide-eyed tourists from across the globe. One look and you want to know everyone's stories. It's a

microcosm of the city's possibilities.

When the ferry gets going, Lower Manhattan's profile slowly reveals the full sweep of its high-rises. At night, office lights suggesting occupancy and work (Deadlines? Big deals signed? Cleaning crews?) pockmark the buildings like Christmas lights. The ferry makes a right turn as the Hudson stretches out in the distance, and the New Jersey side of the river makes its own statement through the ever-growing number of towers in Jersey City and Hoboken.

On your left, low-slung Governors Island, formerly an Army and then Coast Guard base and now a seasonal park and arts space, acts as a barrier from seeing all the Brooklyn waterfront. Depending on the weather, the Statue of Liberty appears in familiar vivid iconic detail or only as disembodied parts looming in the fog. Then there's Bayonne's post-apocalyptic-looking waterfront, where giant cranes hover like a Transformer in mid-metamorphosis. The stout Robbins Reef Lighthouse doesn't look like much, but the story of the woman who tended it for more than 30 years after her husband's death reads like a nautical tall tale: she apparently rowed her children to school on Staten Island and is said to have rescued 50 stranded sailors.

Look down at the churning wake for a sense of the boat's deceptive speed (16 knots, or 30km/h). There's a lot of traffic in the harbour, whether it's police boats zipping past the bow, sailboats on pleasure cruises, or tugs escorting barges stacked with containers on their way to the Atlantic Ocean and beyond.

Staten Island and St George Terminal, overhauled in 2005, come into focus ahead, as does the shiny baseball stadium for the minor league Staten Island Yankees (temporarily nicknamed 'the pizza rats' in 2018 after a fan write-in contest). Construction continues apace on a next-door mall, but plans for the world's largest Ferris wheel appear stalled for the moment. The neighbourhood, lined with some stately, historic government buildings, looks battered only a few blocks away. Many tourists disembark and immediately make their way through the terminal's mini-mall back to the cavernous waiting area to reboard the next departing boat.

Beyond the docked ferry, the city waits to swallow everyone back again.

❷ LIFE ON BOARD

Seats on the eight-ferry fleet are ergonomically inhospitable (three new ships with new seating designs will begin operating in 2020), and not every boat has outdoor promenades and extended foredecks. The largest, the *Andrew J Barberi*, accommodates 6000 passengers, and all but one of the ferries has three levels of seating decks. Each has a basic fast-food-style concession selling snacks, hot dogs, beer and the like, as well as onboard restrooms.

❸ OTHER ROUTES

Visiting the Statue of Liberty and Ellis Island automatically involve short ferry hops. Circle Line offers all the classic New York City sightseeing cruises. NYC Ferry ($2.75, $1 more to bring a bicycle on board), operating only since May 2017, links Manhattan, Brooklyn, Queens and the Bronx; it's an especially popular and scenic way to reach beach spots in Rockaway, Queens.

❹ MAKE IT HAPPEN

The ferry terminal is a short walk away from the 4, 5, 1, R, J and Z subway lines in Manhattan. Departures are every 15 or 20 minutes during rush hour, every 30 minutes to every hour other times. Just walk on board: it's free! Bicyclists enter via the lower level, but

© DROP OF LIGHT / SHUTTERSTOCK

FIRST FERRIES

The first ferries between Staten Island and Manhattan were small sailboats used by farmers, beginning in the 1740s. Competition was fierce and unregulated. In the 1830s, Cornelius Vanderbilt, who would become one of the wealthiest Americans in history, bought control of the dominant ferry company. Vanderbilt instituted a schedule (previously, ferries had left when full) and controlled the route until the Civil War.

 Head to the back deck for a close-up view of the receding Battery Park office towers and One World Trade Center.

 Move on over to the port side for a nice perspective on Governors Island.

 Grab a spot on the starboard side for unobstructed views of Ellis Island and the Statue of Liberty.

ABOVE AND BELOW: The Staten Island Ferry against One World Trade; the Statue of Liberty in New York Harbor. **PREVIOUS PAGE:** Looking out at Lower Manhattan.

the ferry doesn't take cars. You must disembark and reboard in Staten Island. Avoid rush hour, and keep in mind that summertime sunsets are special.

Cheap fast-food items are sold from old-fashioned snack bars on board. For something more substantial after your trip, Enoteca Maria, an Italian restaurant just up the hill from the St George Ferry Terminal, has half its menu designed by a rotating cast of grandmothers cooking dishes from their respective homelands. **MG**

 Peer at Bayonne's industrial waterfront in New Jersey, lined with giant shipping cranes.

 See Robbins Reef Lighthouse, marking the entrance to the area's busiest shipping channel and Newark Bay.

 Study the ballpark for the Staten Island Yankees, seen just to the right as you approach St George.

Niagara Falls Up Close

CANADA

START **NIAGARA FALLS**

END **SAME**

DISTANCE **1.4 MILES (2.2KM)**

DURATION **20 MINUTES**

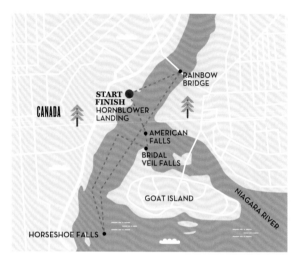

A mighty, misty wall of water plummeting earthward at the rate of a million bathtubs of water a minute, Horseshoe Falls, Niagara Falls' main cascade, is nature in pure show-off mode. This thunderous tide of teal on the US–Canada border is majestic from any vantage point (and there are many), but for an up-close, mist-in-your-face appreciation of its power, there's nothing like a boat ride to the falls' base. Since voyages began in 1846, everyone from Hollywood icons to British royals has seized the chance to sail into the spray – a (potentially) wet and wildly fun round trip that, though just 20 minutes long, will make a lasting impression.

❶ RIDING THE WAVES

In waterfall terms Niagara Falls isn't especially tall – it doesn't even crack the top 500 worldwide – but when it comes to sheer power, few cascades on earth can compete. Roughly 3086 tons (2800 metric tonnes) of water plunge over the edge each second, hurtling at speeds up to 68mph (109km/h) into the Niagara River. The source of this force is the water flowing out of the first four of North America's vast Great Lakes, barreling down the Niagara River from Lake Erie on its way to Lake Ontario and from there

to the St Lawrence River and the Atlantic Ocean.

To get widescreen views of all three cascades – Horseshoe Falls, the smaller American Falls, and Bridal Veil Falls – visitors can head to either Niagara Falls, Ontario, or Niagara Falls, New York, neighbouring towns across the US–Canada border. Each town offers its own take on the original Niagara adventure, via a boat trip with either Maid of the Mist (New York) or with Hornblower Niagara Cruises (Ontario). Since Maid of the Mist first launched in 1846, there have been daring rescues, movie cameos and visits from countless world leaders and celebrities, including Marilyn Monroe, Stephen Hawking, Prince William and Prince Harry. The Canadian-side tour is nicknamed the Voyage to the Falls, but both providers offer a 20-minute, all-ages trip to the foot of Horseshoe Falls and back.

In Canada, this storied journey of rare natural grandeur begins with a red mist poncho. Marilyn probably wouldn't approve, but if you want an open-

BELOW AND RIGHT: The Historic Prince of Wales Hotel in Niagara on the Lake; spray rises from the American Falls. **PREVIOUS PAGE:** The splash zone at Horseshoe Falls.

FROM LEFT: © LES PALANIK / SHUTTERSTOCK; © AIVOLIE / SHUTTERSTOCK

air experience (recommended), discard this freebie at your peril. On board, a panoramic top deck and a lower deck with a glass-walled indoor area give sweeping views as the boat heads into the Niagara Gorge, its rugged cliffs hewn by the Wisconsin Glacier 10,000 years ago.

Immediately ahead at the American Falls, torrential sheets of water break onto a bed of hulking rocks in a tumult of foam and vapour laced with rainbows; separated by a tiny island is the slender Bridal Veil Falls, a lone ribbon of pelting water. They're a taste of what's to come, as the rumbling of Horseshoe Falls grows louder and the falls emerge fully into view, huge plumes of spray filling the sky like steam rising from a cauldron.

Soon enough the boat approaches the falls, inching through frothing blue-green waters towards its curtain of raging torrents, nearly half a mile wide (about

1km) and 197ft (60m) tall. Some posit that the name Niagara may derive from a word of the indigenous Iroquois people meaning 'thundering waters' (it's more widely accepted to mean 'the strait'), and you'll soon get why. It's a sight of visceral power that you'll also feel in the spray soaking your face and the roar in your ears. Varying wind levels make every ride different – you might enjoy clear views or be engulfed by mist, inching forward in a hypnotic haze until the rush of the waterfall feels impossibly near. Heading back, you'll have a chance to take in the scenery along the river as you dry off, including the grand facade of an abandoned, century-old power station, the Space Needle-esque Skylon Tower crowning the Niagara Falls skyline, and the Rainbow Bridge arching between Canada and the USA just downstream. For a 20-minute trip, it packs a punch: you wouldn't be the first to hop right back on and do it all over again.

 Put on your mist poncho and stake out a spot on board at Hornblower Landing.

 Watch the tumultuous American Falls plunge from a height of 187ft (57m) onto churning rocks.

 Look out for the slender Bridal Veil Falls tumbling into the river.

BOAT TRIPS
FROM NIAGARA FALLS, USA

Visitors to the US side of the falls can ride the famed
original Maid of the Mist service. Like its Canadian
counterpart, the 20-minute cruise ventures past
the American and Bridal Veil Falls into the misty
Horseshoe Falls, but it starts and
ends in Niagara Falls, USA.

❷ LIFE ON BOARD

You'll ride on the *Niagara Wonder* or *Niagara
Thunder* or one of their fellows, both 700-passenger
catamarans with two decks; the lower tier also has
an indoor area with retractable glass walls. There are
also two wheelchair-accessible washrooms and seating
for visitors using wheelchairs or with limited mobility,
plus an on-board audio commentary and free wi-fi.

❸ OTHER ROUTES

Hornblower Niagara Cruises also offers three 'light
mist' trips venturing less far into the Horseshoe Falls:
a 20-minute evening trip taking in sunset and the
waterfalls' dusk illuminations; the 40-minute Falls
Illumination Cruise, showcasing the colourfully lit
night-time falls; and the 40-minute Falls Fireworks

Cruise, which also includes an evening display of
fireworks. Both night-time cruises feature music and
an onboard bar offering snacks, craft beer and wine
from the Niagara region.

❹ MAKE IT HAPPEN

Trips depart every 15 minutes rain or shine during
the season, which runs from spring to November 30
(start dates vary considerably according to weather).
Trips run from 8.30am to 8.30pm during peak season
(roughly May to August), with shorter days at other
times. You can book tickets on-site, but it's better to
skip the lines and book in advance online, especially
for often sold-out night-time cruises. Summer brings
fine weather but the longest queues – consider a
shoulder season trip, or beat the crowds by visiting
before 11am or after 4pm. **SM**

Experience the majesty, the mist
and the thunderous roar of the
legendary Horseshoe Falls.

Admire the Rainbow Bridge
linking Canada and the US on
the voyage back.

Toast the trip with the likes of
barbecue, craft beer and Niagara wine
at Hornblower's falls-view hang-out,
the Riverside Patio.

Arctic Circle Cruise

GREENLAND AND CANADA

START **KANGERLUSSUAQ, GREENLAND**

END **IQALUIT, CANADA**

DISTANCE **1650 MILES (2657KM)**

DURATION **11 DAYS**

Skirting coastlines dotted with colourful villages, this trip to West Greenland and Baffin Island on the Vavilov with One Ocean Expeditions allows travellers a brief glimpse into what it takes to call the stark and stunning environment of the Arctic home. To make a life at latitudes that kiss the Arctic Circle is no easy feat, but the special beauty of that life is unparalleled. A trip to the high Arctic also provides a rare connection to the natural world. While environmental damage in the area is visible and undeniable, seeing the endless summer sun glistening on monolithic icebergs is a mystical experience. Visiting this raw place is essential travel for anyone who wants to know what conservationists are working so hard to preserve.

❶ RIDING THE WAVES

The ship's captain expertly navigates hundreds of colossal icebergs through Disko Bay in Greenland, finally coming to a stop near Ilulissat. The expedition leader already has passengers suited up and ready to climb into Zodiacs and cruise through the frigid waters. Glistening blue-and-white tabular bergs tower above as the Zodiac weaves through the maze they create. Later in the day, a trip to shore offers the chance to

hike above town to a viewpoint above the ice field.

The first few days in western Greenland explore quaint Arctic towns and villages. With pops of bright primary colours on some of its buildings, Sisimiut is the first glimpse of Arctic life. One Ocean Expeditions employs Inuit guides and traditional artisans to share knowledge of the region. Sisimiut is home to champion traditional Greenlandic kayakers, who may even demonstrate their skills for passengers.

Two days on board the ship as it crosses the Davis Strait offer the chance to sit comfortably on the bridge with binoculars in hand, hoping to spot fin, humpback and sperm whales. In middle summer, late at night or early in the morning, the midnight sun dips almost to the horizon before floating up again, painting the sky with its pink-gold radiance for a sunset that flows right into sunrise. A late summer trip could yield views of the aurora borealis.

Once across the strait, the ship will stop somewhere around Sunshine Fjord. Passengers have the option to hike or take a Zodiac cruise above 66° 33' north of the equator and cross the Arctic Circle. The sheltered waters of the fjord are also perfect for kayaking.

The ship continues cruising around the rugged Baffin Island coastline down to Cape Mercy. In winter the pack ice is thick in this region, but it recedes in summer, making it an ideal location to watch for polar bears. If one isn't spotted here, Monumental Island and the Lower Savage Islands are also favourite hunting grounds for the bears. The water near the Lower Savage Islands is rich in nutrients that attract a diversity of marine life.

A standout of the trip is time spent in Pangnirtung. This remote Inuit hamlet in Nunavut is surrounded by jagged, frosted peaks and filled with summer wildflowers. It is the gateway to Auyuittuq National Park and boasts a thriving art scene and outdoor opportunities galore. The highlight is the exceptional local art galleries, whose artisans painstakingly create both traditional and contemporary works.

This journey is filled with both stark realities and magical moments. The ice is receding and the water is warming. People who have made their lives here struggle under modern expectations. But there is also awe over the vibrant life carved out in a world better suited for those with fins and claws. An enormous humpback whale is dwarfed by some of the icebergs that casually float through the Davis Strait. Tiny wildflowers grow bravely up the slopes of gigantic mountains. These are the moments when scale and reality morph into an entirely new understanding of the word wild.

❷ LIFE ON BOARD

A daily wake-up call from the expedition leader spurs passengers into motion. On most days there will be two excursions to get travellers off the ship. On sailing

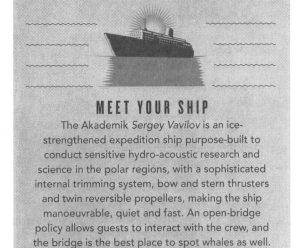

MEET YOUR SHIP

The Akademik *Sergey Vavilov* is an ice-strengthened expedition ship purpose-built to conduct sensitive hydro-acoustic research and science in the polar regions, with a sophisticated internal trimming system, bow and stern thrusters and twin reversible propellers, making the ship manoeuvrable, quiet and fast. An open-bridge policy allows guests to interact with the crew, and the bridge is the best place to spot whales as well.

 See colourful Sisimiut, a charming seaside village that is Greenland's second-largest town, for a first look at Arctic communities.

 Watch giant tabular icebergs erupt from the Jakobshavn Glacier.

 Venture above the Arctic Circle from the Sunshine Fjord.

CLOCKWISE FROM LEFT: An iceberg off the coast of Canada; a Greenlandic puppy. **PREVIOUS PAGE:** A cruise ship moves through the ice floe.

days, passengers attend lectures or spend their time on deck watching for wildlife.

❸ OTHER ROUTES

From Russia's Far East to Spitsbergen and Arctic Norway, there are plenty of routes available to explore the land of the midnight sun. For the goal oriented, a trip to the North Pole or through the Northwest Passage is an iconic journey.

❹ BUDGET/LUXURY ALTERNATIVE

While the *Vavilov* offers one of the more affordable adventures to the North, there are luxury alternatives as well. Polar Cruises (www.polarcruises.com) is a one-stop shop for finding the right combination of ship and itinerary to fit your needs.

❺ MAKE IT HAPPEN

Ships leave from Kangerlussuaq, Greenland. Book trips through One Ocean Expeditions or through a travel service like Polar Cruises, usually six months or more in advance. Many trips have activity options that include kayaking, snowshoeing and photography seminars. All expedition-style journeys to the Arctic are round trip. For western Greenland and Baffin Island, charter flights from Ottawa to the ship ports are included in the cruise cost. All Arctic cruises are scheduled from July to September. **SS**

 Keep your eyes open for polar bears as you cruise around Cape Mercy.

 Visit the remote Inuit community of Pangnirtung, renowned for traditional and contemporary art and crafts.

 Go for a Zodiac cruise and watch Arctic wildlife in the maze of channels around the Lower Savage Islands.

San Juan Islands

USA

START ANACORTES	
END SAN JUAN ISLAND	
DISTANCE 23 MILES (37KM)	DURATION 1 HOUR

 *Tucked away in the extreme northwestern corner of the contiguous US, practically kissing the border with Canada, sits an intricate puzzle of over 400 islands, islets and eagle perches known collectively as the San Juans. Slow-paced, bucolic and largely free of the suburban sprawl that has colonised much of continental America, these sleepy outposts are best accessed by the no-frills but solidly reliable Washington State Ferries system, whose trusty, utilitarian ships make the voyage west out of Anacortes through*

a watery realm where humans and nature have maintained an all-too-rare peace.

❶ RIDING THE WAVES

It would be difficult to stop at all 172 named San Juan islands in one year, let alone one trip. Fortunately, Washington State Ferries narrows the choice by docking at just four: flat, easy-to-cycle Lopez; small, fiercely private Shaw; wild, precipitous Orcas; and the unofficial capital, San Juan Island.

Islands crowd the horizon as you bid adieu to the diminutive port town of Anacortes and start navigating the tree-covered archipelago to the west. If you've just arrived from Seattle or anywhere else with a population of more than 30,000, the feeling of serenity is immediate. It's almost as if you've crossed an invisible line between modern America and a sepia-toned photo from a less frenetic era.

Come summer, a light-hearted holiday atmosphere

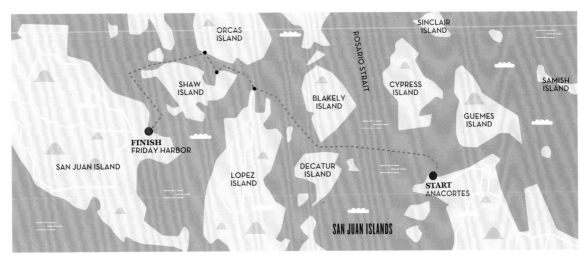

takes hold as vacationers come aboard with their kayaks, bicycles and picnic hampers. Get ready for a rush to port or starboard should a pod of orcas be sighted, as everyone gathers on deck with their cell phones set to camera mode.

The natural geography of the islands favours elegant Douglas firs, sturdy cedars, and rust-red arbutus. Indeed, trees are everywhere in this temperate rainforest, hugging the rocky coastlines or packed densely on steep hillsides. The first islands you pass are lightly populated and largely private. Such houses that exist are discreetly hidden behind foliage, although you'll occasionally spot a chic hideaway perched atop a cliff or nestled in a quiet cove.

Each of the four main islands has a distinct personality, and regular visitors have their favourites. Lopez, the first stop, is hailed as the friendliest and most laid-back isle. Here the local drivers proffer what is known as the Lopez wave – a lazy, two-fingered salute above the steering wheel – while visiting cyclists meander through a patchwork of pastoral fields watched over by the snow-white hump of Mt Baker.

Beyond Lopez the ferry gets closer to the shoreline as it cuts through the narrow channel that divides Shaw from Orcas. Bald eagles perch on towering Douglas firs, and smaller watercraft, including kayaks, start to appear on both sides of the ferry. Recreational boaters love the San Juans for their sheltered waters, deserted beaches and well-maintained marinas.

Orcas' ferry dock is small but well-used. Shaped like a saddlebag and with little flat terrain, the island is a microcosm of the outdoors-embracing Pacific Northwest. You can rent kayaks here, climb the archipelago's highest peak, 2402ft (732m) Mt Constitution, or comb local beaches for shells.

Back at sea, ferries push on to San Juan Island, with sightings of orcas becoming ever more likely.

© PURESTOCK / ALAMY STOCK PHOTO

Friday Harbor, the only settlement that passes for a town in these parts, sports a marina packed with expensive yachts. Marginally smaller than Orcas, 55-sq-mile (142sq km) San Juan Island is a mishmash of leafy hedgerows and pretty clapboard houses where such mainland interferences as traffic lights and fast-food franchises are as foreign as tigers or elephants. Canada is practically pebble-throwing distance from its western shores. The watery international border that runs along the Haro Strait was once a political hot potato that nearly brought the British and Americans to war in the mid-1800s. At the end of your voyage, you can visit an island highlight, a two-section historical park that explains the bizarre military stand-off in full.

 Exchange 'Lopez waves' with the drivers lining up dockside on Lopez Island.

 Watch the small trickle of passengers disembark at the tiny dock on Shaw Island.

 Stop and rent a kayak on Orcas Island.

LEFT: Watmough Head on Lopez Island. **PREVIOUS PAGE:** A boat off Lopez Island.

THE PIG WAR

In 1859 the British and US almost went to war over ownership of the San Juan Islands when an America settler on San Juan Island killed an Irish farmer's pig. Both sides subsequently sent troops and warships to the area and goaded each other with insults. Fortunately, after a tense military stand-off, diplomacy prevailed, and the site is now the home of San Juan Island National Historic Park.

❷ LIFE ON BOARD

While not luxurious, the vessels of Washington State Ferries serve their purpose with comfortable seats, efficient if slightly pricey food concessions, large windows to absorb the magnificent vistas and plenty of opportunity to roam around on deck.

❸ OTHER ROUTES

Hosting the largest ferry system in the US, Washington State has innumerable opportunities to visit other islands in and around Puget Sound. A perennial favourite of Seattleites seeking a bit of weekend tranquility is the Bainbridge Island ferry.

❹ MAKE IT HAPPEN

Ferries for the San Juan Islands leave Anacortes roughly every hour between 4am and 11pm in summer. Reservations can be made through the Washington State Ferries website and are recommended if you're bringing a car. It's not necessary for walk-on passengers to reserve. Fares are collected on westbound ferries only, and foot passengers and cyclists can ride inter-island ferries for free in either direction. To stop at all four islands, change to an inter-island ferry at Lopez. The best months for dry, sunny weather in northwest Washington are July to September. Bring your binoculars to search for orcas en route. **BS**

 Look out for orcas on the approach to San Juan Island.

 Stop for a snack at a farm-to-table cafe in Friday Harbor.

 Visit the fascinating San Juan Island National Historic Park.

Inside Passage Day Cruise

CANADA

START PORT HARDY	
END PRINCE RUPERT	
DISTANCE 315 MILES (507KM)	**DURATION 1 DAY**

Travellers invariably fall for Canada's monumental landscapes. From grand mountains and vast forests to shorelines that open onto broad fjords, there's a jaw-dropping beauty to the country's spectacular wilderness. One of the best ways to experience the full menu of vistas is by taking the Port Hardy to Prince Rupert ferry through British Columbia's glorious Inside Passage. This spine-tingling northbound voyage offers a rolling diorama of coast and crag views, alongside a side dish of camera-enticing wildlife. Best of all is the chance to unwind deeply and snag a front-row seat on some epic Canadian scenery without even trying.

❶ RIDING THE WAVES

It's 7.30am in summertime Port Hardy on the northern tip of Vancouver Island. The sun has been up for two hours, but it's chilly and almost silent on the dew-glistened decks of the MV *Northern Expedition*, a gleaming, white-painted BC Ferries ship that typically carries more than 500 local and visiting passengers.

An ear-splitting klaxon and a rumbling vibration underfoot announce the vessel's on-time departure as deck doors suddenly fling open and camera phones focus on the scene: a shoreline bristling with bald

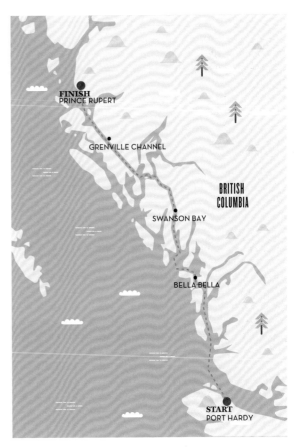

eagles perched on trees and ready to dive for any fish that might be churned up by the ferry's exit.

Alaska-bound cruise ships have been threading alongside the scenic islands and mainland wilderness of British Columbia's Inside Passage for decades. But savvy visitors also know the region's public ferry service covers the same route to the northern BC city of Prince Rupert, delivering breathtaking mountain-framed panoramas for a fraction of the cost.

The day-long voyage is also one of Canada's best ways to relax. After exploring the dining options on board (the seafood-forward buffet is recommended) as well as the small gift shop (go for the books on First Nations heritage), passengers on the modern, German-built vessel soon slide into a slower pace. Time is a nebulous concept on this 16-hour trip, with many of those on board alternating between catlike basking outside and lazy snoozing on comfy vinyl armchairs inside.

There are typically two types of passengers: locals returning home or making far-flung family visits or trip-of-a-lifetime overseas visitors drinking in the views like a restorative tonic. The groups mix well, and there's often a chatty camaraderie on board, especially on the outer decks where guitars are strummed, card games are played and couples entwine to gaze at the scenery.

That scenery is something even the locals can't

keep their eyes off. The vessel slides through glittering waters between multihued peaks that splay out on either side, many of them covered by dense, undulating forests. Sandy bays, red-capped lighthouses and old settlements with intriguing names like Namu and Dryad Point punctuate the shoreline. And there's always the possibility of a wildlife sighting or two.

The captain usually announces any nearby orcas, triggering a sudden rush for the outer decks. Giddy chatter dissolves into silent reverence when the whales are finally spotted, with passengers taking turns for the best photo vantages. But orcas aren't the only locals to watch out for. There are usually seals lolling on sun-soaked rocks plus the occasional gaggle of perky porpoises racing the ship just for fun: they always win.

The languid pace on board the ferry becomes ever more gentle as the day unfolds. Many passengers sun themselves on deck for hours, while others unfurl carefully packed picnics for a leisurely al fresco feast.

© EDGAR BULLON / ALAMY STOCK PHOTO

SCENIC HOTSPOT

Sharp peaks rising up to 3500ft (1067m) flank Grenville Channel, one of the most dramatic stretches of Inside Passage topography. Typically encountered about four hours before you reach Prince Rupert, it is 43 miles (69km) long but just 1400ft (427m) across at its narrowest point. Known as The Slot or the Big Ditch, it's a major thoroughfare for vessels enjoying its calm waters.

© EDGAR BULLON / ALAMY STOCK PHOTO

 Stay on deck to watch the bald eagles as you depart from Port Hardy.

 Watch for Bella Bella onshore, home to one of the region's largest First Nations communities.

 Snap images of the lighthouse at Boat Bluff, one of the route's most-photographed spots.

CLOCKWISE FROM LEFT: BC
Ferries passing Whytecliffe Park; boats
at Port Hardy; wild birds at Port Hardy.
PREVIOUS PAGE: A harbour seal off
Vancouver Island's Fisherman's Wharf.

An all-pervading feeling of relaxed contentment takes over as the afternoon light shifts to a golden early evening sky.

The northern scenery is more rugged by this stage, with clouds casting rolling shadows over the forests and silvery waterfalls forming tentacles down the sides of towering cliffs. When the sun gradually sinks, many passengers retreat inside to sidestep the chill. But some remain to watch the pyrotechnic sunset. It's been a long, life-affirming day, and Prince Rupert is just ahead.

❷ LIFE ON BOARD

Built in Germany in 2009, the MV *Northern Expedition* is a modern passenger and vehicle ferry with a cafe and a summer-only restaurant that includes an all-you-can-eat buffet option. There is plenty of comfortable seating on board first-come-first-serve (window seats are sought after), but small private cabins are also available for an additional fee.

❸ MAKE IT HAPPEN

From mid-June to mid-September, Inside Passage day cruises depart from Port Hardy at 7.30am every other day; the cruises are less crowded at the start or end of the season. The rest of the year, this is an overnight service departing at 6pm on Saturdays only. Book via www.bcferries.com; reservations are essential and early booking is recommended, especially for cabins or vehicle passage. Passengers typically travel one-way from Port Hardy to Prince Rupert or vice versa, with stops possible in Bella Bella or Klemtu. In Prince Rupert, connect to the Haida Gwaii ferry or VIA Rail's train to Jasper, Alberta.

Bring snacks and drinks so you're not reliant on onboard eateries. Binoculars and an extra layer for cooler evenings on deck are also recommended. **JL**

 Search for a brick chimney among the trees, evidence of the old Swanson Bay community.

 Save your camera battery for Grenville Channel, the voyage's narrowest stretch of mountain-flanked scenery.

 Stay in Prince Rupert for a while and don't miss its Museum of Northern British Columbia.

Journey Between the Seas

PANAMA

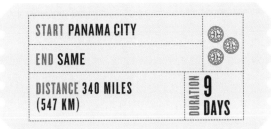

START **PANAMA CITY**	
END **SAME**	
DISTANCE **340 MILES** (547 KM)	DURATION **9 DAYS**

Remnants of old ruins wedged beside a bustling downtown neighbourhood. Dense rainforests just a few miles from the tall glass buildings and paved streets of a thriving metropolis. This is Panama, a dynamic and diverse country that offers adventure in all forms. You can kayak in Gatun Lake, spend an afternoon at Fort San Lorenzo, or snorkel in the waters of the Pearl Islands. Whatever you fancy, the Journey Between the Seas tour with EcoCircuitos, a tourism organisation that promotes ecotourism and education, lets you dive into all things uniquely Panamanian.

❶ RIDING THE WAVES

Cutting through the waters of the Sambú River, up a narrow tributary into the thick jungle, is the only way to come face-to-face with one of Panama's oldest indigenous groups. The Emberá – 'the River People' – have lived in the Darién region for centuries, and for a few hours you can catch an authentic glimpse of the past. The Emberá children lead the way down a muddy path and to a clearing where the village stands. Elders will showcase their intricate carvings and handwoven baskets with pride. Some will invite you into their thatched-roof homes built on stilts, and a few may even ask for a dance during a traditional Emberá song.

From the heat and sweat of the jungle, you proceed to the cool waters of the Pearl Islands. Once known for an abundance of the prized gem, the islands of San Telmo and Mogo Mogo are now a natural playground. Kayaking for the active types, snorkelling for nature lovers or a bit of peace for the weary on the secluded beach: the options are endless.

You won't see the approach to the Panama Canal; the journey is made at night. But once you arrive, you want to stand right at the front of the *Panama Discovery* catamaran. Rain or shine, position yourself directly in line with those giant metal doors to witness something you won't see watching from above at the Miraflores Visitor Center. Nor would you be able to grasp the unique lock system on board a huge cruise shop. A little intimacy goes a long way, especially when those massive doors open and the waters of the Panama Canal (northbound passage) come into view from your catamaran.

From the Panama Canal to the mouth of the

© CANNON PHOTOGRAPHY LLC / ALAMY STOCK PHOTO

© URS HAUENSTEIN / ALAMY STOCK PHOTO

Chagres River, the adventure continues. There's a stillness when you walk around the lush, greenery-covered ruins of Fort San Lorenzo. The breeze is slight, and you barely hear the sound of the Chagres crashing against the cliffs below. Your guide will speak of pirates and gold, of attacks and plunder. But it will be the panoramic views and the dark, cool stone labyrinths of the fort that will stick with you.

There's one more treat in store, and this one doesn't involve a boat. Get your land legs back in style with a trip on the Panama Canal Railway. Perhaps the only things more colourful than the railway's history are the views heading from Colón back to Panama City.

❷ LIFE ON BOARD

The *Panama Discovery* catamaran measures 110ft (34m) and holds 24 guests. It's manned by 11 crew members and outfitted with snorkelling gear and

THE PANAMA HAT SECRET

When you think of Panama, one of the first images that come to mind is those stylish brimmed straw hats. But did you know the panama hat originates in Ecuador? The toquilla straw it's made of grows there. Gold rushers travelling to the West Coast in the 19th century bought the hats en masse on their journey through Panama, and the name stuck.

 Peruse and purchase the unique handcrafted items for sale by the Emberá women.

 Snorkel in the waters of the Pearl Islands, which are filled with aquatic life.

 Stand at the front of the *Panama Discovery* to see how the locks of the Panama Canal work.

CLOCKWISE FROM LEFT:
Fort San Lorenzo near Colón; a
view of the Caribbean; finishing a
Panama hat. **PREVIOUS PAGE:**
A freighter waits to enter the
Panama Canal.

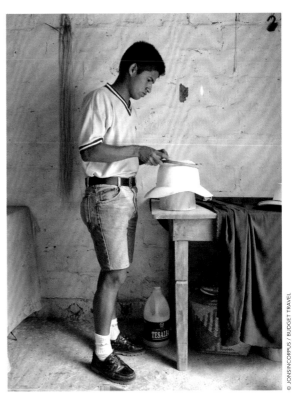

kayaks. Each of the twelve cabins below deck has its
own bathroom and shower. The main deck is indoors
and features large windows and a cosy sofa. There's
a gourmet chef on board serving up three meals a
day and an eager staff to keep your glass filled with
whatever you like.

❸ BUDGET ALTERNATIVE

If a nine-day excursion is not in your budget,
there's always a one-day Panama Canal trip. Panama
Marine Adventures offers partial (four to five
hours) or full transit (10 to 12 hours) northbound or
southbound packages.

❹ MAKE IT HAPPEN

There are departures once a month from March to
June as well as a pair of departures in late October

and November. Tickets should be booked at least a
month in advance. The entire route is pre-planned,
with EcoCircuitos picking up and dropping off
travellers at Tucumen International Airport. The
ideal time to visit is during the dry season (December
through May). However, the tour also runs during rainy
season (June through November). **AJ**

 Look out for *Mimosa pudica*, called
the 'sensitive plant' because its
leaves close when touched, at Fort
San Lorenzo.

 Enjoy the scenery on the
Panama Canal Railway; there
are no bad seats.

 Back in Panama City, go
shopping for your very own
Panama hat.

The Bahamas by Mailboat

THE BAHAMAS

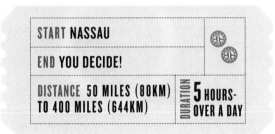

START NASSAU	
END YOU DECIDE!	
DISTANCE 50 MILES (80KM) TO 400 MILES (644KM)	DURATION 5 HOURS-OVER A DAY

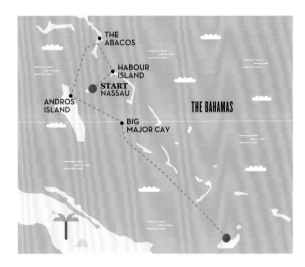

Are you more tortoise than hare? Have more time than money? Love stopping to smell the sea? Then island-hopping the Bahamas by mailboat may be just the ticket for your next 'slow travel' journey. Mailboat travel is a hallowed yet increasingly archaic way of getting around the Bahamas' 30 inhabited islands. It involves long hours – sometimes even days – of sitting on the swaying deck of a cargo ship alongside sacks of mail and pallets of canned peas, just watching the sapphire-blue Atlantic roll by. Does this sound like hell? Then this isn't for you. Sound like heaven? Climb aboard.

❶ RIDING THE WAVES

On the docks of Nassau on the island of New Providence, porters yell to each other as they haul boxes of fresh pineapples, crates of live conchs, massive tins of lard and other local necessities on and off the peeling-paint–hulled vessels. The next piece of cargo is you.

These are the famed mailboats of the Bahamas, connecting the archipelago's far-flung islands for more than 70 years. These days most locals rely on tiny planes to get to where they're going. But the mailboats are still the smaller islands' lifelines, hauling everything from mail, food, schoolbooks and medical

equipment as they travel to places like Ragged Island and Deadman's Cay. The mailboats also still take passengers, whether they choose to journey this way to save money or due to a fear of flying. For the adventurous and patient, mailboats mean seeing the islands the way travellers experienced them decades ago, crossing the Caribbean Sea without the instant gratification of jet travel or wi-fi connection.

Mailboat schedules are highly unpredictable, contingent on everything from crew availability to weather to cargo delays. Maybe you've been hanging around the docks for days, waiting for a specific boat. Or maybe you've decided to hop on the first ocean-bound ship you see, caring more about the journey than the destination.

Once you're aboard, this is a no-frills ride. You're sharing the deck – or a basic cabin, for longer trips – with strangers. But if you're the kind of person to choose a mailboat, you're probably well versed in the pleasures of travelling like a local. Within hours you'll

JO CREBBIN / SHUTTERSTOCK

of water-filled limestone sinkholes and (allegedly) a giant birdlike creature known as the chickcharnee, who will grant you good luck as long as you're polite. Multiple days between inbound and outbound boats give you plenty of time to wander. Wherever you're headed, expect miles of rolling ocean, sunsets that look like oil paintings and silver carpets of stars.

❷ LIFE ON BOARD

There are two main kinds of vessels that ply the Bahamas' mail routes: older, slower freighters and newer, faster catamarans. Freighters offer on-deck

likely be chattering away with new friends, sharing warm Kalik beers and cans of Vienna sausages. Maybe you'll even earn an invitation to dinner when you arrive at your destination.

Where are you going? Maybe you're headed to Harbour Island, where celebrities swan across the pink sand beaches and party all night in tiny local bars. Perhaps you're bound for Long Island, where freedivers brave the chilly depths of Dean's Blue Hole, a 663ft (202m) sinkhole just off the sugar-white shoreline. Could be you're sailing for Inagua, the country's southernmost district, home to an enormous saltworks and some 80,000 flaming pink West Indian flamingos.

Travelling by mailboat, you can see a Bahamas that's a universe away from the casinos and tourist-crowded beaches of Nassau. There's Spanish Wells, a lobster-fishing community populated mostly by the intensely religious descendants of 17th- and 18th-century British settlers. There's Cat Island, where locals still practice obeah, a form of Afro-Caribbean spirituality passed down from the days of slavery. There's Andros, massive in size yet tiny in population, with its pine forests full

© ALPAMAYOPHOTO / GETTY IMAGES

PIRATE LIFE

The same seas travelled by mailboats today were once infested with pirate ships. From the early 1600s, pirates trawled these shallow waters for Spanish galleons to loot. The most famous of all was Edward Teach, best known as Blackbeard. He would tie lit fuses into his ebony beard before boarding an enemy vessel, often terrifying the captain into surrender.

 Watch boats load cargoes of fruit, fish and more at bright, bustling Potter's Cay in Nassau.

 Luxuriate on the pink sand beaches of Harbour Island ('Briland' to locals), a low-key but star-studded destination.

 Go bonefishing in the flats of the Abacos, a favourite of yachties and sportspeople.

seating and spartan cabins, while catamarans may have enclosed passenger lounges with TVs and snack bars. Long hauls offer simple meals like fish and rice 'n' peas.

● MAKE IT HAPPEN

Mailboats technically have schedules, but they are rarely followed. Your best bet is to go down to the docks (in Nassau, this is Potter's Cay) and ask around. Being flexible with your destination helps. Most boats leave around once a week and return between two and six days later. If waiting that long on a small island doesn't appeal, you can sometimes sail there and fly back (though keep in mind that many islands have infrequent air service). Advance booking of mailboats is not necessary, and passenger berths are often not full. Avoid travelling during Atlantic hurricane season, which typically lasts from summer to late fall. Though basic food is served on most boats, bringing your own snacks and water is highly advisable. **EM**

 Dive the continental shelf off Andros, where shallow seas drop suddenly to 6000 ft (1829m) depths.

 Paddle in the gin-clear waters alongside the famed swimming pigs of Big Major Cay.

 Watch thousands of sunset-coloured flamingos on the far-flung island of Great Inagua.

Río de la Plata

ARGENTINA AND URUGUAY

START **BUENOS AIRES, ARGENTINA**

END **MONTEVIDEO, URUGUAY**

DISTANCE **30 MILES (48KM)**

DURATION **2 HOURS**

One of the world's biggest estuaries, the Río de la Plata forms a sprawling natural border between Argentina and Uruguay. Crossing this expansive waterway, which eventually empties into the Atlantic Ocean, transports travellers from the exuberance and energy of Buenos Aires to the (slightly) more subdued and relaxed ambience of Montevideo. After exploring the Argentinean trifecta of tango, football and perfectly grilled pampas-raised beef, ease into the heritage architecture and glorious art nouveau cityscape of the Uruguayan capital.

❶ RIDING THE WAVES

It's not often that you can hop a boat between two major capitals, but with this trip you can soak up the sights, sounds and tastes of both Buenos Aires and Montevideo. Before departing Buenos Aires, visitors may pay homage at the labyrinthine Cementerio de la Recoleta, the final resting place of former Argentinean first lady Eva Perón. Concealed amid the cemetery's ornate mausoleums, the simple plaque remembering her is surprisingly humble. To the southeast, Evita delivered speeches from the balcony of the Casa Rosada in the 1940s, and nearby, Las Madres de Plaza de Mayo (the Mothers of the Plaza de Mayo) hold poignant vigils every Thursday to remember the victims of Argentina's repressive military dictatorship, in power from 1976 to 1983. In today's less fraught times, traditional tango music is still celebrated in the city's milongas (dance halls or dance parties), and lessons are a popular activity for visitors to the city.

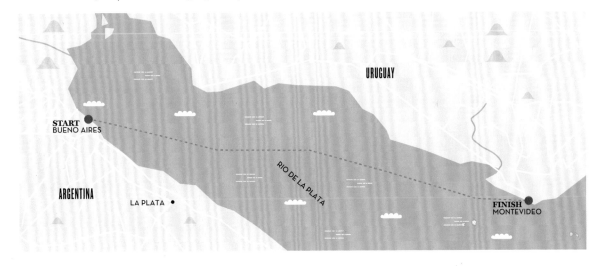

Between turns on the dance floor, watching football and enjoying quite possibly the world's best grilled meat are consistent passions for the Porteños who inhabit this city on the Río de la Plata. On Sunday the weekly San Telmo feria (street fair) combines buskers, antiques and craft stalls, and the opportunity for a leisurely lunch Buenos Aires–style.

Take leave of these delights from Buenos Aires' compact Dársena Norte harbour. Although travellers' final views of Buenos Aires as they depart for Montevideo may be the modern office buildings lining the city's redeveloped Puerto Madero docks, you'll hopefully be taking vivid memories of Argentinean history, culture, sports and cuisine after your time in the city. The entry into the River Plate is marked by passing the Yacht Club Argentino on the vessel's starboard side. Designed by the French architect Eduardo Le Monnier in 1911, the building has a tower, crafted to look like a lighthouse, that offers heritage balance to the boxy modern buildings diminishing in the ferry's wake as it begins its journey to another country.

Expanding to a maximum width of 140 miles (225km) when it enters the Atlantic Ocean, the broad confluence of the Uruguay and Paraná Rivers can resemble a vast sea as the Buquebus ferry makes its way east to Montevideo. On the port bow, the historic city of Colonia del Sacramento in Uruguay slips by on the northern riverbank; the meaning of the Río de la Plata's alternative English name of 'River of Silver' is accentuated when the riverine expanse glistens in southern hemisphere sunlight. Ahead are the considerable distractions of Montevideo.

From Montevideo's restored 19th-century ferry terminal, it's a short walk to the city's Mercado del Puerto. Another of Montevideo's most-loved heritage buildings, the market is packed with parrillas, grill restaurants especially popular with locals during weekends. Recommended form is to begin with a medio y medio aperitivo, a refreshing fifty-fifty split of sparkling and still white wines, before devouring grilled meat, vegetables and seafood.

After a serving of matambre (rolled beef stuffed with hard-boiled eggs, vegetables and herbs), a stroll around Montevideo's Rambla is almost mandatory. Hugging the Río de la Plata for almost 14 miles (23km), the Rambla is often busy with Montevideo locals fishing, walking, running and biking.

❷ LIFE ON BOARD

On board the modern ferries crossing the Río del Plata, there are various passenger classes and experiences. Most affordable is economy class, with seating in a shared cabin, while a slight upgrade to tourist class provides access to a more spacious

 Learn to dance the tango at La Viruta, a popular Buenos Aires milonga.

 Search out bargains at the San Telmo feria to a soundtrack of street performers.

 Ease out of Buenos Aires next to the elegant profile of the Yacht Club Argentino.

LEFT: Puente de la Mujer in Buenos Aires. **PREVIOUS PAGE:** The Barrio Histórico of Colonia del Sacramento, Uruguay.

cabin. Cafes offer drinks and light snacks; a good combination is a café cortado (espresso with a dash of milk) with a medialuna (small Argentinean-style croissant). Business class travellers can expect more comfortable seating, a spacious cafe area, and complimentary coffee, pastries, sparkling wine and snacks throughout the journey. Business class passengers also receive priority boarding privileges. Although the crossing to Uruguay is relatively short, a duty-free shop is open during the journey.

❸ OTHER ROUTES

There are also regular ferry crossings from Buenos Aires to the port town of Colonia del Sacramento, west of Montevideo. Colonia del Sacramento is one of Uruguay's oldest settlements, and the cobblestoned streets of the Barrio Histórico (Historical Quarter) date from the 17th century when the region was under Portuguese rule. Colonia del Sacramento is a popular day trip from Buenos Aires, and it's also possible to reach Montevideo from here by bus.

❹ MAKE IT HAPPEN

Most days there are two or three departures from Buenos Aires to Montevideo. Booking ahead on Buquebus is recommended, especially around weekends and public holidays. Bookings incorporating onward bus travel to the coastal Uruguayan resort of Punta del Este can also be arranged, along with multi-day packages (including accomodation) in Montevideo or Colonia del Sacramento. **BA**

THE *GRAF SPEE*

In December 1939 the Battle of the River Plate was WWII's first major naval battle. Three British Navy ships engaged with the *Graf Spee*, a German vessel attacking merchant shipping in the South Atlantic. The captain of the damaged *Graf Spee* eventually scuttled his ship in the neutral port of Montevideo to avoid further conflict.

 Appreciate the ocean-like expanse of the Río de la Plata as the ferry approaches Montevideo.

 Order up a feast at a parrilla at the Mercado del Puerto in Montevideo.

Join with Uruguayan locals strolling along Montevideo's spectacular Rambla waterfront esplanade.

Lake Titicaca

PERU

START PUNO

END TAQUILE

DISTANCE 22 MILES (35KM) ONE WAY

DURATION 1¹/₂ - 3 HOURS

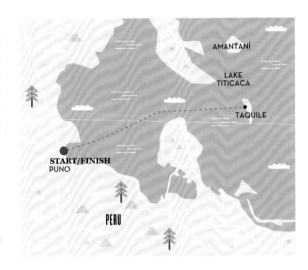

Get a sense of island pace on a boat journey from Puno across Lake Titicaca to Isla Taquile. Your simple boat slides by the human-made Islas Uros (Uros Islands), constructed from reeds, and then it's an hour of water, blue sky and scrolling clouds to ponder. The vast lake spans not only two countries, Peru and Bolivia, but also multiple cultures. Ahead of you is Isla Taquile, the stuff of fairy tales – a hilly island where men, and only men, knit colourful clothing, and women weave intricate waistbands. There may be no electricity, but this digital detox has knockout views in every direction – of the lake, Bolivian mountains in the distance, or stone archways on the island's paths.

❶ RIDING THE WAVES

There is a moment during the crisp morning on the lake when you realise the sun has flicked a switch, and the lake turns into a mirror of the blue sky. The pan-pipe player aboard the boat pauses, and in gentle unison everybody slides back the pleated window curtains to reveal the view. The glints of sunlight on the endless silver-blue water leave you dazzled, before you remember it could also be those 12,467ft (3800m) above sea level. This is Lake Titicaca, the largest lake

in South America and the loftiest navigable lake in the world. The view is all water except for the serrated Andes peaks embroidered onto the horizon.

You brave the boat's wind-chopped roof and witness stands of green reeds on either side, swaying in the wake of the boat. The yellow, human-made reed islets of Uros trickle by. White fishing dinghies bob, propelled among the reed gardens by long rowing poles. Children wave. Then Isla Taquile emerges into view. If you painted the island, you would just need a golden smudge for the hills and flicks of khaki for the kolle trees stretching, arms heavenward, towards a slab of blue.

As you shuffle through a stone archway on Taquile, sun-drenched nostalgia seeps through like a false memory. In the main square, imagine if this were your life. The men: sitting, knitting; wearing black trousers and vests, white shirts, and pom-pom beanies with colours declaring their marital status. The women: perched on a wall, dressed in an hourglass of

colours, crowned with a black headscarf. The lake in every direction, surprisingly high, so that if you gaze towards the horizon, you have to raise your head in reverence. The scent of lake breeze and grass.

Your homestay family give sun-weathered smiles and communicate in Quechua and gestures. The mother cooks a succulent herbed fish and quinoa soup inside a simple house capped in corrugated metal. Tonight there will be chicha to drink and dancing in Isla Taquile's main hall, but first you are led on a tour across the island's Inca-terraced hills. You cross paths with a woman herding sheep and a man skipping thread across knitting needles. You are headed to the most important site on the island, where the goddess Pachamama (Mother Earth) is honoured. You hike higher, sensing how important it is to your hosts that you see this. Bolivia's distant Cordillera Real becomes clearer. And then it appears, the 3000-year-old pre-Inca temple. The ragged, stacked brick walls are as sun-

© SAIKO3P / GETTY IMAGES

© JASON LANGLEY / ALAMY STOCK PHOTO

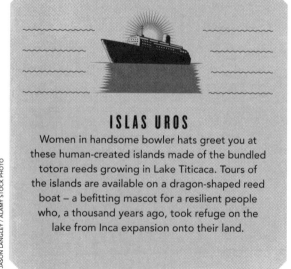

ISLAS UROS

Women in handsome bowler hats greet you at these human-created islands made of the bundled totora reeds growing in Lake Titicaca. Tours of the islands are available on a dragon-shaped reed boat – a befitting mascot for a resilient people who, a thousand years ago, took refuge on the lake from Inca expansion onto their land.

 Clamber to the upper deck for an unhindered view of Lake Titicaca and Puno.

 Step onto a human-created island made entirely of reeds at Islas Uros.

 Ride a dragon boat around Islas Uros for total tranquillity.

CLOCKWISE FROM LEFT: The floating islands at Uros; stone walls on Isla Taquile; hilltop view of Lake Titicaca. **PREVIOUS PAGE:** Uros reed boats and structures.

soaked as the soil around it, and its roof is the heavens above, with a magnificent blue in every direction, blending sky and lake.

❷ LIFE ON BOARD

The flat, ferry-like boats have comfortable seats, large windows and sometimes-windy upper decks. There is no variation in seating class, and different tour agencies can charge very different prices for the same seats. These transport vehicles don't offer food, though tours include lunch on Taquile.

❸ OTHER ROUTES

Speedboats are smaller and take half the time to reach the island, though the jerky movements can be harder going for people who have not acclimatised to the altitude. You can catch a slightly cheaper ferry from Puno port without a tour, but you will still need to pay the small entry fee to Isla Taquile. Be sure to double-check with the captain that there will be a return ferry.

❹ MAKE IT HAPPEN

Boats to Isla Taquile run multiple times a day in the mornings. You can book tickets at any agency in Puno the day before; public ferries from the port do not need to be booked in advance. Most tours stop only for lunch on Isla Taquile, but an overnight with a homestay is more rewarding and also beneficial to the community. Festivities devoted to Pachamama happen in January. June to August will have cold nights, but are dry and days are consistently sunny.

Bring snacks and water for the boat ride. There is no electricity on Isla Taquile, so pack accordingly. **PT**

 Step through stone archways that transport you into a different pace of life on Isla Taquile.

 Eat fresh quinoa soup with a family and learn about Isla Taquile's textile culture.

 Marvel at the starry light-pollution-free sky from a pre-Inca temple to Pachamama.

Amazon Exploration

PERU

START IQUITOS	
END SANTA ROSA	
DISTANCE 298 MILES (480KM)	DURATION 10 HOURS

 *Iquitos is the largest city not to be connected to the outside world by road. Marooned in the watery wilds of the northern Peruvian jungle, Iquitos is all about the boat, and its most interesting river trip just got more accessible. It is now a mere 10 hours' float downriver to the tri-border shared with Colombia and Brazil, and in contrast to the ponderous cargo boats or cramped speedboats of old, CONFLUAM's speedboat ferry transports you there in (relative) comfort, without sky-high cruise ship fees. So enter*

the planet's largest, longest waterway and the 298-mile (480km) finale of its Peruvian portion: brush against some of the most biodiverse areas on earth, spy pink dolphins cavorting on the currents or sloths swinging in the bankside trees, and immerse yourself in the spectacles of the Amazon River.

❶ RIDING THE WAVES

There were the adventuring conquistadors' boats, and the rubber barons' boats, and then, once Iquitos became a big river port, the cumbersome cargo boats, but the latest craft to attempt to master the mighty Amazon in Iquitos is CONFLUAM's high-speed ferry. (It stands for Conscorcio Fluvial del Amazonas.) Provided you can rise at the ungodly hour of 3am to be at port for departure, you can benefit from the change. Luxury, as you may be thinking when you stand rubbing your eyes in the dead of night at the crowded embarkation point, is a misleading moniker

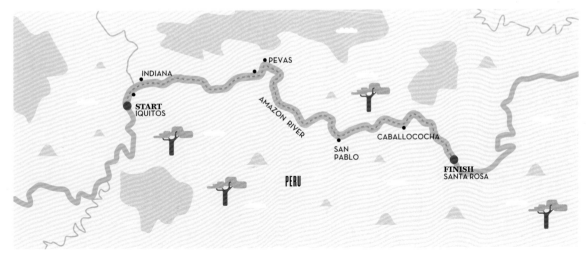

for this trip. It is important to realise, however, that CONFLUAM's boats, with their reclining leather seats, tables and complimentary meals, are a sight more sumptuous than any other vessel to have offered the Iquitos–Santa Rosa route at an affordable price.

Iquitos, the embarkation point, is not a city to leave in a hurry. This energetic, engrossing metropolis, part shanty town and part colonial tiled mansions, will certainly imprint itself on your senses, whether at its swanky river-facing restaurants or at its floating market, Belén, where all manner of jungle products from insect larvae to bottled ayahuasca to shamanic perfumes are vended in colourful, grubby chaos. A sleep-befuddled you might be harbouring doubts about this particular ride while you sit bumped side to side against your dozing fellow passengers. As the ferry revs up and shoots off into the surprisingly chilly night, the last electric light you will lay eyes on for a long while is soon left far behind.

The sheer scale of their country means Peruvians have become accustomed to sleeping on public transport, but despite the well-appointed appearance of the boat, you might not find shut-eye so simple. This is because the Amazon is no gentle river but a raging, muddy torrent over 1 mile (2km) wide at this point, carrying a rapidly rising and falling mass of water, debris as big as large trees, and an indeterminable number of boats sharing navigable space, from indigenous canoes to colossal logging and oil-extraction ships. Keeping a smooth course at the speed CONFLUAM rushes downstream is beyond any captain.

Dawn, arriving after two hours of travel, makes the early start worthwhile. Look out in the rapidly quickening stickiness of the morning for the best wildlife sightings. Pink river dolphins are easily seen dipping and diving ahead of the boat, while caimans occasionally lounge on the muddy banks and sloths languish in the treetops. Because of the boat's speed

RIGHT: A home near Iquitos.
PREVIOUS PAGE: The Upper Amazon Basin. **NEXT PAGE:** An Amazon dolphin; taking an add-on guided tour during an Amazon stay.

and distance from shore, sightings are not what they would be on a dedicated wildlife-watching excursion: this vessel's object is getting you from A to B, pronto. But when the wildlife eludes you, human activity provides the eye candy. Families fish from peki-pekis (canoes with spluttering outboard motors tacked on) and garishly painted, antiquated riverboats shunt cargo ranging from cars to logs to plantains. The foliage sporadically yields to reveal gaggles of clapboard or log-built residences raised on stilts to escape the frequent floods, or cleared areas where the locals are engaged in an impromptu football match.

Few stretches of the river are primary jungle (jungle unaffected by human activity and thus much more wildlife-rich) in the early part of the voyage, although as the ferry nears Pevas, the approximate midway point, you are closing in on zones of exceptionally high flora and fauna biodiversity. Pevas, the most intriguing port of call, is the oldest town on the

Amazon but is best known these days for being the residence of one of Peru's most talented contemporary artists, Francisco Grippa. Grippa's beautiful gallery, displaying paintings inspired by two decades of living in the Amazon, makes for a magical stop.

After Pevas, similar scenes and scenery flash on repeat from port and starboard, until, after a half-day of travel, a red-and-white-striped lighthouse and a 'Welcome to Peru' banner above a cluster of thatched huts emerge from the vegetation. Passengers know that they have arrived at Santa Rosa, Peru's border town: the end of one voyage and the beginning of another, should time and inclination allow pursuit of the Amazon's journey further downriver, to Colombia, Brazil and the Atlantic Ocean.

❷ LIFE ON BOARD

The seating is as comfortable as you will find on any regular river transport in this neck of the woods: it is padded and reclines a long way. Your complimentary breakfast and lunch are served on tables.

❸ OTHER ROUTES

CONFLUAM's ferries are upper end but not top-of-the-line. More sedate luxury cruises, bookable many weeks in advance and for much more money, trawl the same route. These include Aqua Expeditions (www.aquaexpeditions.com) or Rivers and Forest Expeditions (www.rfexpeditions.com). On these trips there will be breaks along the way to take smaller boats up into the Amazon's tributaries.

You could also drop down a comfort zone and grab a berth on a cargo ship departing from Iquitos's Puerto Masusa dock, for a price similar to a CONFLUAM ferry. The voyage takes four times as long (almost two days) but the experience is even more

Discover the chequered history of the region's rivers at Iquitos's Historical Ships Museum, exhibited on a century-old riverboat.

Hit the vibrant bars and restaurants of the malecón (riverside promenade) in Iquitos.

Experience dawn etching itself over the Amazon River.

colourful, as your fellow passengers are locals bound for various intermediate stop-offs and are travelling with their baggage, often of the still-alive variety.

O MAKE IT HAPPEN

Boats depart daily from Iquitos about 4am, from Puerto Enapu. Book tickets the day before at CONFLUAM's Iquitos office. You generally get downriver to Santa Rosa, the Peruvian border settlement, in eight to 10 hours, depending on water levels (lower water means longer runs). Here you can either return by ferry or use Santa Rosa's immigration facilities and switch to other vessels to continue to Leticia, Colombia, or Tabatinga, Brazil. In Tabatinga you can proceed downriver towards the Atlantic Ocean on other craft. Going one-way all the way down is best. In dry season (May to October), water levels are low, but animal sightings are better. **LW**

AL FRÍO Y AL FUEGO

This floating restaurant, moored in the mouth of the Itaya River, serves some of the best food in the Peruvian Amazon in unforgettable surroundings. The dining adventure starts with a magical boat journey from Iquitos. While you wait to sample the restaurant's superb river fish dishes, swim in the pool or admire the city lights glimmering across the water.

 Spy pink river dolphins, sloths, monkeys and numerous birds as you voyage downriver.

 Alight at Pevas, home to one of Peru's greatest living artists.

 Cap off the odyssey by crossing the border by boat into Colombia or Brazil and carrying on downriver as far as the Atlantic.

The Galápagos Islands

ECUADOR

START **SANTA CRUZ**

END **SAME**

DISTANCE **VARIABLE BASED ON ITINERARY**

DURATION **8-15 DAYS**

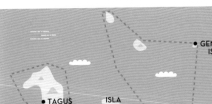

In 1835 a young naturalist named Charles Darwin set foot on a remote archipelago, 600 miles (966km) west of South America's coastline, and was astonished by the weird, wild and wonderful creatures he found there. Nearly 200 years later, a cruise to the Galápagos Islands, which are part of Ecuador, represents the holy grail for wildlife lovers – a once-in-a-lifetime journey into a strange world of swimming iguanas, flightless birds and giant tortoises, where nature still holds the upper hand. It's certainly not cheap, but this is a journey you'll never forget.

❶ RIDING THE WAVES

Discovered by chance in 1535 by Tomás de Berlanga, a hapless Spanish missionary who was attempting to sail from Panama to Peru, for centuries the Galápagos Islands – or the Enchanted Isles, as they were known to early sailors – were only visited sporadically by whaling ships or expedition vessels, such as Darwin's visit in 1835 aboard HMS *Beagle*. Since 1959, 3077 sq miles (7970sq km) of the Galápagos has been a national park, and since 1978 the archipelago has been a Unesco World Heritage Site. Access is now strictly controlled by Ecuador's National Park Service: only a few areas are open to visitors, all vessels must follow

designated routes, and groups must be accompanied by trained naturalists at all times. All these important initiatives are designed to protect the islands' fragile ecosystems, which are threatened on many fronts, from invasive species to pollution, habitat loss and climate change.

While it's possible to visit in your own yacht, the most straightforward way for ordinary mortals to visit the Galápagos is to join an organised cruise. Carrying from around 12 passengers up to 100, cruises are a surprisingly eco-friendly way to explore: by living on board and exploring each island in small Zodiac boats, the environmental impact of each visitor is greatly minimised. Vessels range from liveaboard dive boats to luxurious cruisers complete with cocktail bars, lecture rooms, restaurants and even gyms – all a long way from the *Beagle*, where scurvy and typhus were commonplace, and the evening menu consisted of salted meat, ship's biscuit and the occasional side order of seabird or giant tortoise.

Most cruises last between five and 15 days, leaving from the populous main island of Santa Cruz before heading out into the distant reaches of the archipelago. Here the real exploration begins. After stopping at the deserted island of North Seymour to see colonies of giant tropicbirds and blue-footed boobies, you'll venture onwards to Isabela, the largest island in the archipelago at 60 miles (97km) long, and one of its most volcanically active. Isabela has five active volcanoes, including Volcán Wolf, which spectacularly erupted in 2015. Here, and on nearby Fernandina, boats moor in remote bays and coves for myriad adventures: snorkelling with sea lions and manta rays, wandering dusty trails in search of land iguanas, finches and lumbering giant tortoises, or gazing over black lava fields and rocky cliffs inhabited by tropical penguins and Nazca boobies. Since the animals have little experience (or fear) of humans, it's possible to get astonishingly close to the wildlife. It's like starring in your own nature documentary, only here the animals are right in front of you rather than mediated through a screen or camera lens.

As the days glide by, the treasures of the Galápagos gradually reveal themselves. You'll spend one day watching marine iguanas basking on black volcanic rocks, Sally lightfoot crabs skittering over the sand, and frigate birds skimming low over the beach. The next, you'll be swimming on a rocky reef, surrounded by angelfish, sea turtles and eagle rays. Sadly, not all the islands' wildlife has fared well since human contact: on Floreana, all the island's giant tortoises had already been wiped out by the time Darwin arrived in 1835, while nearby Santa Fe became infamous as the home of Lonesome George, a Pinta Island tortoise that was the last survivor of his species. Since his death in 2012, he has become a figurehead for the fight to save the Galápagos' animals, and a sobering reminder of the fate that awaits them if we fail.

 Watch blue-footed boobies perform their signature dance on North Seymour Island.

 Swim with friendly sea lions at Urbina Bay on Isabela Island.

 Hike up from the old pirates' hideout of Tagus Cove on Isabela Island.

CLOCKWISE FROM LEFT: Pinnacle Rock on Bartolomé Island; a Sally Lightfoot crab; flightless cormorants and marine iguana, Fernandina Island. **PREVIOUS PAGE:** Playing in the waters near South Plaza Island off the coast of Santa Cruz. **NEXT PAGE:** Puerto Villamil snorkelling and diving.

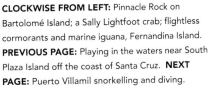

GALÁPAGOS FACTS

Roughly 50% of the land species and 20% of the marine species in the Galápagos occur nowhere else on earth. The Galápagos are home to the only penguin in the northern hemisphere, and its giant tortoises live up to 150 years; the temperature at which eggs are incubated determines their sex. The island's volcanoes are caused by their location between three tectonic plates – the Pacific, Cocos and Nazca.

And then, all too soon, after looping around the southeastern island of Española and the distant northern islands of Pinta, Marchesa and Genovesa, the adventure is over. One morning the big island of Santa Cruz looms on the horizon, and before you know it, you find yourself plunged back into the hectic human world of street traffic, blaring TVs, souvenir sellers and busy markets. After days of open skies, deserted islands and endless horizons, it's a transition that requires a few days of adjustment – and one which, no doubt, Darwin himself experienced.

'The archipelago is a little world within itself,' he wrote in 1839's *Voyage of the Beagle*. 'Both in space

 Watch thousands of frigatebirds, storm petrels, lava herons and red-footed boobies on Genovesa Island.

 See thousands of marine iguanas basking on rocks at Punta Espinoza, Fernandina Island.

 Learn about giant tortoise conservation at the Charles Darwin Research Station, Santa Cruz Island.

and time, we seem to be brought somewhat near to that great fact – that mystery of mysteries – the first appearance of new beings on this earth.'

❷ LIFE ON BOARD

Conditions vary depending on the vessel. Some are basic (bunk berths, shared meals), others surprisingly luxurious (private cabins, on-board restaurants, lecture rooms). Meals are usually included in the price.

❸ OTHER ROUTES

The route described incorporates all the islands, but most trips just explore one group (either eastern, western or northern), lasting between five and 15 days.

❹ BUDGET ALTERNATIVE

If you're on a budget, it's possible to base yourself on Santa Cruz and take day trips to nearby islands such as Rábida, North Seymour, Bartolomé or Pinzón.

❺ MAKE IT HAPPEN

Boats generally depart every couple of weeks. Bookings can be made through many travel agencies; Columbus Travel (www.galapagosisland.net) is a good starting point. Most cruises depart from Santa Cruz, which has regular flights from Baltra to the mainland city of Guayaquil in Ecuador, with onward connections to Santiago, Chile. Some flights and cruises depart from the island of San Cristóbal. For the calmest seas and warmest temperatures, December to May is ideal. Cooler temperatures and choppier waters from June to November can bring good deals.

For advice on travelling responsibly in the Galápagos, consult the Galápagos Conservancy (www.galapagos.org) or the Galápagos Conservation Trust (https://galapagosconservation.org.uk). Most boats provide snorkels, masks and fins, but bring hiking sandals or reef shoes, as there are wet landings on many islands. Crossings can be rough; take seasickness medication if sensitive to motion. **OB**

Patagonia and Tierra del Fuego

CHILE

START PUNTA ARENAS	
END PUERTO WILLIAMS	
DISTANCE 349 MILES (561KM)	**DURATION 36 HOURS**

Exploration has stood at the heart of Patagonia and Tierra del Fuego since the first humans paddled their canoes through these glacier-bound passageways past thousands of craggy isles. To this day the region remains largely roadless and inaccessible by land, which means that boarding a ship is the best way to visit this wild country. The journey brings you in reach of ancient cultures and a fast-changing glacial landscape in Chile. Connecting Punta Arenas to the remote outpost of Puerto Williams, the ferry Yaghan is your no-frills ticket to explore this realm, drawing hale travellers and hikers bound for Isla Navarino.

❶ RIDING THE WAVES

In the south of Chile, the mainland dissipates and the Pacific Ocean scatters the continent into thousands of islands, with narrow channels cutting through forests that have never known the blade of an axe. This same spellbinding landscape was visited by explorer Ferdinand Magellan in 1520 and naturalist Charles Darwin in the 1830s. Long before their arrivals, the dugout canoes of Kawésqar and Yaghan people plied these waterways. Their traditional seafaring lifestyle continued up through the start of the 20th century.

Today you too can make this passage back through

maritime history by boarding the ferry *Yaghan*. From the port of Punta Arenas, the 230 ft (70m) car and passenger ferry travels through the Strait of Magellan to Puerto Williams, the southernmost town before Antarctica – a kind of last stop at the end of the world. Its passengers are varied: a ragtag mix of adventurers clad in Gore-Tex boots and Fuegian passengers burdened with provisions from the mainland, gifts, and even pets returning from a visit to the veterinarian.

For residents of this archipelago, these epic multi-day commutes are a way of life. Even if you don't

"Deep wilderness unmarred by human touch surrounds the ship: snowbound peaks, craggy isles."

speak Spanish, interacting with the locals turns out to be a big part of the trip. In turn, the Fuegians often turn their curiosity on their seatmates. Fewer than a hundred passengers ride aboard, and cafeteria lines become community gatherings as tin trays are filled with hot meals and tables are shared.

It's a cosy scene below decks, but it's what's outside that brought you here in the first place. Deep wilderness unmarred by human touch surrounds the ship: snowbound peaks, craggy isles and silent forests with vegetation too thick to penetrate. With binoculars you can scan the horizon for whales, Commerson's dolphins and sea lion colonies.

The best views come towards the end of the journey. Set your sights on glaciers. La Avenida de los Glaciares, or Glacier Alley, marks the entrance into Beagle Channel. Most of these glaciers in Parque Nacional Alberto de Agostini have names from far-flung Europe: Garibaldi, Pia, Romanche, Italia, España and Holanda. Bookmarked between steep ridges, these tidewater glaciers flow from the remote Cordillera Darwin mountains. Passengers bundle up and hit the decks to observe this awesome spectacle of nature. The views are beautiful but bittersweet, as these glacial fields are in the process of receding before our very eyes. Pried loose by meltwater, great chunks of ice crumble, booming into the sea, creating waterfalls and spewing tiny sunlit bergs.

Gliding further south, the ferry meets up with whatever weather system may be coming off Antarctica. Bright skies can make the whole liquid world shimmer. Or you might find blasting sleet prickling all exposed skin – there's a reason that

Yaghans travelled with bonfires burning on their canoes! Coming here is the only way to truly understand the mastery of these ancient seafarers. Adventurers by nature, Yaghan women skin-dived for mollusks and bathed their children in the numbing waters of the Beagle Channel to fortify them.

The ferry can drop hikers off at Chile's Parque Nacional Yendegaia, established in 2013, on demand. No tame national park, this former estancia (large-scale ranch) on mainland Tierra del Fuego sits in utter isolation. If you choose to disembark, you can hone your survival skills here, but bring your A game: the ferry does not return for days at a time and stops only in decent weather.

At last the destination is reached, well past midnight. In starry darkness the ferry is met by scores of Puerto Williams residents from naval families to guesthouse owners who come to take you to your lodgings in this hospitable, southernmost port of the world.

DETOUR TO DIENTES DE NAVARINO

This rugged five-day hiking circuit circles Isla Navarino's signature sawtooth spires (dientes means "teeth" in Spanish) through an eerie wilderness of secluded lakes and exposed rock. Pioneered by Lonely Planet author Clem Lindenmayer, who also named many of the mountain features, it is the world's southernmost continental trek. Book a guided trip for this hard 33-mile (53km) route with multiple mountain passes.

© BYVALET / ALAMY STOCK PHOTO

 Set sail from windy, wool-boom city Punta Arenas, grabbing a window seat for views.

 Get glimpses of Isla Dawson in the Strait of Magellan, site of a 19th-century mission and later a prison.

 Observe the wonders of Glacier Alley, with close-ups of the glorious Glacier Italia.

CLOCKWISE FROM LEFT: Passing Glacier Alley; colony of king cormorants; Beagle Channel near Puerto Williams at night. **PREVIOUS PAGE:** Beagle Channel. **NEXT PAGE:** Ushuaia port.

 Follow Charles Darwin's route in the HMS *Beagle* while plying the Beagle Channel.

 Consider detouring to remote Parque Nacional Yendegaia for a week of full wilderness immersion.

 Explore quirky Puerto Williams, a welcoming end-of-the-world outpost with outstanding seafood and nature excursions.

❶ LIFE ON BOARD

Built in 2011, the ferry *Yaghan* can take 184 passengers and 70 cars. Capacity on longer hauls is lower, at 75 seats. It's public transit, with both cheaper semi-reclining seats and more expensive Pullman seats that recline almost flat. A downstairs dining hall serves up simple meals, with accommodations made for special diets with advance notice.

❷ OTHER ROUTES

It's a 2.5 hour ferry ride from Punta Arenas to the capital of Chilean Tierra del Fuego, Porvenir, for a taste of the laid-back Fuegian life. It's a good day trip or an overnight to combine with a tour to the region's only king penguin colony. From Puerto Natales, shortcut to the lower end of the Carretera Austral (Chile's famous 'southern road') via the new 41-hour ferry service to Puerto Yungay. It also stops in the World Heritage site of Caleta Tortel, a whole town built on boardwalks. Ushuaia, Argentina is another possible destination.

❸ LUXURY ALTERNATIVE

If a luxury cruise is more your speed, check out Cruceros Australis, whose four-night journeys between Ushuaia and Punta Arenas operate between September and May. Trips stop at Cape Horn to visit the continent's southernmost lighthouse.

❹ MAKE IT HAPPEN

Ferry *Yaghan* has seven departures monthly. You can book online with Transbordadora Austral Broom in Punta Arenas, Chile; for January and February book at least 40 days in advance. The long hours of daylight make this trip extra spectacular in summer, though it's still worthwhile in the quieter but colder off-season. Non-residents must reserve Pullman seats but can switch to cheaper seats if they don't sell out with locals. It's best to travel this route as a one-way and book a one-way flight return, or continue to Ushuaia, Argentina, via motorboat (carry your passport). **CM**

ASIA

AMAZING BOAT JOURNEYS

Komodo National Park

INDONESIA

START **LABUAN BAJO, FLORES**

END **SAME**

DISTANCE **75 MILES (121KM)**

DURATION **3 DAYS**

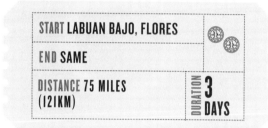

There are a dozen reasons to take one of these voyages through some of Indonesia's most stunning islands, assuming you even need a reason at all: who doesn't want to glide idly past uninhabited islands, bathe in azure water and hike to stunning viewpoints? But in addition to all that, on your tour around the islands of Komodo National Park you might possibly catch sight of a dragon. While the chances are slim that you'll actually get eaten, you'll feel a bit like you're walking behind the professor in Jurassic Park, knowing that a hungry reptile might come crashing out through the bushes. Just don't laugh it off too much – male Komodo dragons can weigh as much as 200 lbs (90kg), and can run faster than you'd expect.

❶ RIDING THE WAVES

There are any number of ways to make the trip through the islands of Komodo National Park, from day jaunts to simple overnights to two-, three-, even week-long (or longer!) excursions that will make you feel like you've got all the time in the world. Many of the medium-length trips begin on the island of Flores, known for coffee and its quiet fishing lifestyle. The airport in Labuan Bajo is only 15 minutes from the

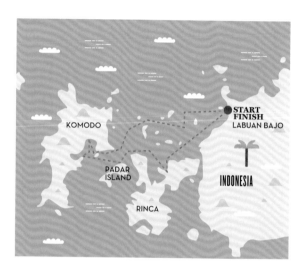

docks; you board your craft, and within moments the motors are humming and you're heading out to sea.

A common itinerary zips you to Manta Point for a swim with these giant underwater gliders, then a stop at Komodo's Pink Beach. Depending on the time of day, Pink Beach may or may not be pink – the colour comes not from the sand but from the sun's angle, the tide and the weather conditions. Without the pink, Pink Beach is just a typical beach; though pretty, it's one of the few stops that you might consider optional. From there, head to a nearby harbour, have dinner and watch as thousands of flying foxes (a fruit-eating bat) emerge from their daytime shelters and head off in search of food. This is not a 'tornado' of bats like some insect-eating, cave-dwelling bats create, but it's a beautiful scene and makes a lovely end to a day on the water.

Day two, done right, will include Komodo Island in the morning, as the lizards are most active and visible when they're hungry. You'll arrive at the dock shortly after breakfast, pay the Komodo National

Park fees and choose a viewing path: short, medium, or long. Though results vary because the animals are wild, chances are you'll soon be taking a selfie with (well, actually behind and a safe distance away from) the famed Komodo dragon. The jungle here is fascinating, filled with unique flora and birds, so even if you only see a few lizards, it's a lovely and interesting visit. Eventually the trail will circle back, and you'll end with the option to buy some T-shirts and souvenirs.

What happens next will depend on the weather, because while you can get up close and personal with the dragons rain or shine, the view from Padar Island's lookout peak just isn't quite the same if it's cloudy, rainy or obscured by fog. If the day is clear and bright, the boat will head here next, and you'll have an unrivalled view of Padar Island's perfect scalloped bays, with turquoise water surrounding green hills so beautiful they seem computer-generated. It's one of the world's greatest views, and your trip won't be complete without it.

On day three, you'll repeat the Komodo dragon

HEED THE RANGERS' WARNINGS

Never venture out into the jungle on your own. Rangers are trained not only in seeing Komodo dragons (which are masters at camouflage) but also in defending against them. In 2017 a Singaporean tourist was badly mauled by a lizard when he tried to enter the Komodo National Park alone to avoid paying the entry fee.

© TAN YILMAZ / GETTY IMAGES

experience but on Rinca Island. Rinca, smaller but more wild, offers a good chance to see lizards if you didn't see them (or didn't see enough of them) on Komodo Island. From here, the boat will chug or sail its way back to Labuan Bajo, arriving in early to late afternoon. Longer voyages will see more, do more, stop more and explore more, but these highlights are the region's crowning glories.

❷ LIFE ON BOARD

Tour operators vary widely. In most cases the tours will not include the Komodo National Park fees, but some of the higher-end ones do. Low-end tours will include a simple cabin room and three meals (simple but tasty Indonesian food), and may or may not have fans for cooling; they will not have English guides. Higher-end trips will include a cabin with air-conditioning, an English-speaking guide/captain, gourmet-quality food, and possibly dive or snorkel equipment. While most boats are motorised, you may want to opt for the quiet serenity of a sailing vessel.

© MARTIEN JANSSEN / 500PX

 Swim with giant manta rays in waters that seem too turquoise to be real off Manta Point.

 If the sun and weather combine in the right way, see why Komodo Island's Pink Beach gets its name.

 Watch flying foxes silhouetted by a coral sunset when the boat stops for the night.

❸ OTHER ROUTES

Another route begins the voyage not in Flores but in Lombok, where you visit some island villages, view boat-making and see other tourist sites before embarking. On the way to the Komodo area, you'll likely stop at Satonda Island, a doughnut-shaped island with an ocean-filled crater in the centre.

❹ MAKE IT HAPPEN

Tours depart daily, weekly, or several times monthly depending on the length and the package. You can book through any number of tour companies, but be careful in your choice as some operators are less than scrupulous. A round trip from Labuan Bajo on Flores is popular; the best time of year to go is March. All visits to the dragons must be done with a guide. **RB**

CLOCKWISE FROM TOP: Padar Island in the Komodo National Park; a Komodo dragon; a beach on Gili Air island.
PREVIOUS PAGE: Boat moored at Kelor Island.

© BARRY KUSUMA / GETTY IMAGES

 Take a selfie up close and personal with the world's largest lizard in Komodo National Park.

Hike on Padar Island to one of the world's most incredible scenic views.

 Snorkel in crystal-clear water at Kanawa Island, seeing fish, turtles and coral galore.

Halong Bay

VIETNAM

START **HALONG CITY**

END **SAME**

DISTANCE **ABOUT 20 MILES (32KM)**

DURATION **2 DAYS**

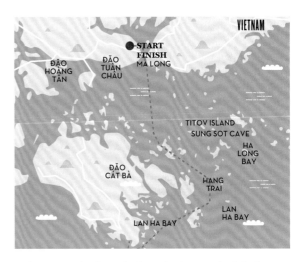

Cruise the emerald waters of Halong Bay, 'where the dragon descends into the sea', a mystical location where limestone peaks soar skyward from the sea. Halong Bay is nature at its most expressive, a dramatic collection of rock sculptures hewn over the centuries and sheltering the Vietnamese coast. Spending a night on board a junk is the perfect way to experience the magic of Halong Bay, undoubtedly the leading attraction in northern Vietnam. There are more than 3000 limestone karst islands scattered throughout the bay, and exploring hidden caves and grottoes by kayak is a natural high.

❶ RIDING THE WAVES

Designated a World Heritage site by Unesco in 1994, Halong Bay is a vision of ethereal beauty and, deservedly, the most well known of tourist attractions in northern Vietnam. Busy Halong City is perhaps not the most glamorous gateway to Vietnam's most iconic attraction, but the views across the water to the monumental karsts rising out of the water are a teaser for what is to come. On a misty day, shadowy shapes loom on the horizon like an invading army of tall ships. On a clear day, you can see a forest of stone sentinels standing guard over the Gulf of Tonkin.

As you cruise into the bay, the karsts shed their uniformity, and their individual characteristics begin to shine. Some are tall and gnarly, like bony fingers pointing to the heavens; others are small and dumpy but conceal secluded caves or lagoons. Here and there are glimpses of the white sand, hidden coves and secret beaches that dot the bay.

Your first stop might be Dau Tien Ong, a karst cave that includes some archaeological relics from early fishing communities that sheltered here in the Hoa Binh era, dating back to 2000 BC. There are gaggles of stalactites and stalagmites, and the usual debate ensues over which are which, let alone how to spell them. Guides point out some formations resembling animals, including a peacock and a crocodile, although you might need to use some imagination to reach the same conclusion.

Depending on the crowds, different caves are featured on the cruise. Hang Sung Sot, or Surprise Cave, is one of the largest, with three immense chambers. In the second chamber is a kitschy, rose-lit,

LEFT: © VICHAI PHUBUBUPHAPAN / ALAMY STOCK PHOTO; RIGHT: © MATT MUNROO / LONELY PLANET

© JUNPHOTO / SHUTTERSTOCK

 Climb 420 steps on Titop Island for great photo ops with a stunning bird's-eye view of Halong Bay.

See Cua Van, a small floating village in the heart of the bay, with colourful houses that are an iconic image.

 Explore the hidden lagoons or sea caves of some of the karsts.

WHERE THE DRAGON DESCENDS INTO THE SEA

Halong translates as 'where the dragon descends into the sea', and legend says that this mystical seascape was created when a great mountain dragon hurtled towards the coast, its flailing tail gouging out valleys and crevasses. As the creature plunged into the sea, the area filled with water, leaving only the pinnacles visible.

CLOCKWISE FROM LEFT: The Sung Sot Cave or Surprise Grotto on Bo Hon Island; a local guide takes a break; views of the limestone karsts are omnipresent. **PREVIOUS PAGE:** Traditional junks on Halong Bay. **NEXT PAGE:** Touring cruise ships.

island, so you have a chance to cool off after the climb.

The boat anchors for sunset, the ideal time to put your feet up and enjoy a beverage. For those feeling more motivated, try out a Vietnamese Master Chef challenge on board. Your chef demonstrates how to make a fresh spring roll, and the guests attempt their best interpretation. After dinner, there is an opportunity for a midnight dip, and nature's light show kicks in. The waters of Halong Bay are home to bioluminescence, caused by tiny glowing algae that light up the swimmers like Christmas decorations.

The next morning, you can explore Cua Van floating village, a cluster of brightly coloured houses set against the backdrop of some dramatic karsts. This is the largest fishing village in the bay, composed of almost 200 households all perched over the water. Most of the fish is farmed in homemade pens alongside the houses.

The highlight of the cruise is kayaking into a hidden lagoon, a secret sea cave that is only accessible during low tide. As you paddle through the mouth-like entrance, there is little sense of what is hidden beyond; it's like discovering Scaramanga's lair from the Bond film *The Man with the Golden Gun*. Swifts flit through the air, the limestone soars into the sky, and the kayaks feel tiny and insignificant as they bob about in the gloaming.

phallus-shaped formation that is revered as a fertility symbol by the Vietnamese.

Hang Dau Go is another gargantuan cave with disco lighting and a surplus of strange stalactites, including an international conference of garden gnomes in the first chamber. The cave derives its name, which means 'cave wooden stakes', from the role it played during the 13th-century battles with the Mongols, when locals stored iron-tipped wooden stakes here, later used in the Battle of Bach Dang to destroy Kublai Khan's invading fleet by impaling their ships.

Titop Island is a busy stop on the Halong Bay circuit for the panoramic views of the bay and its seemingly endless karsts in all their glory. The only catch is that you have to huff and puff up 420 stairs to earn the view, but it is worth the effort. Most of the incredible images you have seen of Halong Bay were taken from here, and this is the vantage point to see them for yourself. There is also a small beach at the base of the

❷ LIFE ON BOARD

A sail with Bhaya Cruise includes all meals with two lunches, dinner and breakfast. Depending on the boat, there are usually between two and 20 cabins on board,

 Watch the sun sink over the horizon in Halong Bay while sipping a gin and tonic on the deck.

 Take a night swim to see the bioluminescence of Halong Bay work its magic.

 Experience 'shock and oar' with a paddle as you kayak around these magnificent karsts.

"The highlight of the cruise is kayaking into a hidden lagoon, a secret sea cave that is only accessible during low tide."

and all have kayaks on board for exploring sea caves. Most leading operators offer the same setup.

❸ OTHER ROUTES

Explore the waters less cruised around Bai Tu Long Bay, an extension of Halong Bay stretching to the Chinese border. Treasure Junk (http://treasure-junk.com) offers affordable exploratory cruises here.

The southernmost part of Halong Bay is Lan Ha Bay, near Cat Ba Island, and this can be explored independently aboard charter boats from Cat Ba town.

❹ BUDGET ALTERNATIVE

The very cheapest Halong Bay cruises are the daily four- to six-hour cruises around the bay, departing from Bai Chay. Sign up here for a mere US$5 and pay entrance fees along the way. The best budget cruise is V Spirit Cruises.

❺ MAKE IT HAPPEN

Boats depart daily from Halong City and usually include transfers from Hanoi. You can book with Bhaya Cruise, or contact another tour operator for an all-inclusive tour. Most people visit Halong Bay as a side trip from the capital, Hanoi. However, independent travellers can connect with Cat Ba Island and Haiphong for onwards travel.

Halong Bay shines its brightest under clear skies, making the best times to go spring (March and April) and autumn (October and November). Summer months can be too wet, with the possibility of typhoons, and winter months are generally too cold.

Vietnam offers visa-free access to Asian nations and some European countries; check in advance. **NR**

Okinawa Islands

JAPAN

START **KAGOSHIMA, KYUSHU**	
END **NAHA, OKINAWA**	
DISTANCE **456 MILES (734KM)**	DURATION **25 HOURS**

Japan conjures up many images – crowded trains, neon lights, geishas, temples and shrines – but it's often forgotten that first and foremost, this is an island country. Besides the main islands that host an increasing number of visitors, there are abundant isolated islets to explore, each with its own fascinating history and culture. Island-hopping from Kyūshū port city Kagoshima to Okinawa is an incredibly rewarding journey that will take you far beyond the tatemae (public face) of Japan that is portrayed to the outside world. Discover the honne (private face) of this amazingly complex country by taking the ferry to its remote southwest islands.

❶ RIDING THE WAVES

This adventure lets you leapfrog across Japan's subtropical southwest islands between Kagoshima (pop 600,000) and Okinawa's main city of Naha (pop 320,000). On the way are stops and potential stopovers on the lovely, isolated islands of Amami-Ōshima, Tokunoshima, Okinoerabu-jima, Yoron-tō, and Motobu port on the main island of Okinawa-hontō. Get off, do some exploring, then hop on the next boat to come by.

Naze (名瀬), on the gorgeous island of Amami-

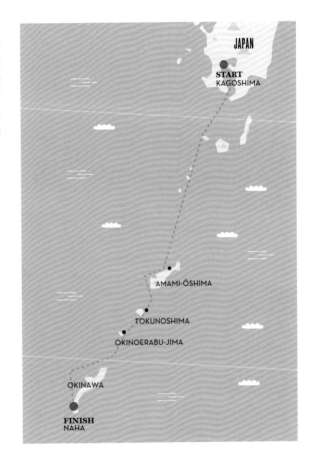

Ōshima (奄美大島), is the first port of call, 11 hours southwest of Kagoshima by ferry. This is the largest and most populous island on the journey between Kyūshū and Okinawa, with around 60,000 residents. Known for excellent beaches, dense jungle and unusual flora and fauna, Amami-Ōshima is home to the endemic Amami black rabbit, tree ferns and mangroves. It's where you can shift to the local island sense of time.

Just over three hours further on, the ferry will drop into Kametoku (亀徳) port on the intriguing island of Tokunoshima (徳之島; pop 23,000), known for its coastal rock formations and the unusual sport of tōgyū, a kind of bovine sumo. Instead of very large men trying to force each other out of a ring, however, these bloodless matches end when one bull retreats. Tōgyū is incredibly popular with locals, and there are 13 official venues on the tiny island.

Two hours down the line, the ferry stops at Okinoerabu-jima (沖永良部島), a sugar-cane-covered island of 13,000 souls, edged with excellent beaches, interesting coastal formations, blowholes and a living limestone cave sporting 1969ft (600m) of illuminated walkways. You'll also find Japan's biggest banyan tree, a whopper on the grounds of a local elementary school.

Yoron-tō (与論島), an hour and 40 minutes onward and within sight of the northern tip of Okinawa's main island, is possibly the most appealing of the islands. Only 3 miles (5km) across and with a population of 5000, it is fringed with white sand-speckled beaches and features spectacular Yurigahama (百合ヶ浜), a stunning stretch of white sand about 1640ft (500m) off the eastern coast that disappears completely at high tide. Small boats shuttle visitors out to Yurigahama when it is above the waves. In keeping with its sister-city relationship with Mykonos in Greece, the island has whitewashed buildings and even a terraced gallery cafe serving gyros.

The ferry drops into Motobu (本部) port, halfway down Okinawa's main island's western coast and 2½ hours onward from Yoron-tō, before making its final two-hour leg to Naha, Okinawa's bustling and colourful prefectural capital.

LOCAL DIALECTS

The Amami and Okinawa dialects of these islands are considered by Unesco to be 'endangered tongues'. Your best chance to hear them spoken is among the incredible number of island elderly: Okinawa and the southwest islands are said to have the highest concentration of centenarians in the world.

Depart Kagoshima under the watchful eye of Sakurajima, the smoking volcano just across the bay.

Explore Amami-Ōshima's dense jungle, tree ferns and fine beaches.

Enjoy Tokunoshima's intriguing coastal rock formations, beaches and traditional 'bovine sumo'.

ABOVE AND BELOW LEFT: A beach on Amami-Ōshima Island; the walls of Naha's Shuri Castle in Okinawa. **PREVIOUS PAGE:** Kagoshima Bay and Sakurajima volcano.

❷ LIFE ON BOARD

As you'd expect in Japan, these ferries are very organised. Second-class tickets will get you a sleeping mat in an open room, and the only leg on which you might think about splurging on a private room is the 11-hour stretch between Kagoshima and Amami-Ōshima. Consider taking your own supplies for the journey, although there is a restaurant, shop and vending machines on each ferry.

❸ OTHER ROUTES

To visit super-remote islands that most Japanese haven't even heard of, take the twice-weekly Ferry Toshima from Kagoshima to the Tokara-rettō (トカラ列島; www.tokara.jp), seven inhabited and five tiny,

uninhabited islands that offer plenty of hiking, fishing, onsen (hot springs) and outdoor opportunities. There are guesthouses on some of the islands, but taking a tent and ample food supplies is advised. Ferry Toshima can take you from Kagoshima via these fascinating tiny islands to Amami-Ōshima, the first port of call on the main Kagoshima–Okinawa route.

❹ MAKING IT HAPPEN

Marix Line and 'A' Line run the Kagoshima–Naha route on alternate days. The ferry company websites are in Japanese, so you may want to book ahead through an agency. There's a ferry heading in both directions each day between the start of May and the end of October. Both Kagoshima and Naha are easily accessed with flights from mainland Japan, so you can fly or train into Kagoshima, island-hop to Naha, and then fly back to wherever you want (or vice versa).

The ferries are large, carrying around 700 passengers, with most people travelling second class in open rooms with sleeping mats. **CM**

 Discover Okinoerabu-jima's impressive viewpoints, limestone cave, beaches and Japan's biggest banyan tree.

 Bathe at offshore Yurigahama, a stunning stretch of sand that disappears at high tide, near Yoron-tō.

 Arrive in Okinawa prefecture's capital, Naha, and explore the colourful, bustling streets and markets.

Kerala Backwaters

INDIA

START **ALLEPPEY**	
END **KOTTAYAM**	
DISTANCE **80 MILES (129KM)**	DURATION **3 DAYS**

The South Indian state of Kerala may be blessed with some 372 miles (600km) of magnificent Arabian Sea coast, complete with countless palm-fringed beaches, but the greatest jewel in its watery crown must be its enchanting backwaters. This 558-mile (900km) system of canals, rivers and glistening lakes gives credence to the state's long-held slogan, 'God's Own Country'. Spending a few days exploring these waterways and the tropical landscapes and villages that line them is one of the subcontinent's greatest experiences. To fully embrace the journey, hire a houseboat converted from a kettuvallam (rice barge) – it enables you to sleep and dine in style en route.

❶ RIDING THE WAVES

It's hard to forget the first time you set eyes on a *kettuvallam*, the boat's fanciful curves and armadillo-

like appearance seemingly jumping from the pages of a storybook. The excitement is only amplified when you step aboard for your houseboat trip on Kerala's backwaters. You'll rush about, quickly touring its confines and marvelling at the novel cabins, quirky spaces and natural materials everywhere. Don't be surprised if you even find yourself leaping onto your bed, gazing out the picture window and fantasising what views you'll wake up to in the mornings ahead.

Things soon get under way, and it's not long before the scenes of swaying palms on the lush banks pull your attention. Although not propelled by punters with bamboo poles as their predecessors were, modern diesel-powered *kettuvallam* houseboats still cruise at a pedestrian pace, which gives you plenty of time to absorb the array of sights on shore. It's a chance to witness the patterns of rural life – often unchanged in centuries – play out in ways you won't have seen in other parts of India. With the knowledge of the boat's crew at hand, you'll also learn the intricacies of the

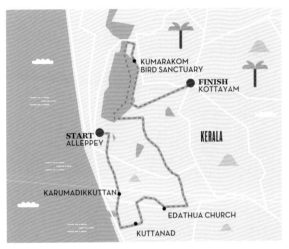

© SCORPP / SHUTTERSTOCK

backwaters' environment, economy and society.

Watch locals defy gravity as they make their way up coconut palm trees, and you'll soon understand why they are known as 'toddy-tappers'; their climb is either a foray to tap the tree and mount an earthenware pot to collect coconut sap, or a later trip to harvest the fermented proceeds. If you're willing to brave the powerful kick of a toddy (palm wine), ask to try some later that evening as there may well be some on board (if not, it won't take long for some to be procured).

Over the coming days you'll marvel at the many more ways these beautiful palms are used in Kerala (a state whose name means 'land of the coconut'). Witness ropes and coir being created from coconut fibre, mats being woven from the leaves, and furniture being manufactured from the wood. And come mealtime you'll appreciate the coconut even more, whether it's creamed into a devastatingly delicious

"Colours are brighter, movements are more pronounced, beauty and birdlife are everywhere."

fish curry, pulped into a tasty chutney or grated over a sweet dessert.

The Keralan cuisine is always a highlight of any houseboat cruise, particularly as it is enjoyed floating al fresco. Besides a bevy of fresh fruit in the morning, breakfasts may include dishes such as puttu (steamed rice powder and coconut), sambar (aromatic vegetable dal) or even dosas with coconut chutney. Lunch and dinner are typically rice-based and focus on a variety of sweet and sour curries spiced with a mix of chilli, ginger, cardamom, mustard seeds, pepper and cumin. Unsurprisingly, fresh seafood, such as pomfret, prawns and kingfish, is a specialty.

 Experience village life in Kuttanad, a region of narrow backwaters and beautiful paddy fields.

 Admire Karumadikkuttan, a 9th-century black granite figure of Lord Buddha that's been visited by the Dalai Lama himself.

 Visit Edathua Church, a key pilgrimage site for Kerala's Christians.

FROM LEFT: Thottada River enters the Arabian Sea; palms line the brackish Kerala lagoons, canals and lakes. **PREVIOUS PAGE:** Traditional *kettuvallams*. **NEXT PAGE:** Chinese fishing nets in Cochin.

FROM LEFT: © DANIEL J. RAO / SHUTTERSTOCK; © WAJ / SHUTTERSTOCK

You'll have no doubt about the ingredients' freshness as you'll have watched your crew doing some of the daily shopping en route, whether buying snapper from a passing fisher's boat or plucking pineapples from one of their own families' gardens. The distance from field to plate is also an incredibly short one as you make your way through the narrow backwaters of Kuttanad, a landscape dominated by picturesque rice paddies, and a place where farming is done below sea level. In areas such as this you'll have the opportunity to stop and wander through villages to further your understanding of Keralan culture. You can also visit important historical and religious sites such as the buddha statue Karumadikkuttan in Karumady.

The channels are so slender in places that you can actually watch the water levels rise ahead of you as the *kettuvallam* pushes its way along. Noticing subtleties such as this is perhaps only possible because of the relaxed pace. As you sit happy and relaxed in your chosen perch on the vessel's edge, your eyes even seem to register more than is usual – colours are brighter, movements are more pronounced, beauty and birdlife are everywhere.

More wonders await when you cross some of the larger lagoons and lakes such as Vembanad, where you'll be faced with some of the most intricate and ingenious fishing apparatuses you've ever seen. These large, cantilevered 'Chinese fishing nets' (as they are known in Kerala) are the unofficial emblems of the backwaters and are perhaps one of its most photographed features.

TIED UP IN KNOTS

Remarkably, the hulls of *kettuvallam* are constructed without the use of a single nail. Created by tying hundreds of long wooden planks together with coir knots, the structure is then waterproofed with coconut fibres and black resin extracted from stewed cashew kernels. Indeed, the literal translation of *kettuvallam* in the local Malayalam language is 'to tie-boat'.

 While in the waters of Vembanad Lake, cruise by Kumarakom Bird Sanctuary for a visual feast of feathered varieties.

 Marvel at the Chinese fishing nets along Kerala's shores, and dine on some freshly caught fish as well.

 Finish in Kottayam to enable your leap into the wilderness of the Western Ghats, protected home of elephants, tigers and more.

No matter what variety of sights and sounds you've encountered during your day, nights follow a gloriously similar pattern. The houseboat ties up alongshore in the midst of the scenery, allowing you time to soak up the sunset (and a drink or two) before dinner is served. Spend the rest of the evening contemplating the day, dreaming of tomorrow or watching a dramatic thunderstorm light up the horizon.

❷ LIFE ON BOARD

Houseboats, either converted from a *kettuvallam* or designed to look like it, are typically 82ft to 98ft (25m-30m) in length and around 13ft (4m) wide. Above the slender and shallow wooden hull is typically a hoop-shaped superstructure covered in delicately woven bamboo mats. This usually houses two or three en-suite cabins, a lounge, kitchen and dining area, as well as quarters for the crew and chef. Some larger varieties also have a raised upper deck with a canopy, enabling a 360-degree vantage point for viewing birdlife and the surroundings. With a captain, chef and well-stocked kitchen on board, you'll be well taken care of – Keralan dishes are always a particular highlight.

❸ MAKE IT HAPPEN

More than a thousand houseboats ply Kerala's network of inland waterways, so there is plenty of choice. Whether you cruise for a day or a week is up to you. Vessels can be chartered through travel agencies, hotels and guesthouses across Kerala, though there is an advantage (if you have the time and patience) to wait until you reach Alleppey, Kollam or Kottayam. These houseboat hubs have a plethora of private operators, and you'll be able to inspect your houseboat and negotiate costs before booking. Food, drink, a personal chef and driver/captain are generally included in the quoted cost. A basic houseboat for 24 hours is about ₹7500 (US$110) per person, with more luxurious options costing around ₹2,000 (US$175); larger, family-sized boats rise upwards of ₹20,000 (US$300). **MP**

Mekong River

VIETNAM AND CAMBODIA

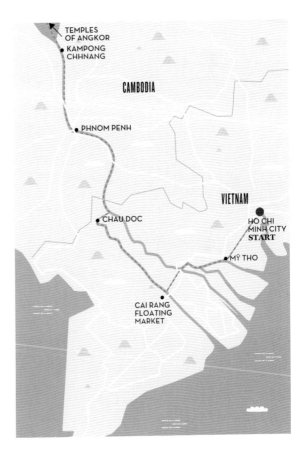

START	HO CHI MINH CITY
END	SIEM REAP
DISTANCE	APPROX. 405 MILES (652KM)

DURATION **4 DAYS**

One of the world's great rivers, the mighty Mekong descends from the Tibetan Plateau, winding its way through China, Myanmar, Laos, Thailand, Cambodia and Vietnam before spilling into the South China Sea, an epic journey of 2700 miles (4350km). Crossing from Cambodia into Vietnam, it splits into many tributaries searching for the sea, giving rise to its Vietnamese name Cuu Long (Nine Dragons). To follow the Mekong River upstream aboard the luxurious Aqua Mekong from Vietnam's commercial capital of Ho Chi Minh City (Saigon) to the ancient Khmer capital of Angkor is to pass through timeless landscapes, bustling towns and floating villages, all framed by the vibrant history and culture of these contrasting countries.

❶ RIDING THE WAVES

As you pull out of the city of Mỹ Tho in the Mekong Delta, river life in Vietnam is enchanting to observe. The bustling waterway oozes life, with traders, fishers, farmers and fruit sellers jostling for space. Even more atmospheric are the congested canals, visible at regular intervals, the 'side streets' of the delta. In a pancake-flat land that is flushed with floods during monsoon season, the rivers are equal to the roads. The Mekong

opens a gateway to the rhythms of an older Asia.

Befitting a commercial centre, Can Tho is ringed by floating markets, and the traders of Cai Rang make this the largest of the region's river malls. It brings together hundreds of tiny vessels selling fruit and vegetables, fish and flowers, and a splash of souvenirs. Observed from above, it's a riot of colour, broken only by the conical hats that protect the sellers from the beating sun.

© MATT MUNRO / LONELY PLANET

Chau Doc is a cultural crossroads where Vietnam meets Cambodia, a border town that is undeniably Vietnamese but has a fair share of Khmer influence. A delve into the history books reveals that the whole of the Mekong Delta region was part of Cambodia as recently as the 17th century, when Saigon was a Khmer village known as Prey Nokor.

Across the border in Cambodia, the Mekong is known as Tonlé Thom (Great Water), as it dominates the country and feeds the population. The riverside landscape is dotted with sugar palms and the sweeping roofs of Khmer temples. The river commerce that defines the delta in Vietnam grinds to a halt, and river traffic dries up here. On a gentle bicycle ride through a local village, you can see that life in Cambodia is lived at a calmer pace than in its bustling neighbours.

The Cambodian capital, Phnom Penh, may feel like a chaotic yet charming collision of Asia's past and present. Its top sights include the impressive National Museum of Cambodia, home to the world's greatest collection of Khmer sculptures, and the Royal Palace with its Silver Pagoda, so named for the 5000 silver tiles that carpet the floor. You can also tour the darkness of S-21 Prison (now the Tuol Sleng Genocide Museum), a former high school that was used by the Khmer Rouge to imprison and torture enemies of the revolution.

Branching off the Mekong River, the *Aqua Mekong* heads north towards the Tonlé Sap Lake and its unique communities of floating villages. Chhnok Tru is a floating village near Kompong Chhnang with all the trappings of a traditional Cambodian village – wooden houses, pens for pigs, a basic school, a petite clinic, even karaoke bars – but it all floats upon the water.

The incredible temples of Angkor, capital of the Khmer Empire, are the crowning glory of this waterborne journey. Home to one of the world's

TONLÉ SAP LAKE

The Tonlé Sap is the largest freshwater lake in Southeast Asia and a vital organ in the body of the Mekong. It acts as the lungs (or gills) of the river, breathing in each year to absorb the torrent of floodwaters that swell the Mekong River each year, acting as a natural flood barrier. A majority of the population around the lake pursue a living by catching fish and rice farming.

LEFT: © GUOZHONGHUA / SHUTTERSTOCK; RIGHT: © BUI LUAN / 500PX

Experience life in the fast lane with a two-wheeled Vespa tour of Ho Chi Minh City.

Rise early to see Cai Rang Floating Market, where all the stalls are boats, at dawn.

Visit the floating fish farms of Chau Doc.

most spectacular collections of temples, Angkor is the sacred skeleton of a vast empire that once stretched from Myanmar to Vietnam, and from Laos to Malaysia. Originally built as a centre of Hindu worship in the early 12th century, it was gradually converted to a site for Buddhist worship by the end of the century of its founding.

Jungle-clad Ta Prohm temple has been abandoned to the elements, a reminder of the riotous power of nature: tree roots embrace the crumbling stone like a muscular snake squeezing the last breath from its

victim. The scale of the great walled capital of Angkor Thom is simply staggering, and at the exact centre lies the enigmatic and enchanting temple of Bayon, the most expressive of Angkor's many monuments. Its 54 towers are each topped off with four faces, which bear more than a passing resemblance to King Jayavarman VII himself, Bayon's builder.

A pilgrimage to Angkor ends at the mother of all temples, Angkor Wat. Rising at 5am, venture forth into the darkness to witness Angkor's magic at first light. The soaring towers are silhouetted against the brightening sky; the stars are slowly extinguished one by one with the inevitable onslaught of the sun's rays.

FROM LEFT: Mekong Delta produce sellers; floating homes on Tonlé Sap Lake; rays on Can Tho, Vietnam.
PREVIOUS PAGE: The gateway to Angkor Thom. **NEXT PAGE:** Phong Dien Floating Market in Can Tho.

❷ LIFE ON BOARD

The spacious *Aqua Mekong* cabins include floor-to-ceiling windows to take in the passing landscapes.

 Discover Cambodia's rich culture at the Royal Palace and National Museum of Cambodia in Phnom Penh.

 Explore the watery world of Kompong Chhnang's floating villages.

 Marvel at the magnificent temples of Angkor, including the fabled Angkor Wat, enigmatic Bayon and jungle-clad Ta Prohm.

"Chhnok Tru is a floating village near Kompong Chhang with all the trappings of a traditional Cambodian village."

All meals (and most drinks) are included on board, and the menu is a delicious mix of local specialties and home comforts.

◔ OTHER ROUTES

It is also possible to cruise the Mekong River in Laos. With Luang Say Cruise, you can travel from Luang Prabang to the Golden Triangle with an overnight in Pak Beng. Another option is to explore the 4000 Islands area of southern Laos aboard a converted rice barge with Vat Phou Cruise.

◔ MAKE IT HAPPEN

The *Aqua Mekong* has around 50 departures per year ranging from three to seven nights. Book this luxurious ship via the website at www.aquaexpeditions.com. The best itinerary is the four-night high-water trip that operates from Ho Chi Minh City to Siem Reap from July to November. The most popular time to travel is usually the dry season (November to March), but the high-water wet season from July to November is rewarding for river cruising, as the rice fields are lush. There are many options to cruise the Mekong. *Blue Cruiser* is not a cruise but an affordable speedboat travelling daily between Phnom Penh, Cambodia and Chau Doc, Vietnam, while Pandaw Cruises was the first company to operate luxury cruises on the Mekong River.

Vietnam offers visa-free access to Asian nationals and some European countries. Other nationalities should arrange a visa in advance. A 30-day visa-on-arrival (US$30) is available to all visitors to Cambodia.

You can often save by opting for a May to August departure during low season. **NR**

© FILMLANDSCAPE / SHUTTERSTOCK

Mahakam River

INDONESIA

START **SAMARINDA**

END **LONG BAGUN**

DISTANCE **334 MILES (538KM)**

DURATION **2 DAYS**

Floating up the Mahakam is the closest you'll come to time travel. Starting from the sprawling city of Samarinda, a trip along each bend in Indonesia's second-largest river takes you further back in history. Eventually you're penetrating deep into the jungle, spotting proboscis monkeys, river otters and kingfishers on your way to the next indigenous village. The waterways snaking out of Borneo's thick rainforests long defined human existence here, but asphalt and buses are rapidly killing off river travel.

The double-decker kapal biasa *trip is the last of an era, a relic of a simpler time when people lived in concert instead of conflict with nature.*

❶ RIDING THE WAVES

The lower reaches of the Mahakam River in East Kalimantan can be jarring. The loaded *kapal biasa* ferry, with short-term passengers on the lower level, leaves Samarinda to churn its way slowly through a maelstrom of development and a traffic jam of barges heavy with timber or coal. Over half of Borneo's lowland forests have been cleared in recent decades. As you begin your search for the rainforested 'Heart of Borneo' a line of tugboats quietly hauls that heart downstream to sell to the highest bidder.

The former sultan's palace in Tenggarong, built by the colonial Dutch in the 1930s and now the Mulawarman Museum, marks the first step back in time. Its modern architecture is an imposing reminder of the occupying forces who once waged battle for

Indonesia's resources – arguably starting today's accelerated pace of exploitation.

As the boat moves upstream, passengers disembark with the spoils of commercialism: bundles of plastic wares and shiny new motorbikes to ride through towns with no roads. In Muara Muntai, some 12 miles (20km) of weathered ironwood walkways connect houses on stilts. Villagers are rapidly widening the boardwalks, initially built for foot traffic, to accommodate mopeds.

Muara Muntai also marks the beginning of the lake region: endless marshlands teeming with more than 75 species of birds. In the middle of Lake Jempang, the village of Jantur appears to float on the water under a blanket of drying fish. At the far end of the lake, the Dayak villages of Tanjung Isuy and Mancong maintain a spiritual connection with their disconnected roots – despite the new road that brings more visitors on motorbike than by boat to their historical longhouses. The tiny town of Tering serves as the terminus of the

© GEORGE MARTINUS / ALAMY STOCK PHOTO

LAST CHANCE TO SEE

As mining and logging roads claw their way deeper into the heart of Borneo, the romance of river travel gets abandoned for the cheap utility of dusty buses. The ferry may eventually shut down – go now while there's still wild Borneo to see, and river boats to see it from. The jungle's biodiversity includes endemic species like the proboscis monkey and Mahakam River dolphin.

paved road, and above it the river, forest and villages change palpably. The current speeds up, communities spread further apart, and the forest thickens. This region rewards the resourceful traveller. Stop at any of the settlements, negotiate a homestay, hire a fishing boat and explore the countless creeks that spiderweb through the forest.

The *kapal biasa* route ends at Long Bagun, at a sharp bend in the river between the misty foothills of the Muller Mountains. Here women tie intricate beadwork for their child's next dance. A shirtless shopkeeper melts gold from nearby mines. A fisherman casts his net in a spiralling arc. The pace of life is more relaxed, but even here, bulldozers are chewing through the forest on the edge of town. Change is coming.

The truly adventurous can take the small boats that head further upriver and even deeper into Borneo's living past. The journey is treacherous – the rapids

 Explore the region's history at Mulawarman Museum in Tenggarong.

 Stay in Muara Muntai, a quiet fishing village connected by kilometers of elevated boardwalk.

 Take a side trip across Lake Jempang to the longhouse villages of Tanjung Isuy and Mancong.

LEFT AND BELOW: Baitul Muttaqin Mosque in Samarinda; boats on the river. **PREVIOUS PAGE:** On the Mahakam.

claim several lives each year – but the experience is priceless. For the rest of us, returning the way we came is a bittersweet float back to the bustle of modern life.

❷ LIFE ON BOARD

All spaces are shared on the ferry, with the downstairs deck (no chairs) reserved for day-trippers; the upper deck's long bench of mattresses accommodates overnight travellers. A small kitchen prepares prepackaged noodles (bring snacks), and toilets consist of a hole in the floor. Score a spot on the roof above the captain's bridge for optimal river-life viewing.

❸ LUXURY ALTERNATIVE

Although the ferry is the best way to connect with the local culture, an increasing number of tour operators run private houseboats. Having a guide explain what you're seeing while a kitchen staff prepares hot meals can be a less stressful (if more restrictive) way to explore the river's highlights.

❹ MAKE IT HAPPEN

Two ferries head upriver from Samarinda daily, departing at 7am. Arrive early to secure your optimal spot, and pay on board: there is no advance booking. You can and should hop off at any point to wait for the next day's boat, paying for each segment as you go. During the dry season (Jul–Oct), the ferry may not be able to make it to Long Bagun, but motorboats will haul you as far upriver as you're willing to pay. The return trip is typically faster, especially during the rainy season. You'll want a thin blanket for sleeping on the boat. Note the ferry doesn't linger at village ports. **LB**

 Stay anywhere north of Tering in the Upper Mahakam for an immersive, off-the-beaten-path adventure.

 Watch merchants melt down gold from nearby mines in the misty mountain village of Long Bagun.

 Continue upriver through deadly rapids to Tiong Ohang, the start of the Cross-Borneo Trek.

Star Ferry

HONG KONG, CHINA

START **TSIM SHA TSUI, KOWLOON**

END **CENTRAL PIER, HONG KONG ISLAND**

DISTANCE **1.3 MILES (2KM)**

DURATION **8-10 MINUTES**

Hong Kong may be the alpha feline of Asia's tiger economies, but millions navigate this futuristic cybercity the old-fashioned way, on the ferryboats of the Star Ferry Company. These beloved green-and-white tubs have been crisscrossing the channels between Hong Kong's islands since 1880; indeed, some of the ferryboats in use today are almost old enough to remember the days when China was a monarchy and Britannia ruled the waves.

❶ RIDING THE WAVES

The air-conditioned trains of the Mass Transit Railway (MTR) system can whip you from Hong Kong Island to Kowloon in seconds, but where's the fun in that? Better by far to ride the bobbing boats of the Star Ferry Company, for a journey back through the decades as well as across Victoria Harbour. These venerable steamer-style commuter boats have been upgraded with modern tech, but as you plop onto a hard wooden bench and take a deep breath of harbour air, you can almost feel yourself whisked back to an era of starched shirts, sampans and the frisson of geopolitical espionage. Connecting with the past is a big part of the Star Ferry experience; each of the ferryboats still has 'star' in its name – *Radiant*

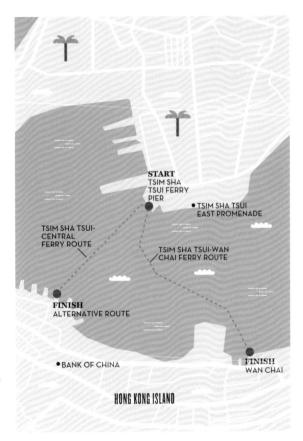

Star, Celestial Star and *Twinkling Star* are firm local favourites – as a tribute to the original *Morning Star* that pioneered the service.

Back in the misty days when Hong Kong was the fulcrum between colonial West and imperial East, steam propelled the Star Ferries across Kowloon Bay. Today electricity and diesel do the job, but the experience of being on board has changed only superficially. Locals still gaze contemplatively out

across the bay from the hard wooden benches; the same cooling breezes still blow in across the South China Sea. What has changed is the Hong Kong skyline, with iconic skyscrapers rising up from the water like props from *Blade Runner*, transforming the eight-minute commute between Hong Kong Island and Kowloon into an architectural sightseeing cruise.

Needless to say, the Star Ferries are a popular vantage point for viewing the nightly Symphony of Lights show in the harbour, when the island and Kowloon skylines are illuminated by a barrage of lights and lasers, like a music video for a 1980s synth-pop band. Never one to miss an opportunity, the Star Ferry Company runs a dedicated Symphony of Lights cruise with snacks and drinks rolled in, but you'll get a pretty good view from the standard Tsim Sha Tsui–Wan Chai ferry for just a few dollars if the departure time coincides with the flicking of the switch at 8pm. The fact that you are watching this space-age spectacle from a tin tub that wouldn't seem out of place in a vintage detective novel only adds to the fun.

The allure of the Star Ferry isn't just about nostalgia. In an era of robot concierges and check-in by tablet,

HONG KONG QUEEN

The Star Ferry Company's iconic green livery wasn't an accident. In the years after WWII, paint shortages limited the city's painters to three basic colours – white, green and candy-apple red. White was the Chinese symbolic colour of mourning and red the colour for celebration, leaving green as the default shade for workaday utilitarian purposes such as public transport.

there's something humanising about travelling from A to B in a vehicle open to the elements. Sure, there's an air-conditioned cabin upstairs, but the real Star Ferry experience is in being exposed to the harbour air, with a babble of Cantonese conversations in your ear.

 Take in the commercial buzz and bright lights of Tsim Sha Tsui, and the view across Victoria Harbour to the even brighter lights of Hong Kong Island.

 Wobble down the ferry gangplank at Tsim Sha Tsui and stake out a vantage point on the upper deck for the view.

 Feel those cooling harbour breezes as you enter the open water between Kowloon and the island.

❷ LIFE ON BOARD

Iconic to Hong Kong, these green vessels are throwbacks to an earlier era. Although the Star Ferry fleet has been upgraded over the years, the boats still feel like outtakes from the 1950s, complete with hard bench seats, strip lights and life preservers roped to the handrails. With the exception of the special ferries used for harbour cruises, food and drink are not allowed to be consumed on board.

FROM LEFT: The high-rises of Hong Kong along the harbour; crossing Victoria Harbour. **PREVIOUS PAGE:** The Star Ferry against the night lights of Hong Kong.

❸ MAKE IT HAPPEN

Ferries run from 6.30am to 11.30pm between Tsim Sha Tsui and Central piers and from 7.30am to 11pm on the Tsim Sha Tsui–Wan Chai route. The rechargeable Octopus card is valid on the Star Ferry, but it's more fun to use the dinky plastic tokens, brought in to replace the much-missed metal Star Ferry tokens with their star-shaped centre hole. Fares are a dollar higher at weekends. There are also different fares for the upper and lower deck (upper costs a bit more), but only the upper deck is available on the Tsim Sha Tsui–Wan Chai route, and most people head to the upper deck anyway for the harbour views. Ferries depart every eight to 20 minutes, so locals treat the Star Ferry like a shuttle bus across the harbour. **JB**

 See the Bank of China Tower leading a parade of landmark skyscrapers on Hong Kong Island.

If you time your evening trip right, use the journey to watch the spectacular daily light show.

 Look back towards Kowloon, with its rival garden of skyscrapers, as you disembark at Wan Chai.

Yangtze River

CHINA ●

The Yangtze is much more than just the longest river in Asia. It's a fount of Chinese civilisation, making the surrounding valley rich and productive and allowing for trade with distant regions. Its murky waters bear legends of the distant past and carry cargo to the modern future. Explore this rich history with a cruise from Chongqing to Wuhan or all the way to Shanghai and the East China Sea, passing Ming dynasty temples, terraced hill villages and deep green gorges before going through the locks of the world's highest capacity dam.

❶ RIDING THE WAVES

It's nearly midnight, and everyone should be long retired to their cabins. But the decks of the cruise ship are alive with passengers hustling towards the bow, cameras in hand. Find an empty spot by the railing, below the vast, looming steel doors that look like gateways to a world of giants. These are the locks of the Three Gorges Dam, the vast hydroelectric project that changed the face of the upper Yangtze when it opened in 2003, displacing millions of residents,

| START CHONGQING |
| END YICHANG OR SHANGHAI |
| DISTANCE UP TO 1400 MILES (2254KM) | DURATION 3-10 DAYS |

flooding archaeological sites and destroying thousands of acres of wildlife habitat, while also providing clean energy to replace coal.

Passing through the locks that raise and lower boats across the upper and lower portion of the Yangtze is one of the highlights of this epic river journey. A display of human might, the process takes four hours, during which passengers stand rapt on deck, watching one gate after another slowly swing open in the moonlit darkness.

By the time you reach the locks, you're either nearly at the end of the journey or somewhere in the middle, depending on how far you're going. Passengers climb aboard near Chongqing, a sweltering metropolis in

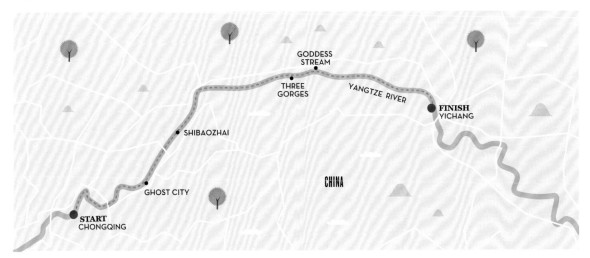

GODDESS STREAM

THREE GORGES

YANGTZE RIVER

FINISH
YICHANG

SHIBAOZHAI

CHINA

GHOST CITY

START
CHONGQING

© KIJJA PRUCHYATHAMKORN / SHUTTERSTOCK

THE THREE GORGES

The three gorges from which the dam gets its name run for nearly 200 miles (322km). The shortest but most scenic is 5-mile (8km) Qutang Gorge, its rust-coloured cliffs topped with vegetation, and often fog. Elegant 25-mile (40km) Wu Gorge has mountains of foliage that glow red in autumn. The longest gorge, Xiling, has peaks that have inspired poetry for thousands of years.

© HENRY WESTHEIM PHOTOGRAPHY / ALAMY STOCK PHOTO

"Alight in Shanghai, perhaps China's loveliest and most cultured city, to walk the Bund."

southwestern China. Though not a traditional tourist draw, Chongqing is well worth a couple days before the cruise. Wander the narrow Ming dynasty streets of Ciqikou Ancient Town while watching traditional artisans and snacking on chilli-oil–slicked street noodles; ride the cable car across the shallows of the Yangtze to drink in the modern bars on the north side; or visit the lush local parks and shrines.

Yangtze cruise boats generally depart at night, in a festive atmosphere complete with welcome cocktails and lantern-lit paths. For several days thereafter, you'll drift along the muddy brown waters, stopping to visit pagoda temples and shrine villages or to board smaller vessels for side trips down narrow

gorges dripping with vines. For some of the journey you'll be passing through farmland – patchwork vegetable fields and flooded rice paddies gleaming in the sun. For other stretches you'll cruise through deep gorges, their rocky surfaces hidden in shadow. You'll see villages perched vertiginously high on sheer mountainsides, some of them moved from now-flooded lower areas.

When you're not watching the scenery, the ship offers some uniquely Chinese entertainment. Learn about acupuncture, qigong or jade jewelry during on-deck lectures. Compete in cheesy talent shows in the ship's bar. Have a hurts-so-good acupressure massage at the spa (or just opt for a pedicure). Wail your favorite Cantopop tunes in the private karaoke rooms. Most of your fellow passengers will be middle-class Chinese citizens, with a sprinkling of tour groups from other Asian countries and the odd Western traveller. English-speaking staff are available on mid-

© MARTINHO SMART / SHUTTERSTOCK

 Fill up on tongue-numbing hot pot, loaded with red chillies and Sichuan peppercorns, in Chongqing.

 Climb the scarlet-coloured 12-storey pagoda of Shibaozhai Temple, which has watched over the river since 1650.

 Explore the eerie shrines at Fengdu Ghost City, with statues and paintings depicting traditional Chinese visions of the afterlife.

CLOCKWISE FROM LEFT: Food vendors in Ciqikou Ancient Town; Three Gorges Dam; Tiger Leaping Gorge. **PREVIOUS PAGE:** The bend in the Yangtze at Lijiang. **NEXT PAGE:** The Shennong tributary; a canal in Wuxi city off the Yangtze.

range and high-end ships. For food, expect buffets of both Chinese and Western food, and an on-board convenience store well stocked with instant noodles.

Most cruises are two to three days, ending just past the gorge, with passengers shuttled to the nearby megacity of Wuhan to catch flights or trains. A handful of trips press on as far as Shanghai, which takes 9 to 10 days in total. The lower portion of the river is less famed for its beauty, but you'll have the chance to see modern cities like Jingdezhen, Chizhou and Yangzhou.

Alight in Shanghai, perhaps China's loveliest and most cultured city, to walk the Bund, explore the elegant colonial buildings of the French Concession, shop for cheongsams and tailored suits, and stuff yourself silly on fried dumplings.

❷ LIFE ON BOARD

The tourist vessels plying the Yangtze vary from mid-range companies serving mainly local Chinese clients to higher-end trips with a more varied international clientele. Boats have comfortable private cabins with satellite TV, communal dining rooms, glitzy hotel-style lobbies and a range of entertainments from small movie theatres to spas. Higher-end boats may offer more luxurious suites, 'captain's table' VIP dining rooms and swimming pools. As a general rule, the more expensive the trip, the more English will be spoken by staff. Food is rarely anything to write home about, but you won't go hungry.

 Wind through the vertical cliffs of the Three Gorges, their tops shrouded in forest.

 Board small wooden boats to travel down narrow, jade-coloured Goddess Stream.

 Use your last night on board to engage in rollicking karaoke and carousing.

© NORMAN POGSONG / ALAMY STOCK PHOTO

❸ BUDGET ALTERNATIVE

If you speak Chinese and don't mind speeding past the scenery, local passenger boats travel some of the same routes as the cruise ships. You won't get shore excursions, food may be limited to paper plates of noodles, and bunks and bathrooms are shared. But it'll barely dent your wallet, and, language barrier or not, you'll probably pick up a local card game from your fellow passengers.

❹ MAKE IT HAPPEN

Most cruises start in Chongqing and leave on a weekly or biweekly basis. The majority end in Yichang, near the city of Wuhan, but some go all the way to Shanghai. Book tickets online through a travel agent or via the cruise operator – there are many, so research your options online. Cabin prices vary by size and deck; lower decks are cheaper. The most pleasant times to travel are spring or fall, with prices rising accordingly. You'll need a visa to visit China, which must be arranged well in advance of your flight. **EM**

Along the Ayeyarwady

MYANMAR

START **MANDALAY**

END **BAGAN**

DISTANCE 114 MILES (184KM)

DURATION **10-16 HOURS**

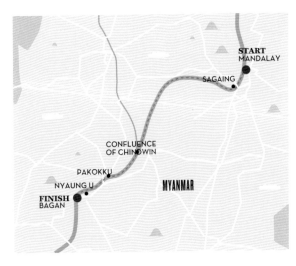

A slow boat along the Ayeyarwady River (also called the Irrawaddy) is the stuff of legend. Sure, Kipling sang the praises of the road to Mandalay, but anyone who knows anything will tell you that the only way to travel in Myanmar is by river. The mighty Ayeyarwady carves a mud-coloured path southwest from Mandalay to Bagan and on to the Bay of Bengal, setting up one of Asia's classic river journeys – a snail's-pace drift past riverbank villages, forests of stupas, bobbing boats of every imaginable shape and size and misty ranges of jungle-clad hills.

❶ RIDING THE WAVES

You don't take the boat to Bagan to save time. In fact the sluggish pace of the journey is precisely the appeal, matching as it does the slow, lazy flow of the Ayeyarwady River itself, which ultimately serves as the metronome by which all rhythms in Myanmar are set.

Even in a comfortable tourist boat, the Mandalay to Bagan trip takes 10 hours or more, and luxe boats transform the trip into a multi-day cruise, with detours on shore, spa treatments, fine dining and other indulgences of the kind insisted on by the colonial classes when Burma was an outpost of the

British Empire. At the other end of the spectrum is the aging, rust-bucket slow boat, which is suspended more often than it runs, and stretches the journey to 16 hours, with luxuries limited to a rustic tea stall and space on deck to set out a plastic chair or a blanket.

But the Ayeyarwady is a great leveller. Whether in deluxe class or economy, the journey downstream to Bagan offers a window onto the Burmese soul: fisherfolk hauling catfish into shovel-shaped rowboats; ribcage-shaped bullock carts hauling logs along the riverbank; farmers tending rice paddies in handloom-woven longyis (sarongs) and banana-pith hats; women with cheeks circled with thanaka (a white cosmetic paste) selling bananas, pastries and peanut brittle from head-carried baskets; and endless chains of novice monks heading out on the morning mission for alms. It's a timeless tableau of Southeast Asian life that is rarely glimpsed through the windows of an air-conditioned bus or a speeding train.

Then there's the drama of departure, wiping sleep

"On the Ayeyarwady the journey itself is the destination."

from your eyes as you make your way to the jetty in the chilly, pre-dawn darkness, and trading the harsh light of flickering fluorescent tubes for the slow, orange glow of dawn over the Ayeyarwady, which lights up the hills of Sagaing like a just-uncovered treasure trove, glinting off the golden stupas that decorate every hilltop. When you travel the Ayeyarwady, the country opens up in front of you like a butterfly unfurling its wings, while you sit back on deck under a canvas shade and enjoy the show. On the Ayeyarwady the journey itself is the destination, but it would be remiss not to mention the sense of anticipation as you approach Bagan, when every structure peeking through the foliage could be the first glimpse of the great plain of temples, ravaged but not diminished by the Mongol armies of Kublai Khan.

❷ LIFE ON BOARD

The level of comfort on the Mandalay to Bagan journey depends on the depth of your wallet. Boats used for luxury multi-day cruises are practically floating hotels, offering private cabins with every imaginable comfort for thousands of dollars per passenger. There's arguably more atmosphere on the rickety steel riverboat run intermittently by the state-owned Inland Water Transport company, where passenger amenities are limited to a toilet, a stand selling snacks and drinks, and an area of deck space where you can watch the river slip by. The more regular and reliable tourist boats fall somewhere in the middle, with better-quality drinks and meals, cleaner toilets and an actual chair to sit in, plus the luxury of a warm indoor lounge on some services (handy for cold early morning starts).

❸ MAKE IT HAPPEN

From October to March, boats leave daily from jetties along the Ayeyarwady in Mandalay, departing between 5.30am and 7am. The journey downstream takes 10 hours or so; it's 12 hours or more if you travel against the flow from Bagan to Mandalay. Services slow to a trickle outside of the tourist season (September through April, to take advantage of high water levels from monsoon season). There's only a single class on most boats; book tickets at least a day in advance at the ticket booths by the boat jetties. Reliable operators include Malikha (www.malikha-rivercruises.com) and MGRG (www.mgrgexpress.com). Services on the aging craft of the Inland Water Transport company (www.iwt.gov.mm) operate only sporadically. In general, spending more on a better-appointed boat is the way to gain more comfort. You should also bring a shawl or a blanket for the chilly dawn start. **JB**

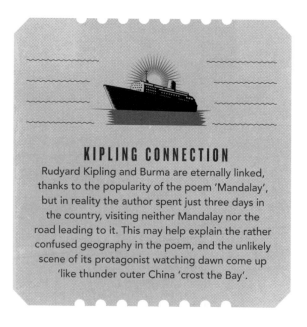

KIPLING CONNECTION

Rudyard Kipling and Burma are eternally linked, thanks to the popularity of the poem 'Mandalay', but in reality the author spent just three days in the country, visiting neither Mandalay nor the road leading to it. This may help explain the rather confused geography in the poem, and the unlikely scene of its protagonist watching dawn come up 'like thunder outer China 'crost the Bay'.

 Anticipate boarding at dawn while Mandalay sleeps.

 Marvel from the boat at the garden of zedis (stupas) at Sagaing, the monastery-studded city southwest of Mandalay.

 Hear the buzz of river traffic where the Ayeyarwady meets the Chindwin River near Yesagyo.

CLOCKWISE FROM TOP LEFT: Temples on Sagaing hill; an Ayeyarwady dolphin; boy collecting driftwood on Ngwe Saung Beach. **PREVIOUS PAGE:** Riverboat *Katha Pandaw*.

 See the hawkers balancing baskets of fruit as they wade and paddle out to meet the boats and vend their wares around Pakokku.

 Feel the excitement of approaching Bagan and spotting the red-brick spires of ancient stupas looming above the trees.

 Explore Bagan's over 2000 Buddhist temples, pagodas and monasteries.

Bangkok's Chao Phraya River

START NONTHABURI OR PAK KRET	
END WAT RAJSINGKORN	
DISTANCE 13 MILES (21 KM)	**DURATION 2-60 MINUTES**

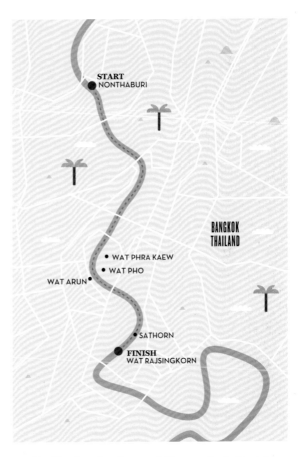

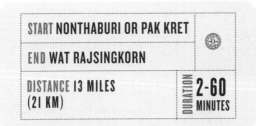

For many first-time travellers to Bangkok, the backpacking district around Thanon Khao San can seem like the whole world. But when new arrivals are ready to feel the real vibrations of Thailand's capital, more often than not that journey begins on the boats of the Chao Phraya Express. These reassuringly regular boats have cut a trail along the Chao Phraya River since 1971, carrying an eclectic cargo of global backpackers, Bangkok commuters, traders hauling goods to market and monks transiting between monasteries. The boats link iconic Bangkok landmarks together like a string of pearls.

❶ RIDING THE WAVES

The sensation of boarding the slender riverboats of the Chao Phraya Express is an apt metaphor for the experience of stepping out of the traveller bubble at Thanon Khao San and into the unfamiliar and exotic streets of downtown Bangkok. These impetuous riverboats pause at stops for just moments, engines reversing in a noisy burst of diesel smoke as passengers leap aboard from wobbly pontoon jetties, bounding over the brown, water hyacinth–clogged waters of the Chao Phraya River. Then, with a blast of the conductor's whistle, you're off, leaving the familiar world of backpacker bars and Skype cafes behind for the frantic hustle and bustle of Bangkok proper.

The first journey may be a short one – perhaps the cruise from Phra Athit, near the dainty whitewashed fort at the top end of Banglamphu, to Tha Chang, backing onto the rear walls of the Royal Palace and Wat Phra Kaew. Or it might be a crosstown expedition, riding south to meet the elevated Skytrain at Sathorn, or jumping off at Si Phraya, where generations of

travellers made the pilgrimage in the days before email to pick up poste restante letters from the post office on Charoen Krung Road. Perhaps you take the Chao Praya to the stop at Oriental to enjoy high tea at the nearby Mandarin Oriental Hotel. Whatever the trip, the sense of leaving behind the Bangkok arranged for travellers and entering the Bangkok arranged for Thais is palpable.

Despite the popularity of the boats with tourists, a trip offers a genuine glimpse of what makes Bangkok tick. Orange-robed monks with begging bowls and parasols add colour against the turgid waters of the Chao Phraya. Commuters pause to wolf down bowls of rice porridge and chicken noodle soup. The mosaic-covered prangs (spires) of Wat Arun rise ancient and archaic above the rooftops of Bangkok Yai. Chains of river barges go past carrying unknown cargos, with crew members roasting fish on braziers or washing laundry on deck. Rickety stilt homes line the riverbanks in the heart of the metropolis.

Then there's the breeze. That blissful, balmy airflow that takes the sting out of the tropical heat and blows away the nostril-stinging fug of traffic fumes, drains

and durians. While first-timers line up for the dawn pilgrimage to Wat Arun via the pint-sized connecting ferry that plies back and forth from Tha Tien jetty, savvy travellers come late in the day, when the breeze kills off the afternoon swelter, and the low afternoon light slips under the clouds to paint the city in licks of bronze and gold. Choose a vantage point on Wat Arun's perimeter wall, kick off your shoes and feel the rhythms of a city exhaling at the end of another frantic day; then reboard the Chao Phraya Express as the city lights come on and another frantic Bangkok night begins.

❷ LIFE ON BOARD

The boats of the Chao Phraya Express are big on character, low on comfort – think wooden bench seats and open windows in place of air-conditioning. There is only one class of travel, with no snacks or drinks available on board. Be sensitive to local sensibilities

KO KRET

For a real river odyssey, ride the Chao Phraya Express north to Nonthaburi, then charter a river taxi to Wat Sanam Neua at Pak Kret, where tiny ferries shuttle over to the sleepy island of Ko Kret. This slice of village life transplanted into urban Bangkok has potters' workshops, a wonky Burmese pagoda and Bangkok's best unauthorised craft brewery.

 Rub shoulders with monks, merchants and Bangkok commuters as you board at Sathorn.

 Glimpse the golden rooftops of Wat Phra Kaew near Tha Chang pier.

 Detour onshore at Tha Tien to inspect the supersized reclining Buddha at Wat Pho.

CLOCKWISE FROM LEFT: Thai architecture on the riverbank; garlands on a water express boat; Bangkok skyline from Lumphini Park; decorative ceramic tiling at Wat Arun. **PREVIOUS PAGE:** Wat Arun temple.

© LUCIANO MORTULO - LGM / SHUTTERSTOCK

© PETER EASTLAND / ALAMY STOCK PHOTO

when taking photos; monks in particular are not keen on being mobbed by paparazzi-like snappers.

❸ MAKE IT HAPPEN

Standard 'no flag' and 'orange flag' boats run between Nonthaburi and Wat Rajsingkorn every five to 20 minutes between 6am and 7pm; boats flying flags of other colours have more limited hours. See the timetables at www.chaophrayaexpressboat.com. Be sure not to confuse the Chao Phraya Express with the more expensive 'blue flag' tourist boat. Tickets can be purchased at jetties or on board (unlike cross-river shuttles, where you can only pay on the jetty); a conductor with a ticket book will come along the cabin. Most travellers use the ferry like a hop-on hop-off bus. Avoid the peak morning and afternoon rushes and position yourself near the single entrance and exit at the back of the boat for short trips. **JB**

 See the sublime pinnacles of Wat Arun, Temple of Dawn, rising dramatically above the riverbank.

 Stop off for high tea in the colonial-era Authors' Lounge at the elegant Mandarin Oriental Hotel.

 Return to exploring Bangkok's delights refreshed by the river breeze.

Cigarette Boat on the Tonlé Sap

CAMBODIA

START	PHNOM PENH	
END	SIEM REAP	
DISTANCE 191 MILES (308KM)		DURATION **3 HOURS**

 *Impatient travellers fly. Parsimonious travellers take the bus. But thrill seekers in Cambodia still prefer the bullet-shaped boat that zips across the Tonlé Sap from Phnom Penh to Siem Reap. This erratic back route to Angkor is low on luxury, big on energy – a headlong dash across the still waters of a monsoon-swollen lake on a boat that wouldn't look out of place in an airplane boneyard. What the trip lacks in serenity, it makes up for in thrills and spills, and waiting at the end are the temples of Angkor, ancient and immaculate in the jungle.*

❶ RIDING THE WAVES

When Cambodia first reappeared on the travel map after the long, dark years of the civil war, the 'cigarette boat' from Phnom Penh to Siem Reap was a traveller rite of passage, a perilous charge across the open waters of the Tonlé Sap, and the preferred 'safe' option for crossing territory still partly controlled by the Khmer Rouge until the 1990s. Today the conflict has been consigned to history books, and cheap road and air travel have stolen the thunder from the ferry ride to Siem Reap, but a small cohort of hardcore travellers still ride the waters as a tribute to the days when Cambodia was backpacking's wild frontier.

Sure, there are more scenic boat rides in Asia. There are certainly more comfortable and relaxing boat rides. But something about this hell-for-leather sprint across the mirror-flat waters of Cambodia's biggest lake tickles the sense of adventure and satisfies a primitive need for speed. At times the scenery – if that word can be used to describe the vast, empty expense of the Tonlé Sap – can be almost monotonous, but the relentless pace of the journey conjures up images of Captain Willard surging upriver in pursuit of Colonel Kurtz in Francis Ford Coppola's 1979 film, *Apocalypse Now*.

Some of the drama comes from the vehicles used for this high-speed water chase. The classic Tonlé Sap ferry looks more like a wingless airplane than a vehicle suitable for travel on water: a long, bullet-shaped cabin flanked on either side by a handspan-wide footplate. Boarding passengers rush to grab the limited areas of outdoor space, where the thrills are to be had, clinging to the side of a racing speedboat with only a tiny rail on the roof to prevent them from being hurled off into the wake. Those who arrive late at the dock are condemned to ride indoors in the chilly air-conditioning, watching straight-to-DVD horror movies on the TV at the end of the cabin.

The beginning and end of the ride offer two contrasting visions of Cambodian life – the chaotic crush of the city as you leave Phnom Penh, and

> *"Traffic dwindles, apart from scattered fisherfolk in long-tail boats, casting their nets."*

the easygoing calm of the countryside on the final approach to Siem Reap. Once you're out on the open waters of the lake, traffic dwindles, apart from scattered fisherfolk in long-tail boats, casting their nets in lonely solitude on the silent water. The lack of obstacles also allows boat drivers to open up the throttle, providing a dousing of spray for anyone at the front of the deck.

There's a certain lawlessness to boat operations on the Tonlé Sap. Life jackets are a relatively new phenomenon, and emergency exits are rare enough to make riding up top in the baking sun the safest option. And the ferries are undeniably overpriced.

© ALEKSANDR TODOROVIC / SHUTTERSTOCK

© MARCUS LINDSTROM / GETTY IMAGES

LAKE OR RIVER?

Literally translated, Tonlé Sap means 'big, not salty river', so is this vast body of water a river or a lake? Well, technically it's both: a long, snaking channel, connecting with the Mekong River at Phnom Penh, and a seasonal lake that swells from a dry-season low of 965 sq miles (2500sq km) to a staggering 6178 sq miles (16,000sq km) at the height of the monsoon season.

 Experience the moped madness and mercantile energy of Phnom Penh, Cambodia's eclectic capital.

 Observe concrete city blocks give way to clusters of wooden stilt houses beyond Preaek Pnov.

 Enter the open expanse of the Tonlé Sap lake at the stilt village of Chnok Tru.

But for those who don't mind mixing a little danger with their overland travel, this bone-shaking boat ride is still the definitive way to ride to Siem Reap.

❷ LIFE ON BOARD

Tonlé Sap ferries are thin on luxuries – amenities are limited to a TV and DVD player, an air-conditioner, and a toilet that can become rather unappealing by the end of the trip. Canned beers, water and soft drinks are sold during the journey but not snacks, so stock up from street food vendors before you board. If you ride on deck, there's no shade, so bring sunscreen and a wide-brimmed sun hat that won't get blown off in the wind. The arrival/departure point in Siem Reap is the floating village of Chong Kneas, but its location moves as the level of the lake rises and falls; if you buy your ticket through a

CLOCKWISE FROM LEFT: Independence Monument, Phnom Penh; the crowded streets of Pub Street in Siem Reap; traditional Cambodian curry; a floating Cambodian village.
PREVIOUS PAGE: Me Chrey villagers retrieving fishing nets on Tonlé Sap.

guesthouse, a transfer to the jetty is included in the price. From here, it's off to Angkor Wat.

❸ MAKE IT HAPPEN

Boats run daily, or every other day, from August to March, when the waters of the Tonlé Sap are swollen by the monsoon; trips are suspended for most of the dry season because of low water levels. Departure is at 7am from either Phnom Penh or Siem Reap. Buy tickets a day ahead from travel agencies, through your hotel, or directly with the boat company. **JB**

 Welcome the return of river traffic as you leave the open water for the muddy inlet at Chong Kneas.

 Disembark at Siem Reap and beat a trail to the stunning temples of Angkor.

 Head to the remote Preah Ko (Sacred Bull) temple 10 miles southeast of the main temples to escape the crowds.

EUROPE

AMAZING BOAT JOURNEYS

Danube Cruise

GERMANY TO HUNGARY ●

START PASSAU, GERMANY	
END BUDAPEST, HUNGARY	
DISTANCE 364 MILES (586KM)	DURATION 8 DAYS

No other river in the world runs by as many capital cities as the Danube, and cruising down this mighty European waterway along the stretch that links three of them – Vienna in Austria, Bratislava in Slovakia and Budapest in Hungary – is an itinerary like no other. With stylish travel practically mandatory as you voyage through some of Central Europe's most sophisticated cities, sign up for waltzing in Vienna and spa basking in Budapest. In between, take in views reminiscent of paintings by the Old Masters. Whether or not you

add on the Danube's fourth capital of Belgrade, Serbia, this will be a trip of a lifetime.

❶ RIDING THE WAVES

The scenes visible on a glide down this dignified river may remind you of the celebrated canvases of the continent's great artists or call up the strains of a waltz, given that some of Europe's most iconic artists took their inspiration from these landscapes. The Danube's dramatic vistas have sparked many a monumental work of art, from paintings by Albrecht Altdorfer to music by Johann Strauss.

Cruises tend to begin in opulent Passau, a German city made wealthy as a trade centre at a joining point for three major rivers, the Inn and the Ilz as well as the Danube. From the stunning church of Dom St Stephan, home of the planet's largest church organ, to the imposing fortress of Veste Oberhaus, it is a fitting point from which to embark on a trip that takes a

slice through a storybook Central Europe.

Soon after, the river surges into Austria. Stop in the capital of Upper Austria, Linz, with its haughty Habsburg architecture ushering you through its Old Quarter, studded by seminal buildings such as the Mozarthaus where Mozart himself once wrote a symphony.

The next section of the adventure, through the verdant Wachau Valley, is perhaps the most scenic on the western course of the Danube. The fertile valley slopes yield Austria's best wines, and many cruises alight here for vineyard tours or an excursion to the vast Unesco-listed Benedictine monastery of Göttweig. This major religious complex has a history spanning most of the last millennium and is still a functioning monastery, sublimely located in wooded hills overlooking the river.

Your cruise understandably tarries in Vienna, undeniably one of Europe's loveliest and best-preserved baroque cities. Whether you are absorbing as much of the astounding architecture as possible – such as the grandiose Schönbrunn Palace, raised by the Habsburg Dynasty to rival Versailles – learning the steps of the waltz or sampling a Viennese coffee in the city's iconic cafes and coffee houses, your free time here quickly evaporates.

Downriver, the craggy castle of Devín announces your arrival into Slovakia. The waters here, now plied leisurely by tourist boats, were where residents of Eastern Europe once risked their lives to cross into the West during the Communist era. There is time enough to linger in the Slovak capital, Bratislava, its Old Town crested by a castle and centred on a cathedral where the monarchs of Hungary were once crowned.

In Hungary, you wind past Esztergom, a beautiful ecclesiastical centre capped by the country's largest cathedral, before arriving, after a week of cruising,

© ERIC NATHAN / ALAMY STOCK PHOTO

into Budapest. As with Vienna, superlatives do not immediately come to mind that can describe the cosmopolitan breadth of this enthralling metropolis flanking both banks of the Danube with its domes and turrets. Budapest provides its own special places for contemplation, though. The city obligingly stands on some of Europe's best natural thermal waters: gravitate to one of the wonderful bathhouses here to relax and reflect on having completed one of Europe's most epic river trips.

❷ LIFE ON BOARD

Whichever cruise company you select, this is high-end travel offering most of the trappings of luxury. There is comfortable, private on-board accommodation, invariably with suites available, and cruises include all meals. Extra costs could include wine tastings, cooking classes, live entertainment, beauty treatments and more. The real highlight, of course, is the easy access to shore points.

 Wander around Passau, a photogenic, historic city at the confluence of three rivers: the Inn, the Ilz and the Danube.

 Dine al fresco on deck while some of Europe's most quintessential scenery slides by.

 Explore Austria's Wachau Valley at the hilltop monastery of Göttweig.

ABOVE AND RIGHT: At one of Budapest's restorative baths; looking down Fisherman's Bastion in Budapest. **PREVIOUS PAGE:** The renowned Chain Bridge over the Danube.

❸ BUDGET/LUXURY ALTERNATIVE

Many cruise companies feature the Danube as an itinerary; it's one of Europe's most popular river cruises. All are high-end, but despite the competition, prices vary substantially. The difference in quality between the lowest- and highest-priced options is not pronounced, but more expensive itineraries may include more interesting stops with better excursions.

❹ MAKE IT HAPPEN

There is a cruise departing on this route almost every day during the spring, summer and autumn. The most famous operators include Viking River Cruises and Amadeus River Cruises, while the rising U by

OTHER DANUBE CRUISES

This is but one stretch of the Danube, which has its origins near Donaueschingen, Germany, and empties into Romania's Danube Delta, 10 countries and 1727 miles (2780km) later. After Budapest, the highlight section is the Iron Gates cliffs on the border of Serbia and Romania. To see the cliffs, take a longer cruise from Passau or begin your Danube adventure in Budapest.

Uniworld line is specifically millennial-focused. Any cruise can be booked via the operator's website. Check the details: operators find innumerable variations on the theme to distinguish their trips from those of rival companies. Passau is the typical starting point for cruises on this section of the Danube, and although some cruises offer out-and-back trips, going one-way allows for more time to enjoy the route as it traverses Germany, Austria, Slovakia and Hungary. **LW**

 Learn to waltz in the city that invented the dance, Vienna.

 Enjoy a memorable first foray behind the old Iron Curtain by exploring Bratislava's beautiful Old Town, backed by wooded hills.

 Enter Budapest and end the cruise by luxuriating in one of the city's inviting bathhouses.

Llangollen Canal

UK

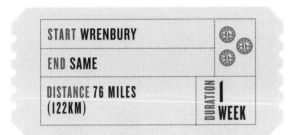

START **WRENBURY**	
END **SAME**	
DISTANCE **76 MILES (122KM)**	DURATION **1 WEEK**

Britain's canal network is unrivalled anywhere else in the world, and the Llangollen Canal is one of its prime stretches. Here it is your job to navigate. No deferring to a driver, no reliance on a guide. You will be at the tiller taking your historic-style narrowboat through the canal up to the thrilling highlight: the point when the surrounding ground falls away into a deep valley and your craft inches over the Unesco-protected Pontcysyllte Aqueduct. The canal that cemented the name of Thomas Telford among the greatest civil engineers of all time has its beguiling, bucolic scenery heightened by a masterful sequence of these tunnels, locks and aqueducts.

❶ RIDING THE WAVES

The Llangollen Canal is one of the loveliest arms of the Shropshire Union Canal, which historically connected the Midlands with the big northern English cities of Liverpool and Manchester. The canal is generally considered to begin at Hurleston Junction, and your journey begins 6 miles (10km) southwest at Wrenbury, prettily clustered around one of the country's finest village greens.

Steady your sea legs with a drink at the pub at Wrenbury Mill, right by the marina you will be embarking from. Here you can see just how singular the vessel you will voyage on actually is. The narrowboat is a breed of boat especially designed to fit the inland waterways of the UK, and it was originally

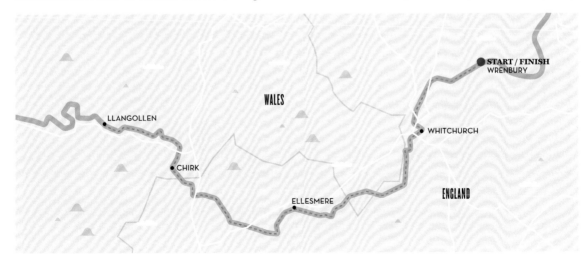

introduced during the Industrial Revolution in the 19th century to connect key towns for commerce. Narrowboats were built as long as the average British canal lock to maximise the goods they could carry, and narrow enough to fit the average British canal. Their use today is more for tourists than trade, but most are still made in elegant, old-fashioned style. Your narrowboat will be no exception, with bedrooms, a kitchen and a common area in place of where, in the past, coal and limestone would have been heaped for transportation to the ports of Chester and Liverpool.

That you are making this trip in such a beautiful vessel, and piloting it yourself, is a big part of the appeal, but far from the only attraction. Once you have mastered the ungainly steering of your craft, settle down to enjoy a route connecting seldom-visited little market towns. These truly special landscapes range from lazy pasturelands to blanket bog, woodlands

THE MARCH

The journey along the Llangollen Canal was once part of the March, a buffer zone between England and notoriously 'barbaric' Wales. Powerful and brutal Norman-English barons known as Marcher Lords established power bases throughout the region in the 11th to 13th centuries. Exempt from the king's writ, the March became an independent but immensely dangerous zone.

 Hone your lock negotiation skills on the flight of three locks at Grindley Brook.

 Moor bankside by old country pubs, wharves, woods and wetlands en route.

 Alight right on the England–Wales border to see stupendous Chirk Castle.

FROM LEFT: Narrowboats along the Canal; Dinas Bran Castle in Wales. **PREVIOUS PAGE:** Historic narrowboats at their moorings.

19 lofty, magnificent arches straddle the River Dee far below. Crossing it, the waterway forges a little deeper into the Welsh hills to wind up at Llangollen. This dynamic, artsy small town hosts a world-class festival, the annual International Musical Eisteddfod, and in the wooded uplands close by are a 12th-century castle and a 13th-century Cistercian abbey.

Then, you turn your vessel around and live the route all over again.

❷ LIFE ON BOARD

ABC Boat Hire's narrowboats are gorgeous historic-style, wood-panelled vessels: pleasing places to sleep, eat and live on for the week. Bedrooms are small, but the deck areas and overall boat space are quite substantial. The Llangollen Canal route is no wilderness. Along its course Whitchurch, Ellesmere, Chirk and Llangollen have shops, pubs and restaurants. Still, bring some supplies with you for setting out, including food to cook if desired, as boats have well-appointed kitchens. The locks should be treated with respect, as accidents can happen. Have someone fit and strong on board to operate the locks.

❸ MAKE IT HAPPEN

Saturdays are departure days for reserved narrowboats. Book at least several weeks ahead to secure your desired departure date; ABC Boat Hire has a base at Wrenbury Mill, the journey's starting point. Boats vary in size from four beds up to 10 beds, but standards of comfort are always high. **LW**

and dramatic valleys. A canal like the Llangollen represents the synthesis of rural and urban: its raison d'être was getting raw products from the countryside to city-dwelling consumers.

Whitchurch is the first town up, after you have eased through a triumvirate of locks at Grindley Brook, followed by Ellesmere: traditional old market towns sporting timber-framed buildings and quirky independent shops. If you stop for one snack en route, make it a heavenly savoury pie from Stokes of Ellesmere. In this area you also traverse one of Britain's most important raised bogs, the wildlife-rich wetland of Fenn's Whixall and Bettisfield Mosses. The canal hits the border with Wales at Chirk. Here, detour to Chirk Castle, a bombastic 13th-century castle which has overseen more than 700 years of British history. Continue on and the longest, highest aqueduct in Britain, Pontcysyllte, rears into view. Its

 Cruise across one of 19th-century engineering's greatest feats, Pontcysyllte Aqueduct.

 Relax in Llangollen, a vibrant, artsy town hosting several major festivals, at the canal's end.

 Explore two masterpieces of medieval architecture outside Llangollen at Valle Crucis Abbey and Dinas Brân castle.

Dalmatian Coast

CROATIA

START SPLIT	
END DUBROVNIK	
DISTANCE 150 MILES (241KM)	DURATION 8 DAYS

The Dalmatian Coast runs for 300 miles (483km) along the Adriatic Sea, where the Mediterranean reaches up between Italy and the Balkan peninsula and glints between Croatia's 1246 islands. The southeastern European nation has more shoreline than Portugal or France, with beaches to prove it. Although there are a bevy of ways to travel this country's increasingly popular coast, the best is topside, skipping across the water with wind filling the sails above you. Along the way – slaloming between the wedge of mountainous mainland and part of an archipelago strung from Italy and Slovenia to the north and Montenegro, Albania and Greece in the south – you'll throw anchor within swimming distance of bistros and lounges, Unesco heritage sites and ancient ruins.

❶ RIDING THE WAVES

Standing on the stern of a two-masted *gulet* sailboat as the ancient outline of Split fades into the distance and the afternoon sun plays on the mainland's Mt Mosor, you may feel a palpable sensation of leaving too soon. Croatia's second-largest metropolis is, after all, one of the country's top destinations. This main coastal city is centred around Diocletian's Palace – a former Roman emperor's town-sized retirement villa built in the 3rd and 4th centuries – which has been repurposed over the last two millennia as part of a bustling urban core with edgy boutiques, bars, cafes and inventive restaurants. As your week-long, island-to-island sailing

CROATIAN WINE

Dalmatia produces outstanding wine.
On the island of Hvar, search for a red variety called
Ivan Dolac, made from the region's indigenous
plavac mali grapes. On Korčula, look for pošip, a
delicious white. And the Pelješac Peninsula,
north of Dubrovnik, produces arguably the country's
best full-bodied red, known as dingač. Viticulture
here stretches back almost 2500 years.

 Visit Diocletian's Palace, a Roman emperor's retirement villa and Unesco heritage site, in Split.

 Admire the fortress (Fortica) and its walls, on a site more than 2500 years old, above Hvar Town on the island of Hvar.

 Pay homage to the 15th-century St Mark's Cathedral and Marco Polo's reputed birthplace in the centre of historic Korčula Town.

CLOCKWISE FROM LEFT:
The Franciscan monastery and
harbour of Hvar; residents of
Prožura; Mljet harbour at night.
PREVIOUS PAGE: A sailboat
near Dubrovnik's old city walls.

nearby Pakleni archipelago before you spend the afternoon and evening investigating historic Hvar Town, where yachts frame a buzzing nightlife.

Croatia is small but dense with culture; each island has its own ancient and proud history. 'We are very lucky to have such incredible islands and nature in Croatia,' says Veselka Huljić, the founder of AndAdventure, a Split-based travel operator offering this eight-day itinerary in the region. 'Every day, we find great food, wine, history and tucked-away bays waiting for sailors.' The next port of call, Korčula, was also a strategic stop for the Greeks, Illyrians, Romans and Venetians. According to perhaps apocryphal local legend, Marco Polo was born here in the 13th century.

The following day, sail along the Pelješac Peninsula, where many of Croatia's most famous red wines are produced with the help of basket-toting donkeys carrying grapes from steep, sea-facing hillsides. The boat sets anchor off the coast of lush and green Mljet island, the western third of which is a national park. On the final two days, the boat feels the tug of Dubrovnik's gravitational pull. Before heading to the 'Pearl of the Adriatic', however, you visit the Elafiti archipelago, a string of satellite islands, with a layover on Šipan, an isle dense with vineyards and olive groves. The odyssey ends in Dubrovnik. Here, atop the town's ramparts, enjoy a celebratory glass of wine while taking in views of the glittering sea and the just-visible specks of islands on the horizon.

charter across the Adriatic kicks off, waving goodbye to a daily embarrassment of riches will become part of a routine that includes diving into the cobalt blue water, sleeping with the sea's rhythm, sampling rich red Croatian wines and forgetting about life on land.

From Split, the 98ft (30m), six-cabin schooner tacks southwest to the isle of Brač for the first of seven stops along the coast of Dalmatia, as Croatia's southern half is known. The next morning, the crew shoves off for Vis, the furthest island from the mainland, once closed to the public because of its importance to the Yugoslav military. Today sailors are again free to explore its hidden coves and remote beaches. From this secluded isle, the trip moves to Hvar, one of the most popular Croatian islands and home to the Stari Grad Plain, whose vineyards were established by the Greeks more than 2400 years ago. The ship will anchor on the quiet western tip of the

 Drink in the sight of the Pelješac Peninsula's steep, sun-soaked vineyards, where grapes are harvested with the help of donkeys.

 Explore one of Croatia's most beautiful and remote national parks on the island of Mljet.

 Walk around the famous walls of Unesco-protected Dubrovnik, the 'Pearl of the Adriatic'.

❷ LIFE ON BOARD

Sailing vessels in Croatia range from bareboat (without crew) to premium crewed charters on yachts. A multi-masted *gulet* typically has six cabins and is built for 12 guests and four crew members, though vessels vary. Before shoving off, staff stocks up on groceries to cook during the trip, topping up rations in ports along the way. Most guests will also explore local restaurants along the way. This journey includes seven breakfasts, six lunches and two dinners prepared by the crew. Travellers looking for self-guided options (or ones without a tourism operator) can book directly with a charter company such as Orvas Yachting (http://orvasyachting.com) or Ultra Sailing (https://ultra-sailing.hr).

❸ LUXURY ALTERNATIVE

There are a host of package options, from type of boat to level of service and privacy. The above example is a 'shared' and static itinerary that can be booked by an individual or couple and has guaranteed, scheduled departures. You can also find private, custom journeys on offer – costlier but completely tailored – in which one group 'rents' the entire vessel, based on the number of people.

❹ MAKE IT HAPPEN

Most sailboat rentals in Croatia run from Saturday to Saturday. Because of the demand, it's recommended to book your cruise months (even half a year) in advance. If reservations on *gulet* cruises are all booked during your dates, an alternative is the ferries that routinely ply the coast. The one-way route sails between Split and Dubrovnik, with seven island stops: Brač, Vis, Hvar, Korčula, Mljet, Šipan and Lopud. Though the trip is offered from April to October, May and September are the ideal months to avoid the summer heat and crowds. To skipper your own boat, a maritime certification, like one from International Yacht Training or Royal Yachting Association, is necessary for safety purposes. **AC**

Queen Mary 2

USA TO UK ⬤

START NEW YORK CITY, USA	
END SOUTHAMPTON, UK	
DISTANCE 3500 MILES (5635KM)	DURATION **8 DAYS**

'Transatlantic crossing': the phrase has an indelible air of romance, and that's precisely why the Queen Mary 2 exists. You could fly from New York to London for less than US$300 if you catch a lucky fare, but despite this (or maybe, given the indignities of flying on budget airlines, because of it), there persists the allure of a far more impractical journey aboard an elegant ocean liner. When you choose a week-long voyage over a six-hour flight, you're travelling not just to another continent, but to another time. The Queen Mary 2 and its rich heritage may be the ultimate example of the enduring romance of travel by water.

❶ RIDING THE WAVES

On an airplane you'll never see a film about a plane crash. On the *Queen Mary 2*, however, *Titanic* is not taboo. In fact it's an inspiration. The world's largest ocean liner, with capacity for nearly 3000 passengers and a staff of more than 1000, was built after the 1997 Kate-and-Leo blockbuster spurred demand for ocean-going glamour.

You may not be able to stand on the bow of the *QM2* with your arms outstretched, but at a formal reception

on the second night, the captain will congratulate you for carrying on a grand tradition of travel. Then you can pose for photos in front of a backdrop of the *Titanic*'s grand staircase. And when the captain announces that the ship is passing the site where the 'unsinkable' ocean liner went down in 1912, you can stare out to the horizon and feel the weight of history.

The *QM2* is the only passenger ship that crosses the Atlantic regularly, and it takes this responsibility seriously. The giant ship is a kind of floating museum,

its warren of wood-panelled, brass-trimmed hallways hung with oil paintings of great ocean liners past and information panels about Cunard, the operating company, established in the UK in 1840. The ship goes both directions, of course, but the eastbound journey seems more fitting: you're heading back to Mother England, tucking into kippers for breakfast, nibbling cream scones at afternoon tea, and dressing for dinner with a kind of seriousness that seems to exist only in Jane Austen novels. (Never mind that the ship is

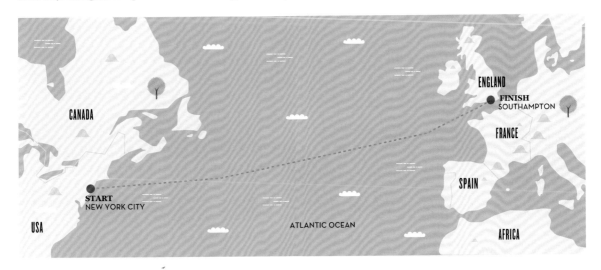

now flagged in Bermuda, and Cunard is part of a multinational cruise corporation.)

For those who like a floating resort, the ship has shuffleboard, a spa, a casino, a disco after dinner and karaoke in the English-style pub, plus activities such as singles mixers and pop-song singalong hour. Prefer a stately escape from the world's hubbub? The ship can be a peaceful retreat, where you can get a massage and catch up on your reading. The hushed library is surprisingly well stocked; savvy passengers make a beeline there the first afternoon. World news arrives only via the chipper daily newsletter, there's no phone reception, and the wi-fi is so slow and expensive as to be no temptation at all. Your only real obligation all week is to bring your passport to the dining room one afternoon for a most leisurely immigration process.

There is, of course, a certain artificiality in the experience that is part of its unique charm. The reality of a week-long trip shows near the end of the week, when the lavish food begins to lose its fresh vegetables. Yet despite this, it's an indulgence to take the trip, and the lowest fares can be surprisingly reasonable, less per night than a typical hotel room in New York City or London.

Once you're out in the middle of the Atlantic, you are truly out there. The only view is sea and sky. The *QM2* is built for its job, extra heavy and stable. If you do hit a few swells, then, to quote one captain, it's only proof of the ship's mission: 'Real ocean weather for a real ocean liner — something to savour.'

❷ LIFE ON BOARD

The *QM2* has four classes of service. Britannia is the most basic, followed by Britannia Club, Princess Grill and Queens Grill. Each class has its own dining room (more intimate as you go up), and Grill-level staterooms and suites are larger. Buffet-style dinner service is also an option in every class, and the one place the evening formal dress codes don't apply.

❸ OTHER ROUTES

The most common variation in the transatlantic crossing is an extension to Hamburg in Germany, after the Southampton stop. Occasionally the ship will take a longer route, via Iceland or Canada, say, or run the crossing in six nights instead of seven. Additionally, themed programming, such as performances by the UK's National Symphony Orchestra, will dominate a particular crossing.

 Wave at the Statue of Liberty as you leave New York City.

 Head to the top deck to watch the *QM2* just squeeze under the Verrazzano-Narrows Bridge.

 Remember the *Titanic* sinking as the ship passes near the wreck site.

AMAZING BOAT JOURNEYS

CLEARING THE BRIDGE

The *QM2* was built to one specific measurement: the height of New York City's Verrazzano-Narrows Bridge, which crosses the bay near the Brooklyn Cruise Terminal. Even with the ship's funnel a bit shorter than normal, it cuts close. At high tide the ship clears the bridge by only 13ft (4m). When built, it was the longest suspension bridge in the world.

❶ MAKE IT HAPPEN

The *Queen Mary 2* makes about 25 crossings year-round. For the best pricing and room selection, book several months in advance (in June for a September trip, for example); cruise agents can sometimes offer discounts or on-board ship credits, beating the prices at www.cunard.com. The lowest price quoted is for interior rooms, with no view; occasionally this lowest fare also includes sea-view rooms. If you're concerned about rough seas, avoid October to December, though storms can strike anytime. Rooms mid-ship and closer to the water are the most stable. And do pack your tuxes and floor-length gowns: people take the dress code very seriously. **ZO**

TOP TO BOTTOM: Jacuzzis on deck add decadence; ocean lore lovers can also visit the RMS *Queen Mary* at its permanent home in Long Beach. **PREVIOUS PAGE:** The *QM2* in profile.

© MAURITIUS IMAGES GMBH / ALAMY STOCK PHOTO

 Make yourself at home in the luxe library and binge-read the classics.

 Be dazzled, after a week of blue, by the vivid green of England's shore at Southampton port.

 Disembark in Hamburg's 19th-century Speicherstadt, a Unesco-protected zone of neo-Gothic brick warehouses.

Venice's Grand Canal

START **PIAZZALE ROMA**

END **SAN MARCO ZACCARIA**

DISTANCE **2 MILES (3.5KM)**

DURATION **50 MINUTES**

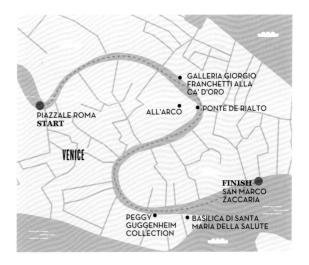

There is no city in the world that can rival the boat trips on offer in Italy's enchanting 'floating city',
Venice. Built on a lagoon, the city has a daily rhythm that takes place largely on its network of charming canals. None is as lively or spectacular as the Grand Canal – a 2-mile (3.5km) stretch snaking its way through the heart of Venice. Trade the touristy and expensive gondola ride for the city's line 1 water bus, the vaporetto, *which will glide you past a roll call of some of the city's most magnificent architecture and under its scenic bridges on a 50-minute trip down this iconic waterway.*

❶ RIDING THE WAVES

Seagulls soar overhead, locals and tourists jostle for the best positions on the boat, and the engine starts to rumble as the *vaporetto* pulls away from its floating platform to join the congested traffic on the Grand Canal's teal-coloured waters. Kicking off the journey from Piazzale Roma, the *vaporetto* cruises under the glass-and-steel Ponte della Costituzione (aka Calatrava Bridge) and past the imposing facade of the Venetian-Byzantine-style Fondaco dei Turchi, which now houses the Natural History Museum, before continuing past the first of what will be a slideshow of majestic

palazzos – some 50-odd on the entire journey – Palazzo Vendramin, home to the Venice Casino.

The *vaporetto's* pace is languid, perfect for taking in the beauty of the pastel-hued Venetian architecture and marble palaces that line the canal's banks, water lapping at their crumbling foundations. Even though the journey has only just begun, it's tempting to hop off on dry land at San Stae station and nab an outdoor seat at Al Prosecco, specialists in unfiltered, natural-process wines, to enjoy a glass of its namesake drink.

Forging ahead, the *vaporetto* chugs past the Gothic 15th-century Galleria Giorgio Franchetti alla Ca' d'Oro, a building whose beauty manages to stand out among some impressive competition, before arriving at the famous Rialto Mercato and Pescaria (fish market) in the neo-Gothic colonnaded building. If the sight of people dining al fresco on fresh seafood and sipping Aperol spritzes is too tempting, disembark and head to osteria All'Arco to taste some of the city's best *cicheti* (Venetian tapas) made using produce from the market.

Back on the water, the *vaporetto* competes for space with other *vaporetti* zigzagging between stations, locals zipping by on luxury boats, and gondolas gliding across with striped-shirt gondoliers steering happy tourists off the Grand Canal and disappearing through tiny crevices between buildings into a maze of back-alley waterways. A shadow is cast over the *vaporetto* as it moves under the engineering feat that is the Ponte di Rialto stone bridge, dating back to 1592, and on past the Renaissance splendour of the Palazzo Corner-Spinelli. As the boat manoeuvres around the next bend, it's a palazzo onslaught on each bank that will have you twisting your neck and agreeing as to the appropriateness of the Grand Canal's name. Standouts include the Venetian-classical-style Palazzo Grassi art museum and the baroque brilliance of the Ca' Rezzonico.

As the *vaporetto* passes glossy black gondolas bobbing and swaying in their moorings, the journey continues under the final of the Grand Canal's four bridges, the beloved wooden Ponte dell'Accademia, and past the palatial home of the Peggy Guggenheim Collection, an incredible art museum. As the *vaporetto* nears the end of its journey, the Grand Canal opens up to the lagoon, creating a feeling of being out at open sea. The water ripples start to form actual waves that look big enough to topple any gondola. The white dome of the Basilica di Santa Maria della Salute glows in the city's pinkish hue; it's next door to the customs-house-turned-art-museum the Punta della Dogana, standing sentinel on the last tip of land on the Grand Canal's south bank.

The journey culminates with the sublime Gothic Palazzo Ducale and the popular landmark Bridge of Sighs before the *vaporetto* pulls into the busy San Marco Zaccaria station, where passengers wait to climb aboard. Find your land legs again and head to the nearby legendary Caffè Florian in Piazza San

© PHILIP LEE HARVEY / LONELY PLANET

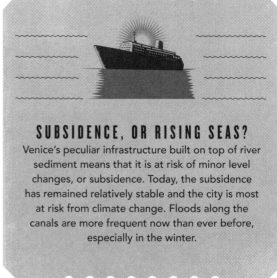

© GIVAGA / SHUTTERSTOCK

SUBSIDENCE, OR RISING SEAS?

Venice's peculiar infrastructure built on top of river sediment means that it is at risk of minor level changes, or subsidence. Today, the subsidence has remained relatively stable and the city is most at risk from climate change. Floods along the canals are more frequent now than ever before, especially in the winter.

 Admire the Gothic architecture of the Galleria Giorgio Franchetti alla Ca' d'Oro.

 Make a detour on land to sample Venice's best *cicheti* at All'Arco.

 Glide under the arch of the magnificent bridge the Ponte di Rialto.

CLOCKWISE FROM LEFT: Basilica di Santa Maria della Salute; the Natural History Museum; colourful Burano. **PREVIOUS PAGE:** A *vaporetto* in motion.

© SERGEY NOVIKOV / SHUTTERSTOCK

Marco. Relax in a piazza seat and raise a toast to one of the most scenic and romantic public transport trips in the world.

❷ LIFE ON BOARD

Vaporetti are flat-decked, single-level boats that have an indoor seating area, though you can test your sea legs in the standing section in the middle. Older boats also have a few open-air seats in front, the most coveted spot for sightseeing.

❸ MAKE IT HAPPEN

Line 1 Grand Canal departs every 10 minutes during the day and every 20 minutes after approximately 8.45pm. Tickets can be purchased at *vaporetti* ticket booths at most station platforms. Travel Cards can

be purchased online through Vènezia Unica (www. veneziaunica.it). It's recommended to travel one way and then, if you have time, walk back. But it's easy enough to just do the trip return if you're not keen on walking.

Boats on line 1 can get overcrowded; try to avoid riding during rush hour. A great time to take the trip is in the evening, when it's less crowded and you'll see the city lit up at night. If you're going to be using the *vaporetto* frequently, opt for a Travel Card, which gives you unlimited travel (24 hours, €20).

Though the Grand Canal section of the line 1 *vaporetto* ends at San Marco Zaccaria, the route continues further to the last stop, Lido. This 7-mile-long (11km) sandbar 'island' is Venice's playground on a hot summer day, with a number of beaches open to the public among the privately owned areas reserved for resort guests. **KM**

 Stop off to admire the art at the Peggy Guggenheim Collection and Galleria dell'Accademia.

 Take your first glimpse of the Basilica di Santa Maria della Salute's grand dome as you round the bend.

 End the journey with an al fresco drink in Piazza San Marco at Caffè Florian.

Volga River

RUSSIA

START **ASTRAKHAN**

END **SAMARA**

DISTANCE **627 MILES (1009 KM)**

DURATION **3-4 DAYS**

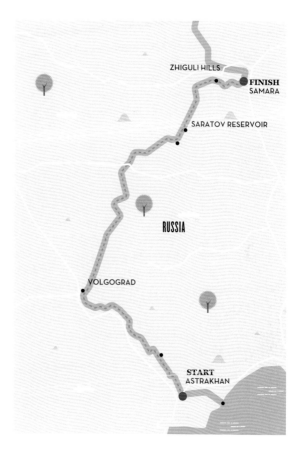

To voyage along Europe's longest river is to journey through the very lifeblood of the Russian psyche. As enigmatic as her homeland, волга-матушка (Mother Volga) slowly wends through her artists and dreamers, writers and revolutionaries, explorers, dictators, invaders and unyielding defenders before dissipating elusively into the Caspian Sea. From May to mid-October, passenger vessels ranging from the latest luxury tourist liners to modest, aging rust buckets ply her historic waters. Whether you prefer sipping Russian bubbles and knocking back sturgeon eggs in your own aquatic penthouse or sharing tomato, cucumber and shot-for-vodka-shot with the locals in steerage, there's a level of comfort (and adventure) to suit all travellers on this route.

❶ RIDING THE WAVES

Astrakhan is Russia's Central Asian gateway, with the waters of the fabled Caspian Sea still 37 miles (60km) away. Thanks to Ivan the Terrible, who cleared the area of pesky Golden Horde Mongols in the mid-1500s, 'modern' Astrakhan sits on the upstream edge of Europe's largest river delta; his rout opened the Volga (and Russia) to Far Eastern trade and Central Asian Нефть (oil). While historically an outpost, Astrakhan

today is one of Russia's most culturally diverse cities. Nature lovers shouldn't miss the Astrakhan Biosphere Reserve, a protected area of wetlands in the lower delta, rich in bird and aquatic life. This is one of the few places in the world where the Caspian lotus grows.

During the Soviet era numerous dams and reservoirs constructed along the Volga's entire 2193-mile (3531km) length widened the river so extensively in places that it resembles an inland sea. Each dam sports an ingenious

© LUXERENDERING / SHUTTERSTOCK

double-lock system to ensure river traffic moves freely in either direction. At other times the river fragments into channels, navigation lights marking the route and testing captains' skills.

After you leave Astrakhan, the first day is spent sinuously cruising along the Volga's main channel through the reeds and marshes of the upper delta until you reach Volgograd the following morning. In 1942–43 during WWII, the city, then called Stalingrad, became the site for one of history's most nightmarish battles. Hitler's relentless eastern advance was finally halted on the Volga's western bank by a depleted but determined Red Army. With winter approaching and both sides forbidden to surrender, fighting degenerated into increasingly desperate door-to-door skirmishes until the Russians eventually outflanked, encircled and finally wiped out the Nazis. Russian casualties counted over a million, and a large memorial on a small hill, Мамаев курган (Mamaev Kurgan), above the town pays tribute. The crowning Родина-мать зовет (The Motherland Calls) statue of Mother Russia wielding a lethal-looking sword is the largest female sculpture in the world. Most ships allow time to visit the memorial. Back on board, stay on deck as you head north past Mamaev Kurgan, as Mother Russia and her sword are clearly visible, the national anthem is played, and every Russian on the boat will be standing, silently watching, many with tears running down their cheeks.

The first of the Volga reservoirs is now negotiated as the ship enters the lock system via a canal off to starboard, where the water level is raised to match that behind the dam wall. Once you are through the locks, the Volga widens dramatically, up to 3 miles (5km) in places, and now is perhaps the right time for a round of Russian Bingo in the lounge.

Saratov, once a closed town in Soviet times when it was off limits to foreign visitors, is reached the next day, and is pleasant though not overly enticing unless you want to escape the on-board disco by jumping a train to Kazakhstan. Space nerds will appreciate the Gagarin Museum, dedicated to Yuri Gagarin, the first man in space, who studied here and even landed nearby when Vostok 1 returned from orbit in 1961.

The river now heads northeast under two massive bridges, winding around low-lying islands before another lock system cleaves the heavily industrialised town of Balakovo in two, below Saratov Reservoir. Abandon bingo for deckside as the scenic, wooded ridges of the Zhiguli Hills mark the sharp, final bend into bustling Samara, once the domain of river pirates. The cosmopolitan city makes the most of its Volga-side location with a popular cafe-lined promenade and a sand beach to rival any on the Black Sea. It also boasts Russia's oldest brewery and has excellent onwards transport connections.

 Spot exotic wildlife in the Astrakhan Biosphere Reserve in the lower Volga delta.

 Relish the myriad channels of Europe's largest river delta.

 Visit the atmospheric and sobering Mamaev Kurgan at Volgograd.

LEFT: The Volga near Samara.
PREVIOUS PAGE: Cathedral of St Vladimir in Astrakhan.

❷ LIFE ON BOARD

Basic shared cabins below deck have one to four beds and 'partial amenities' – a sink and power socket. 'Full amenity' cabins contain a shower and toilet. Expect several restaurants, a bar, and a lounge hosting Russian bingo that morphs into a дискотека (disco) after dark.

❸ OTHER ROUTES

With the right boat and linking canals, it's possible to sail all the way to Moscow (10 nights) or the Black Sea via Rostov-on-Don (three nights from Volgograd). Alternatively, one extra night upriver from Samara brings you to Kazan, home of the Tartars, and a possible three night extension of your trip on the Kama River to Perm, near the Ural Mountains.

❹ MAKE IT HAPPEN

Boats depart every few days from May to mid-October and vary in quality and price. Cabins range from budget-price four-berths to expansive upper-deck suites; the price can include or exclude meals. Either direction works for the trip. Book in advance; Russian websites (in Russian) www.infoflot.com or www.rech-vokzal.ru will be cheaper than ones aimed exclusively at international tourists, but you may need a helping hand to navigate them. Cheaper last-minute tickets may be available from the local речной вокзал (river station). Citizens of most Western countries require Russian visas; some cruise operators will arrange these. **SW**

WHAT'S IN A NAME?

Volgograd, known originally as Tsaritsyn for around 400 years, was renamed Stalingrad after a decisive battle in the Russian Civil War, to honour its famous Bolshevik defender. After Stalin died, Khrushchev, wanting to bury his predecessor's murderous legacy, renamed the city Volgograd. In recent years veterans' groups have lobbied to revert to its WWII name.

 Experience the intricate lock system at Volgograd and Balakovo.

 Join in organised games, like Russian bingo, while crossing Saratov Reservoir.

 Admire or hike the woodlands of the Zhiguli Hills at the bend near Samara.

Bosphorus Strait

TURKEY

START	**EMINÖNÜ**
END	**SAME**
DISTANCE 30 MILES (48KM)	**DURATION 6 HOURS**

Dividing Istanbul, one of history's most influential cities, and the very continents of Europe and Asia, the Bosphorus is the only waterway linking the Mediterranean and the Black Sea. Ferry boats depart regularly from bustling city docks to bring commuters between the European and Asian shores, but they also usher visitors on full Bosphorus cruises from the heart of the city to the mouth of the Black Sea. Your destinations include heritage palaces, imposing fortresses that reinforce the immense strategic value of this storied waterway, and quiet fishing villages worthy of an afternoon's exploration.

❶ RIDING THE WAVES

Spanning three millennia of history and previous incarnations as Byzantium and Constantinople, Istanbul is the only city to bestride both Europe and Asia. The echoes of the Ottoman Empire linger in the gilded halls and harems of Topkapı Palace, and mighty Hagia Sophia celebrates a 1500-year history as a site of pomp and splendour and the one-time seat of the Patriarch of Constantinople before its conversion to a mosque and, later, museum. A template for the modern shopping mall, the Grand Bazaar is a pleasingly disorienting labyrinth of traders hawking

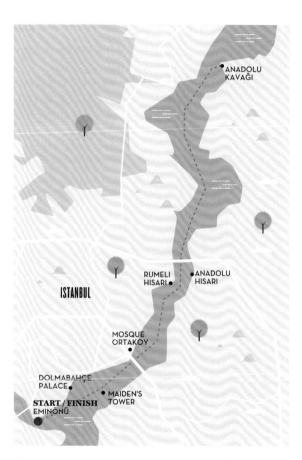

silver, oriental carpets and antiques, while the Spice Bazaar overflows with stalls piled high with fragrant saffron, cumin and chillies. Street vendors proffer sesame-encrusted simit from towering stacks of pastry, and nearby at the busy Eminönü docks, floating cafes dispense Istanbul's iconic *balık ekmek* (grilled fish sandwiches) to commuters embarking on Bosphorus journeys. Amid the tangle of Istanbullus making the short transcontinental hop from one side of Istanbul to

the other or further afield to the Princes' Islands, one of the world's best-value ferry services also makes a six-hour return journey from Eminönü to Anadolu Kavaği near the entrance to the Black Sea. The most used carrier is Şehir Hatları, which provides passengers with an audio guide that narrates the sights en route.

As the cruise approaches its first stop at Beşiktaş, the imposing waterfront profile of Dolmabahçe Palace comes into view. Built around the mid-1850s as a contemporary and European-influenced alternative to Topkapı Palace, this elegant structure was the official summer residence of Kemal Ataturk, the founder of the modern Turkish republic, from 1924 to his death in 1938. From Beşiktaş the boat then crosses to Üsküdar on the Asian side of the Bosphorus. Nearby on its own compact island is Kız Kulesi (Maiden's Tower), originally dating from the Byzantine era in the 12th century and more recently featured in two different James Bond films.

© HAKAN IPEKCI / ALAMY STOCK PHOTO

MANSION LIVING

Some of Istanbul's finest examples of prime real estate are the superb wooden mansions (yalı) lining the Bosphorus. Traditionally these were where moneyed Istanbul families would move to during the warmer months of summer. Most of the surviving heritage mansions with elegant verandas and turrets date from the 19th century; many others unfortunately succumbed to fire over the years.

Passing under the soaring towers of the Bosphorus Bridge, opened in 1973 as the first bridge to link Europe with Asia, you can imagine the spectacle it must have been when Venus Williams played an exhibition tennis match on the broad span in 2005. Further north, just before 1988's Fatih Sultan Mehmet Bridge, the banks are framed by two medieval fortresses. Built by the Ottoman Empire to aid the eventual conquest of Constantinople in 1453, Rumeli Hisarı on the port side is now a museum and used for concerts and events. On the ferry's starboard side, Anadolu Hisarı dates from 1394. Occupying both imposing structures, the Ottomans were able to effect a successful blockade of Constantinople at one of narrowest points of the Bosphorus. Linking the Mediterranean with the Black Sea, the Bosphorus has been a significant strategic prize throughout history, and freighters and container ships from around the world are common sights as

 Take in the busy ebb and flow of Istanbul's ferry traffic around busy Üsküdar and Karaköy.

 Admire the elegance and 19th-century style of Dolmabahçe Palace on the Beşiktaş shore.

 Secure a good spot to observe the perfectly compact Maiden's Tower near Üsküdar.

LEFT: Passengers cross from the east to west side of Istanbul. **PREVIOUS PAGE:** Istanbul's Ortaköy Mosque.

best views are from the vessel's starboard side. As the ferry approaches Eminönü at dusk, the minarets of the Süleymaniye mosque shine before a blood-red sky.

❷ LIFE ON BOARD

The Bosphorus cruise is run by Istanbul's workhorse ferry companies, not a separate luxury line; you'll share your passage with not just other tourists but locals transiting between Istanbul and its suburbs. On the all-day round-trip journey to Anadolu Kavağı, you can explore the passing scenery from a variety of viewpoints. The top deck combines excellent views with cooling Bosphorus breezes. Drinks and snacks including *çay* (Turkish tea) or *ayran* (a refreshing drink made from yogurt) are available from vendors.

❸ OTHER ROUTES

Frequent ferries leave from Eminönü to many other places, including the lively Kadıköy neighbourhood, and the relaxed and scenic Princes' Islands.

❹ MAKE IT HAPPEN

The round-trip ferry along the Bosphorus to and from Anadolu Kavağı runs throughout the year with four departures daily. The one-way journey takes around 90 minutes and it's worthwhile to spend at least three hours at Anadolu Kavağı before returning to Eminönü. Tickets are available at kiosks on the Eminönü waterfront; booking ahead is unnecessary, but you can get tickets a day in advance. **BA**

the journey continues towards the Black Sea.

Around the journey's next brief stop at Kanlıca, where locals may come on board to sell the renowned specialty yogurt made in the neighbourhood, the shores of the Bosphorus feature the upscale 19th-century summer mansions of the city's historical elite. Housed in an especially notable 1925 mansion, the Sakıp Sabancı Museum here includes a world-renowned calligraphy exhibition.

Following stops at the small towns of Sarıyer and Rumeli Kavağı, the cruise continues to Anadolu Kavağı, close to the top of the Bosphorus Strait. Seafood restaurants crowd the shore, perfect for a leisurely lunch, and a walking track meanders uphill to the castle remains of Yoros Kalesi and wide-ranging views down the expanse of the Bosphorus and to the Black Sea.

Heading back to Istanbul from Anadolu Kavağı, the

 Consider the history-making importance of the fortresses of Rumeli Hisarı and Anadolu Hisarı.

 Spend a few leisurely hours enjoying seafood and Turkish meze (traditional savoury snacks) at Anadolu Kavağı.

 Be enveloped by an Istanbul dusk as the ferry docks again at Eminönü.

The Canal du Midi

FRANCE

START **TOULOUSE**	
END **SÈTE**	
DISTANCE **149 MILES (241KM)**	DURATION **6-8 DAYS**

There are few finer ways to experience the glories of the French countryside than from the deck of a canal boat – and when it comes to canals, they don't come grander than the majestic Canal du Midi, which runs for 149 stately miles (241km) between the rosy-red city of Toulouse and the sultry southern town of Sète. A journey down this engineering wonder, now honoured by Unesco, is an intimate look at France, with plenty of gastronomical sightseeing possible en route from the Garonne to the Mediterranean.

❶ RIDING THE WAVES

The canal's origins date back to the mid-17th century, when Louis XIV (the Sun King) was looking for a safer way to transport goods across France without having to brave the coastline, which was notoriously prone to pirates and blockades. A link between France's Atlantic and Mediterranean coastlines had been dreamed of since Roman times, but it took 1600 years for someone with the vision, ambition and engineering expertise to deliver it. That man was Pierre-Paul Riquet – a wealthy farmer, property owner, tax inspector, gifted mathematician and engineer. Having drawn up his plans, Riquet received the commission to build the canal in 1666. Along with the Canal du Garonne, it was to form part of the monumental Canal des Deux Mers, which, once completed, would offer uninterrupted passage from the Atlantic to the Mediterranean.

Unfortunately Riquet underestimated both the

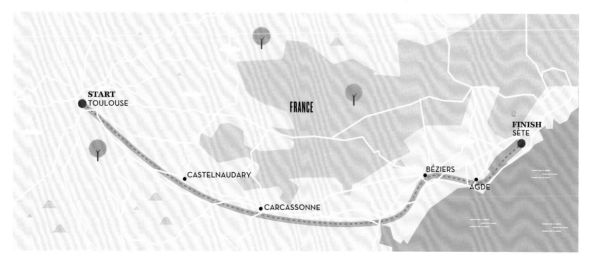

START
TOULOUSE

FRANCE

FINISH
SÈTE

CASTELNAUDARY

BÉZIERS

AGDE

CARCASSONNE

difficulty of the terrain and the incredible engineering challenges required to overcome them. More than 12,000 people were employed in its construction, and a fiendishly complicated system of aqueducts, dams, bridges, locks and tunnels was needed to facilitate its passage. Despite spiralling debts, impatient investors, countless accidents and the threat of bankruptcy, Riquet completed the project, against the odds, just 15 years later in 1681. Sadly the canal's mastermind didn't live to enjoy the fruits of his labour; he died a few months before its official opening.

Three-and-a-half centuries later, the Canal du Midi remains the oldest working canal in the world, listed as a World Heritage Site by Unesco since 1996. Its commercial importance waned following the arrival of the railways in the mid-19th century, and these days it's mainly the preserve of pleasure vessels and traditional narrowboats, known as *péniches*. Most people head from north to south, and several weeks are required to traverse the entire length of the canal, although it's possible to do shorter sections too.

As you putter along at a constant speed of 5mph (8km/h) – a shade above walking pace – life shifts down into a slower gear. Underscored by the chug of the boat's engine, visions of the French countryside glide by: quiet villages, riverside markets, fields of lavender. Avenues of plane trees line the canal banks, casting dappled shade onto the water. There are country markets to shop at and handsome towns to wander; at riverside restaurants you can moor up at the water's edge and while away the afternoon with a *pichet* (jug) of wine, a fresh baguette, a plate of oysters and some homemade cassoulet. There are engineering marvels galore, including 40 aqueducts, 90-odd locks, France's first water tunnel and a famous series of seven staircase locks near Fonséranes, which enable the canal to drop 71ft (22m). At its southern end, past the medieval citadel of Carcassonne, the

canal meanders through wetlands frequented by flamingos, herons and wild ibis. Whether you cruise it for a day or weeks at a time, there are few lovelier ways to experience old France than the Canal du Midi – a waterway and a way of life, rolled into one.

❷ LIFE ON BOARD

The most authentic way to travel is aboard a traditional péniche, although you need to be confident in canal skills such as steering, mooring and so on. Most have accommodation for several people and a fully equipped kitchen.

❸ BUDGET ALTERNATIVE

A cheaper alternative is to hire a small motorboat and stay at hotels along the canal's route. Alternatively you could just hire a boat for a day, for example in Agde,

PLATANES

Elegant plane trees line much of the Canal du Midi's length; the oldest date to the 1830s. Planted to stabilise the banks and provide shelter from the heat, they're a rare example of industrial engineering and landscaping working in harmony. Sadly, many of the trees have been felled due to a killer fungus likely brought over by US ammo boxes in WWII. Replanting disease-resistant trees is under way.

 Visit the fascinating Cité de l'Espace space museum in Toulouse.

 Try authentic cassoulet (a traditional sausage and bean stew) in Castelnaudary.

 Admire the 'witch's hat' turrets of the medieval citadel of Carcassonne.

Béziers or Narbonne, or cycle a section of the Canal des Deux Mers cycle route.

◉ MAKE IT HAPPEN

For small motor cruisers, try LeBoat (www.leboat.com), Locaboat (www.locaboat.com) or Caminav (www.caminav.com). For narrowboats, try Minervois Cruisers (http://minervoiscruisers.com). Prices vary depending on the season and boat size, but expect to pay between €900 and €1400 a week for a four-person boat, or upward of €350 per day for a fully restored péniche. Keep in mind that summer in the south of France can be fiercely hot (and busy), so autumn is a cooler, quieter time to travel.

No licence is required to pilot a boat, but it's worth taking the time to become completely familiar with your vessel before you set out. Most companies offer training sessions on how to steer, stop, moor, use locks and so on. **OB**

CLOCKWISE FROM TOP LEFT: A sunset aperitif in France; moored canal boats; a meal at Le Colombier restaurant. **PREVIOUS PAGE:** Steering a narrowboat along the Canal du Midi.

 Negotiate the seven staircase locks of Fonséranes.

 Sample local Languedoc wines in Béziers.

 Pass through the famous 95ft-wide (29m) round lock near Agde.

Aran Islands Pilgrimage

IRELAND

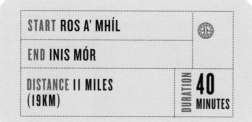

START **ROS A' MHÍL**	
END **INIS MÓR**	
DISTANCE 11 MILES (19KM)	DURATION **40 MINUTES**

The Aran Islands are places that have retained their uniqueness in a world of increasing conformity. Lying at the edge of western Ireland, the three islands are the epitome of isolated island life, where traditional culture has survived and thrived away from the hectic pace of the mainland. A mere 40 minutes by boat from the mainland, the islands feel a lifetime (or two) away, places of living history and utter wildness. This is not a journey for those who want to cram their days with activities. It's for those who crave a reconnection: with others, with the past, with a harsh but bewitching landscape or with themselves.

❶ RIDING THE WAVES

Stepping onto the ferry to Inis Mór, the largest of the islands, doesn't seem like the beginning of a journey to a romantic, rural Ireland. Couples drag their wheelie suitcases loudly along the metal plank,

the wheels hammering over the bumps with a thud. Families push to stay together, harriedly looking around to ensure no little one is lost. Luggage is hastily taken and stored in haphazard fashion. But as you settle down into your seat – or hurry to grab a vantage point outside – you might spot a little clue that you're in a portal to a different world. Emblazoned on the shirts of the crew are examples of the Irish language; for many travellers, this will be the first time experiencing it used as someone's first language. The ferry is within an Irish-speaking area – a *Gaeltacht* – and travellers are now on their way to the region where the language is strongest.

Stand closer to the crew, and you'll even snatch a piece of conversation as *Gaeilge* (in Irish). The meaning may be unintelligible, but there's no mistaking the steady drumbeat the language flows with. The sounds swoop between harsh and melodic and may be interspersed with the occasional English word as the speakers fluently switch mid-sentence.

"The bright, colourful buildings of the cafes and pubs offer a cheerful, inviting contrast. "

If you're not excited yet, the tingle of adventure is beginning in the pit of your stomach right now.

Whether the seas below you sparkle with reflected sunshine or the skies overhead darkly swell with rain, if you choose to stake your claim on a vantage point on the deck, you'll almost certainly be whipped and battered by the strong winds of the Irish west coast. Even on the brightest of days, prepare to shiver as the wind howls around you. It may steal your breath away, but persevere to get the best view.

As you sail, you'll have an excellent vantage point on both sides of the barren Connemara mainland you're leaving behind. The expanse of Galway Bay stretches out on the left, leading all the way back to Galway city. By now you should see the beginnings of the Inis Mór coastline coming more sharply into focus. With the ferry navigating the waves, all excited eyes on board will be peering towards the strip of land you're heading towards, its rugged terrain seeming to bob up and down before your eyes. Between the wind and the swells, few can stand the entirety of the short journey outside. Many people prefer to scurry indoors to the comfortable seats where they can enjoy the journey in peace, but if you can brave the elements, you'll be rewarded. Slowly, slowly, the three core elements of the Aran landscape become clear: the low, limestone walls, the green of the grass and the grey roofs of the houses of the mere 840 inhabitants.

There are also surprises on your approach. A soft golden, sandy beach in a sheltered outlet of turquoise water looks like it would be more at home in the Caribbean than in this rocky outpost of Europe. For

many travellers the coastline is bigger than they imagined, and this glimpse is just the beginning of the adventure. The approach by water hides one of Inis Mór's most famous features on the other side, the epic cliffs with the spectacular Dún Aonghasa proudly on top.

As the ferry glides into the port, the bright, colourful buildings of the cafes and pubs offer a cheerful, inviting contrast from the neutral colours of the landscape, promising pints, food and shelter from whatever the weather might have in store. Signs of life begin to bustle into view; the passengers queueing for the return ferry, a horse and trap or one of the few vehicles lined up to take passengers to their accommodation or on a whistle-stop tour of the island's highlights. In the still waters of Kilronan Harbour, the winds begin to die down and it's time to take your last gulp of sea air before setting foot on Inis Mór.

© MICHELLE MCMAHON / GETTY IMAGES

 Brave the wild winds of Ireland's west coast to get the full experience by staying on deck.

 Say farewell to your last sight of the Connemara mainland on both sides.

 Enjoy the glory of scenic Galway Bay as seen from the ocean.

LEFT AND BELOW: A thatched cottage on Inis Mór; an Inis Mór donkey. **PREVIOUS PAGE:** An Inisheer Island beach. **NEXT PAGE:** Stone fences on the Arans.

THE ICONIC DESIGNS OF ARAN

Internationally, the islands are best known for Aran jumpers (sweaters). There are enduring legends that the stitches represent Irish mythology and that each family has a unique stitch, but neither is true. Most garments are hand-loomed, but you can still find traditional hand-knitted ones in smaller stores; the latter are generally better quality. Woollens are a typical souvenir purchase, and handy extra layer.

 Hurry to the deck to get a view of the islands as they appear on the horizon.

 Have cameras at the ready for capturing the full expanse of the Inis Mór coastline.

 Disembark at Kilronan Harbour for your first taste of island life (and a pint to wash it down).

❷ LIFE ON BOARD

There is no food or drink on board, so bring some if you think you'll need it. However, with seasickness often affecting even the most seasoned travellers on this wild side of Ireland, it may be best to abstain. The seats inside are comfy but there is little seating out on deck, so if you want to spend the journey outside, wear comfortable shoes and ensure you have warm clothing and rain gear.

❸ OTHER ROUTES

Inis Mór is the first stop on the Aran Islands ferry and has the most visitors and facilities, but you can also continue on to the other islands, Inis Meáin and Inis Oírr. You also have the option of a ferry to and from Doolin.

❹ LUXURY ALTERNATIVE

For a high-end day trip to Inis Mór, you can rent your own luxury yacht from Charter Ireland. Your skipper will be included in the price, and up to seven people can set sail. Food will be served on board, and you'll get the afternoon and evening to explore the island at your leisure before returning the next morning.

❺ MAKE IT HAPPEN

Aran Island Ferries depart twice a day from October to March, with three sailings a day between April and September. You can book your ferry online to depart from Ros a' Mhíl (www.aranislandferries.com) or Doolin (www.doolin2aranferries.com); be sure to book in advance during the high summer season. If you don't have your own transport, you can also include a bus transfer from Galway to the ferry port in Ros a' Mhíl. Inis Mór is the most popular stop, but you can also use the ferry to travel between the islands.

The seas can be a bit rough at any time of year but tend to be worse during winter. No special permits are required for the journey, though you may want to leave room in your luggage for woollens. **AMM**

Santander to Portsmouth Ferry

SPAIN TO UK

START SANTANDER, SPAIN	
END PORTSMOUTH, UK	
DISTANCE 652 MILES (1050 KM)	DURATION 24 HOURS

Driving from Spain to the UK would take two days of mindless motoring. Sailing, however, takes just 24 hours; it is also probably the closest thing to a cruise holiday that a journey from A to B can be. The trip is comfortable and thoroughly enjoyable, whether you want to catch up on sleep or make the best of the entertainment offered on board. It is also the chance to sail in and out of two superb harbours and across the Bay of Biscay, which offers whale sightings in summer and mighty seas in winter.

❶ RIDING THE WAVES

The MV *Cap Finistère* car ferry sails out of Santander at 8.30pm, and as the ship slowly pulls out from the dock, you can see the evening bustle along the seafront and the myriad small sailing boats heading back to port. As it enters open water, look back on the city with its mountainous backdrop, the Cantabrian Range, which stretches from the Pyrenees to Galicia. It's thanks to these mountains that northern Spain is so green.

As evening continues, passengers settle down for their meal. You can go for a sit-down meal or have something lighter for an al fresco dinner on deck. Afterwards, the choice is yours: cinema, quiz or a drink in the well-stocked, panoramic bar at the back.

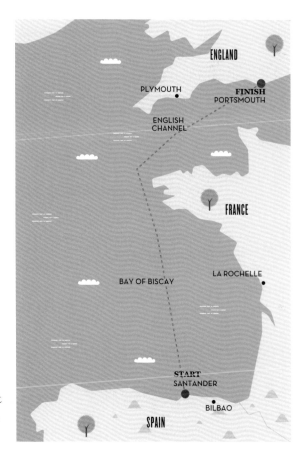

Whatever you choose, you'll sleep well: the berths are comfortable, and the soft whir of the engine and gentle rocking of the boat are guaranteed to lull you.

The *Cap Finistère* usually reaches Brittany on the French coast around 7am or 8am, so you can enjoy a breakfast with views. This rugged coastline, notoriously tricky to navigate, is punctuated by hundreds of lighthouses that have become attractions in their own right. Make sure to look at the beautiful illustrated map

at the information desk to orient yourself.

The French coast starts to disappear from view in the late morning, when it's open sea again as the ship sails through the English Channel. This is your chance to go for a nap or settle down with a book on a sunny deck or in one of the cosy lounges. Book a massage or go to the cinema later that afternoon. As the ship gets closer to its destination, traffic on the Channel intensifies: there are huge container ships, fishing vessels, cruise ships, oil tankers and sailing boats, creating quite a spectacle, especially for children.

The chalk cliffs of the Isle of Wight come into view in the evening. As the *Cap Finistère* skirts the island and enters the Solent (the strait separating the Isle of Wight from mainland England), you can discern Portsmouth and its distinctive Spinnaker Tower, a stunning sail-shaped observation tower at the heart of Portsmouth harbour.

The harbour itself is huge and beautiful. Its historic centre has been redeveloped into a lively neighbourhood, and the commercial docks on the other side are teeming with activity. Portsmouth is also one of the UK's largest naval bases, so you'll see plenty of military vessels, including the aircraft carrier HMS *Queen Elizabeth*, which dwarfs everything else in the harbour.

After one mighty reverse parking manoeuvre, the ship docks and unloads. You can now resume your journey on land, refreshed from your convenient, relaxing sea crossing.

❷ LIFE ON BOARD

Cap Finistère is a relatively small vessel, carrying just under 800 passengers. There is plenty to do during the crossing, with quizzes, live music and talks in the bar area, a cinema, a beauty treatment room and a pool (open May to September). There are also TVs in various areas of the ship. Kids are well catered for with a playground, a kids' corner and dedicated activities.

The cabins are tiny but functional, with good storage, en-suite bathrooms and comfortable beds. If you want more space, upgrade from standard cabins to Finistère Club or De Luxe.

You'll be spoiled for choice for food, from the formal Restaurant du Port to the cafeteria-style Le Café Salad

 Grab a seat on the rear deck and admire Santander and the Cantabrian Range.

 Join whale-watching volunteers along the way and you may well get lucky with a sighting.

 Fall asleep in Spain and wake up in France fresh as a daisy.

LEFT, FROM TOP: Brittany's Quiberon Peninsula; yachts in the 'Round the Island' race around the Isle of Wight. **PREVIOUS PAGE:** Waves breaking on Pointe du Millier, Finistere.

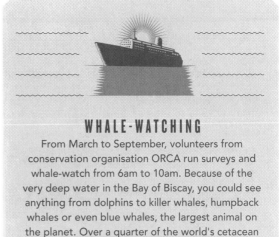

WHALE-WATCHING

From March to September, volunteers from conservation organisation ORCA run surveys and whale-watch from 6am to 10am. Because of the very deep water in the Bay of Biscay, you could see anything from dolphins to killer whales, humpback whales or even blue whales, the largest animal on the planet. Over a quarter of the world's cetacean species have been seen here.

Bar, which offers hot meals as well as salads, and the excellent Petit Marché, which focuses on light takeaway bites such as sandwiches and salads.

The onboard shop sells basic toiletries as well as books, newspapers and the usual assortment of duty-free products.

The only downside is the rather unreliable and weak complimentary wi-fi. If you really can't do without it, then pay for the premium service (€5 to €25, depending on the amount of data you need).

❸ OTHER ROUTES

Brittany Ferries operates a couple more routes between Spain and the UK: Bilbao to Portsmouth (Bilbao is just 31 miles/50km from Santander), and Bilbao or Santander to Plymouth in Devon, in the southwest of the UK. The *Cap Finistère* works on all routes along with the huge *Pont-Aven*, which can carry 2400 passengers. Apart from their difference in size, the ships offer the same level of comfort and great facilities.

❹ MAKE IT HAPPEN

The *Cap Finistère* sails twice a week between Bilbao and Portsmouth, and once a week from Santander to Portsmouth. Tickets can be booked online (www. brittany-ferries.co.uk); summer crossings are very busy, so book ahead. Cabins come with two or four berths; inside cabins are cheaper than those with windows.

The ship sails year-round but summer crossings are the best for obvious reasons: the sea is calm; you can use the pool and sunbathe on the decks; and it's light both when you leave and arrive so you get to marvel at the harbours of Santander and Portsmouth. **EF**

 Count and compare the numerous lighthouses dotting the Brittany coastline.

 Enjoy a spot of ship-spotting: they come in all shapes and sizes.

 Head to a starboard deck for incredible views of Portsmouth harbour.

Aegean Islands

GREECE

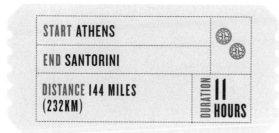

START **ATHENS**

END **SANTORINI**

DISTANCE **144 MILES (232KM)**

DURATION **11 HOURS**

The very name Santorini evokes daydreams of whitewashed cube-shaped houses clinging precariously to the cliffside against mesmerising sunsets. Sure, you could get here via a quick plane hop, but it's vastly more rewarding to take the scenic, wallet-friendly route on a slow ferry from Athens's Piraeus port, discovering other destinations in the Cyclades island group along the way. That's one of the wonders of the Cyclades: each island has its own distinctive character. From the hedonistic beach bars of Ios and the ancient catacombs of Milos to the atmospheric hillside capital of Folegandros and remote, quiet Sikinos, there's something to tempt every traveller.

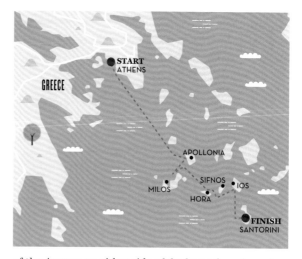

❶ RIDING THE WAVES

The first rays of the sun are barely grazing the boxy apartment buildings of Piraeus when the ferry gives a deep hoot, answered by cheers on deck. A celebratory atmosphere prevails; for many passengers, it's the start of a long-anticipated holiday. As the bustle of the port recedes, tranquility descends. Passengers settle into a rhythm: sleeping in their seats or haunting the deck, staring dreamily into the froth churned up by the propellers.

Steep, scrub-coloured hills soar above the deep blue of the Aegean on either side of the horseshoe-shaped bay, the gleaming white and brilliant blue of Cycladic churches in stark contrast to the brown hillsides, as the ferry pulls into Kamares port on Sifnos. Agios Symeon monastery perches precariously on top of the steep hill on the port side. On Sifnos, as on most Cycladic islands, hundreds of small churches and chapels dot the land, often dating from the Byzantine era, and many are located in inaccessible places such as remote bluffs and caves. Those who built them were motivated by devotion; they sought to be far from distractions and closer to God. With so many people making a living at sea on these islands, many of the churches are dedicated to the patron saints of sailors and fishers.

However, what Sifnos is really renowned for is its food, ever since the first Greek cookbook was written here in the early 20th century by the island's most famous son, Nikólaos Tselementes. Traditional, slow-cooked revithada (baked chickpeas) and mastello (lamb with dill and red wine) in Kastro and Artemonas compete for attention from foodies, along with the fusion restaurants of Apollonia and spiny lobster straight from the sea at Heronissos beach.

Further along in the Aegean, the undulating coastline of Milos appears, its multicoloured hills displaying their barite, alum, obsidian and sulphur, the latter drawn from hot springs. The yacht-studded bay of Adamas, Milos, is the next stop, but it's far from the island's only draw. Some travellers prefer to head for the labyrinthine hilltop villages of Plaka and Trypiti with their converted Cycladic windmills turned guesthouses. The imposing fortress, intact Roman theatre used for summer performances, and Greece's only Christian catacombs are a short walk from there, as is the location where the *Venus de Milo* statue was found (it has stood proudly in the Louvre since the 19th century). Descend to the sea from the catacombs and you hit the traditional fishing village of Klima, its tiny, colourful *syrmata* (boathouses) wedged between the waves and the cliffs. Heading in the opposite direction from Adamas, other travellers take off for the fishing village of Pollonia, which becomes a foodie enclave in summer, or towards distant beaches – the sandy crescents of Kampanes and Nerodafni, the white-rock slabs of Sarakiniko, the golden sand of Provatas.

Some days, stopping just short of Milos, the ferry docks at tiny Kimolos instead, with its soporific capital village, picturesque syrmata and magnificent white-sand beaches. To reach these, you have to trundle along unpaved, dusty roads.

Folegandros comes into view soon after that, the whitewashed houses of its hilly little capital, Hora, clustered around three tiny squares on the hillside above the bay of Karavostasis. The handful of disembarking passengers won't find picture-perfect white-sand beaches here. However, if you trek through the rugged interior, past the island's many remote churches, and scramble down rocky footpaths from Ano Meria, the smaller of its two villages, you'll come

© SIVAN ASKAYO / LONELY PLANET

SANTORINI'S FIERY BIRTH

Five islands known collectively as Santorini – Thira (main island), Thirasia, Aspronisi, Palea Kameni and Nea Kameni – were formed as a result of multiple volcanic eruptions. The most powerful occurred in 1620 BC, destroying a thriving Minoan civilisation and creating half-moon-shaped Thira, the outer edge of a sunken volcanic crater; it was one of the largest volcano eruptions of the past 10,000 years.

© SIVAN ASKAYO / LONELY PLANET

 Feast on imaginative Greek fusion cuisine in Apollonia, the heart of Sifnos.

 Seek out Milos' best swimming spots, from the bottle-green Papafragas to the white-rock slabs of Sarakiniko.

 Stay in Hora in Folegandros and make a sunrise pilgrimage to the Panagia church.

upon secluded little pebbly coves, such as Libadaki and Abeli, and will likely have them to enjoy in private. If you're wise, on your way back to Hora you will stop at Ano Meria's tavernas to sample the local specialty of *matsata* (rabbit or goat stew with homemade pasta).

The few passengers who disembark at the little

CLOCKWISE FROM TOP LEFT:
Outdoor cafe seating in Plaka's backstreets; Agios Nikolaos chapel in Pollonia; a typical lunch of Greek salad and sardines. **PREVIOUS PAGES:** Fishing boat moored near Milos harbour.

port of Alopronia, Sikinos, are mostly locals. It's hard to imagine that an island barely touched by tourism exists in full view of Ios and Santorini, two of the Cyclades' most popular islands. Steeply terraced fields lead up from the port to the two interconnected villages, Horio and Kastro, the latter flanked by the shells of old windmills. A quiet, pastoral life reigns, and footpaths lead through the interior to ancient Roman ruins and the once-fortified monastery of Moni Zoödochou Pigis, where villagers once sought shelter during pirate raids.

By contrast, as the ferry pulls up by the dock at Ios, a large, garrulous group of backpackers prepares to descend on Gialos beach, one of the island's loveliest stretches of golden sand. The beach bars that flank Gialos begin to to pulse with dance beats as the Cycladic capital of youthful hedonism kicks off one

 Immerse yourself in village life in Kastro on low-key Sikinos.

 Party till dawn on the beaches of Ios, then sleep off the hangover on pristine white sand.

 Grab yourself a seat on deck to greet Santorini.

© SIVAN ASKAYO / LONELY PLANET

"Revellers climb the hairpin bends to the tiny port of Hora, a labyrinth of cube-like houses and narrow lanes with a lively main pedestrian street."

of its al fresco parties that last late into the night. All-terrain vehicles and taxis full of revellers climb the hairpin bends to the tiny port of Hora, a labyrinth of cube-like houses and narrow lanes with a lively main pedestrian street and square lined by bars that turn into one big alcohol-fuelled celebration come sundown.

As the sky begins to redden, heralding the advent of one of Santorini's hypnotising sunsets, the ferry finally reaches the sheer cliffs of Thira, its final destination.

❷ LIFE ON BOARD

Zante ferries are spacious and comfortable. Passenger seating ranges from deck space and seats in air-conditioned economy to plusher Zeus and Apollon seating. For extra comfort, passengers may book a berth in four-bed cabins. There is at least one cafe on board that serves Greek standards, fast food and coffee.

❸ MAKE IT HAPPEN

Zante ferries (three weekly, 11 hours) are the slowest and most atmospheric of the five ferry companies that run the Piraeus–Thira route. Seajets (three daily) and Hellenic Seaways (seven weekly) are the fastest (5½ hours) but stop only at Sifnos and Ios, while Blue Star Ferries (16 weekly, 7½ hours) and Anek Lines (two weekly, 8 hours) are slower and make more stops. Book tickets at www.directferries.co.uk or via individual ferry company websites. Book your space two to three weeks in advance in high season (July and August), and a few days beforehand the rest of the year. Late spring, June and September are the nicest months for travel, with smaller crowds. **AK**

On the Thames

UK

START **WESTMINSTER**

END **GREENWICH**

DISTANCE **6¹ᐟ² MILES (10KM)**

DURATION **45 MINUTES**

At its heart, the Thames Clippers RB1 is a commuter service, ferrying passengers between central London and eastern London's riverine neighbourhoods of Canary Wharf (London's financial centre), Greenwich and Woolwich. But not only has it elevated commuting to an art form – fresh coffee, incredible views, no face-in-armpit overcrowding and definitely no signal failure or traffic jam – it has also become an attraction in its own right. The river Thames flows past the majority of London's top sights, and

while most tourist boats chug along the same route, Thames Clippers' catamarans power between stops commentary-free, letting you revel in the skyline and the thrill of its speed.

❶ RIDING THE WAVES

Boarding at Westminster, you couldn't hope for a grander start: on the north bank, the iconic Big Ben, with the Houses of Parliament; on the south bank, the modern grace of the London Eye. It's hard to know which to look at the longest – hang out the back to make the most of the view.

As the boat approaches the bend in the river, move to the front, where views of St Paul's Cathedral, the Tate Modern and the City unfold. As you sail under the pedestrian Millennium Bridge, the capital's idiosyncratic (and quirkily named) skyscrapers come into view: the Gherkin, the Walkie-Talkie and the Cheese Grater to the north, the impossibly tall Shard to

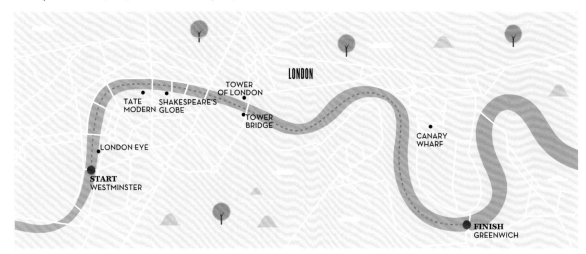

© MICKEY LEE / ALAMY STOCK PHOTO

the south. These new buildings have radically changed London's skyline since 2003 over the past 15 years and may be a sign of things to come: London has around 510 buildings over 20 stories high in the pipeline.

As you sail past Bankside and London Bridge City, the boat comes up to HMS *Belfast*, an old light cruiser that served in WWII and the Korean War. City Hall lies behind it, a building that has been variously compared to an onion, Darth Vader's helmet and a woodlouse.

Next stop is the Tower of London. The building looks rather underwhelming against the modern backdrop of skyscrapers but don't be fooled: the Tower looms large over British history, packing in nearly a millennium of conquests, reigns and executions in its walls. Even today it is the repository of the Crown Jewels, which only make appearances on special occasions, such as the opening of Parliament or a coronation.

Before you've even had the chance to think about how you might look in a crown, the boat is off again, coming head-to-head with one of London's great icons, Tower Bridge. Being on the river is the only chance you get for a full-frontal picture: this is your Instagram moment.

Tower Bridge marks the end of central London and its top sights. As you sail on, you enter the realm of the Docklands, which have undergone a staggering transformation since 1945 from busy port to industrial wasteland to prime real estate. Many of the old wharves and warehouses have been converted into desirable apartment buildings, turning old cranes and pulleys into architectural features.

The speed limit on this stretch of the river is much higher than in central London, so the catamaran flies. Before you know it, you're squaring up to Canary Wharf, London's financial heartland. From there, it's one final push to Greenwich, home to the Meridian and Greenwich Mean Time (GMT, now UTC) and a smattering of maritime history sights:

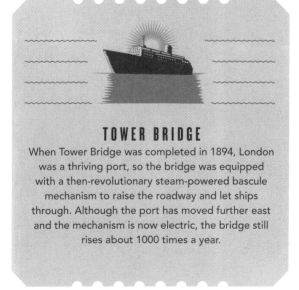

TOWER BRIDGE

When Tower Bridge was completed in 1894, London was a thriving port, so the bridge was equipped with a then-revolutionary steam-powered bascule mechanism to raise the roadway and let ships through. Although the port has moved further east and the mechanism is now electric, the bridge still rises about 1000 times a year.

the Old Royal Naval College, the National Maritime Museum and the *Cutty Sark* clipper ship.

❷ LIFE ON BOARD

With its fleet of powerful catamarans, Thames Clippers is public transport at its best: comfortable leather seats, big windows to take in the view, climate control so that you don't freeze in winter or sweat in summer, an outdoor deck at the back, a

 Hang out the back of the boat to enjoy Big Ben and the London Eye.

 Name-check London's weird and wonderful skyscrapers.

 Get your camera ready for the best view of Tower Bridge.

© HELEN HOTSON / 500PX

FROM LEFT: The Thames Clipper service; Westminster Bridge and Big Ben reflected in the waters of the Thames. **PREVIOUS PAGE:** St Paul's from the South Bank.

licensed bar serving hot and cold drinks as well as snacks, and toilets. There are even free newspapers on board and wi-fi at selected piers. The boats and almost all piers are fully wheelchair-accessible.

➌ OTHER ROUTES

At weekends, the RBX1 offers an express service between Westminster and Greenwich, skipping Bankside and the stops between Tower and Greenwich, shaving 10–15 minutes off the journey.

Culture vultures will love the RB2 service, which runs from Battersea Power Station to London Bridge City. Known as the Tate to Tate, it stops at Millbank outside the Tate Britain and at Bankside outside the Tate Modern. Visitors can therefore move seamlessly

from seminal British art history to world-class contemporary art.

➍ MAKE IT HAPPEN

Boats leave every 20 minutes on weekdays, every half hour in the evenings and at weekends. Tickets can be purchased at every pier; alternatively, book online or use your Oyster card (the public transport smart card) as you would on any other public transport. It's easy and a third cheaper than standard fares.

The bulk of commuters use the Thames Clippers to connect central London with Canary Wharf; tourists tend to move between central London and Greenwich. You can also use it as a hop-on hop-off service with a River Roamer day pass.

Dusk is particularly lovely on the river, when the lights switch on and skyscrapers twinkle against the evening sky. People-watching is also a spectacle on mornings at Canary Wharf. **EF**

 Admire the splendid converted wharves and warehouses in the Docklands.

 Take in Greenwich's rich scientific and maritime heritage.

Finish your trip by standing on the GMT/UTC Meridian.

Blue Cruise

TURKEY

This is the Mediterranean at its grandest. Backed by the hazy profiles of the Taurus Mountains' snowcapped peaks, Turkey's Teke Peninsula tumbles down in blankets of thickly forested slopes to coves scooped out of the jagged shore. To take in the full scope of this landscape, you're going to have to get on the water. Blue Cruises follow this wrinkled coastline between Fethiye and Olympos, looping between scatterings of tiny islands and dropping anchor for swim breaks at hidden inlets along the way. It's travel taken to its laziest, most sun-soaked extreme.

START FETHIYE	
END DEMRE	
DISTANCE 124 MILES (200KM)	DURATION 4 DAYS

➊ RIDING THE WAVES

For hundreds of years *gulets* were laden down with the day's catch as local fisherfolk came into shore. Today though, their wooden decks are more likely to welcome travellers on board at Fethiye for what is known as a Blue Cruise (in Turkish, *Mavi Yolculuk*). As the *gulet*

glides out of the harbour and salt spray settles onto your arms, the bustling town recedes from view, to be framed by the huge Lycian tombs chiselled into the cliffs above. Hugging the shore of the Yedi Burun (Seven Capes), you sail past green-topped specks of islands just offshore. Under the turquoise water, the ruins of ancient Simena's harbour are glimpsed.

Yes, it's possible to explore the harbourside towns and villages of Turkey's Teke Peninsula by bus, but to discover the full spectacle of this coastline's dramatic contours, hop on a *gulet* – a traditional wooden Turkish yacht – and take the watery three-night route heading south. On day one *gulets* stop at Butterfly Valley, hemmed in between towering cliffs, before cruising on to Ölüdeniz's sheltered lagoon. Here the wide sandspit stretches its finger out into the sea, with the green flanks of Babadağ (Mt Baba) soaring up behind. This is where many Blue Cruise passengers choose to take in a bird's-eye view.

Ölüdeniz is one of the world's top places to try out

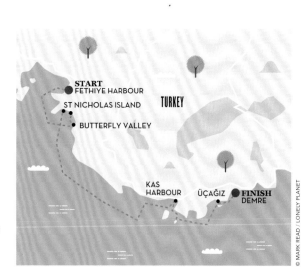

© STUNY / GETTY IMAGES

tandem-paragliding. Fling yourself off the summit of Babadağ to swoop over the slopes with the Mediterranean, a glimmering wash of aqua merging into a deep azure blue, below. After landing on the beach, adrenaline buzz done and dusted for the day, head back on the boat to St Nicholas Island, where Blue Cruises moor for the evening. Hiking boots are donned to explore the island's tumble of Byzantine church ruins onshore; then sit back on deck as the stars come out and the *raki* – a potent aniseed-infused grape spirit – begins to flow.

The *gulet* strikes out further south on day two, the long stretch of cruising broken up with swim stops while moored just off rocky islets where squawking gulls swoop and dive. Follow their lead and plunge off deck into the cool sea for a short, sharp shock after the blasting Mediterranean heat. Later you sail into Kaş harbour to explore the cobblestoned alleys and admire how the town's red-tile roofs clamber up the slope, facing the green hills of the Greek island of Kastellorizo just offshore.

With the *gulet* moored at the waterfront village of Üçağız overnight, wake up just before dawn to witness the swirling mist swathing the sea and the shadowy profiles of other *gulets* slowly appearing like ghost ships as the sun rises. The sea on the edge of Kekova Island is so clear that the remnants of this Lycian port city, toppled by an earthquake in the 2nd century AD, can be easily pointed out as you skim across the surface. Sail past a half-submerged Lycian sarcophagus marking the entrance to Kaleköy harbour and disembark here to explore this dollop of a village with its stone houses clinging to the craggy slope. Wobbly sea legs get exercised sweating the way up to the hill to the Crusader fortress at its tip. From these fortifications, built by the Knights of Rhodes, the view back across the sparkling blue water to the rugged hills of Kekova Island beyond is the stuff of Mediterranean dreams.

Afterwards, sitting atop the summit of Kaleköy in late afternoon, with just one night left on board, you and your fellow Blue Cruise passengers will all agree that this remarkable feast of Mediterranean views sums up Turkey's long, meandering coastline in one small bite. You'll be raising your *raki* glasses to that.

❷ LIFE ON BOARD

Blue Cruise *gulets* generally take between seven and 14 passengers, who are allotted a bed in (usually) twin-berth cabins. All cabins have bathrooms and some have air-conditioning. In the height of summer, if a boat does not have air-conditioned cabins, many passengers choose to sleep on deck due to the stuffiness below. Although this is a yacht, the motor will be used more

 Throw yourself off the summit of Babadağ to paraglide over Ölüdeniz's lagoon.

 Explore the Byzantine remnants on St Nicholas Island before a sunset swim.

 Soak up cobblestoned quaintness amid the winding old-town alleys radiating from Kaş harbour.

FROM LEFT: Butterfly Valley, one of the typical Blue Cruise stops; sunken Lycian ruins off Kekova Island. **PREVIOUS PAGE:** A traditional *gulet* boat. **NEXT PAGE:** Frequent stops mean regular chances for a swim.

©MARK READ / LONELY PLANET

often than the sail because of the distances covered.

The forward deck is laid out with mattresses for sunbathing, while the aft deck is used for dining and lounging, with a shaded table area and cushioned seating. Most *gulets* are stocked with snorkelling equipment as well as other recreational kit such as water noodles and fishing lines. Meals are included in the trip cost and are cooked by the crew. Water, soft drinks and alcohol are extra. As *gulets* provide a full bar, passengers are usually not allowed to bring any of their own drinks on board.

Fethiye. Due to the shorter distances these *gulets* don't have to rely on their motors, meaning there's more actual sailing time. A typical three-night itinerary would include Tersane Island, Ağa Limanı Bay and Cleopatra's Bay. Before Lunch Cruises (www.beforelunch.com) runs this route.

❸ OTHER ROUTES

A less common sailing route from Fethiye is a three-night cruise around the islands of the Gulf of

❹ LUXURY ALTERNATIVE

Don't fancy sharing your *gulet* experience with strangers? The more expensive option is to charter an

 Dive directly off the deck into the blue at one of umpteen swimming stops.

 Hike up to Kaleköy's fortress for panoramic views of forest-clad hills and islands offshore.

 Wonder over the sunken buildings lying under the clear waters off Kekova Island.

THE LYCIAN LEAGUE

Ancient Lycia was a fiercely independent federation of city-states on Turkey's southwest coast, dating back to the 12th century BC. When the Romans marched into Anatolia, they granted the Lycians self-rule; the Lycians went on to establish the Lycian League, the world's first known democratic union. Later Hellenised, the Lycian League nonetheless went on to influence the US Constitution.

entire skippered yacht yourself with family or a group of friends. This way you can also set the itinerary and route. Popular charter embarkation points are Göcek and Kaş. Fethiye-based company Ocean Yachting Travel (www.gofethiye.com) is a good first point of call for information on yacht charters.

❶ MAKE IT HAPPEN

Boats depart approximately three times weekly from late April through May and September to October. From June to August, there are daily departures. Book directly through local operators; one reputable agency is Alaturka Cruises (www.alaturkacruises.com). Steer clear of booking through touts or agencies and hotels in Istanbul as they add on hefty commissions.

The usual way to travel this route is Fethiye to Demre one-way (then travelling on to Olympos by bus). You can also do it in reverse, starting in Olympos. Check if your transfer costs to Olympos are included in the trip price when booking. June to September is the best Blue Cruise time.

Check your operator out thoroughly. Some Blue Cruises are party boats; some are cheap but scrimp on food quality. **JL**

Northern Isles

UK

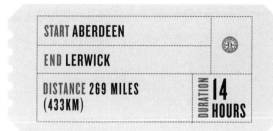

START ABERDEEN

END LERWICK

DISTANCE 269 MILES (433KM)

DURATION 14 HOURS

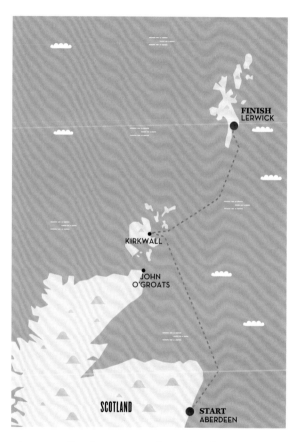

The longest boat trip in British waters, this choppy crossing ushers you from Scotland's third-largest conurbation, Aberdeen, out to two of its remotest, most northerly archipelagos, the Orkney and Shetland Islands. This 14-hour ferry ride packs in cracking sights and experiences, from the idyllic ochre-hued beaches rimming Aberdeen to the stomach-churning swirls of some of the planet's most treacherous tides in the Pentland Firth. It passes the biggest natural harbour on earth, Scapa Flow, and Britain's most isolated inhabited island, Fair Isle. For much of the year, taking this boat means leaving the big city at dusk and waking up to dawn over lonely green islands studded with rocks, crofts, sheep, ponies and barely any other humans, an entire world apart from your departure point.

❶ RIDING THE WAVES

From modern Aberdeen, a city buoyed by oil money and replete with fancy hotels, restaurants and galleries, it seems inconceivable that you could board a boat that transports you to an island group where sheep and ponies regularly outnumber people. Even as you stand across the quay from the ferry terminal, outside Aberdeen Maritime Museum with its multimedia displays charting the city's seafaring past,

a journey of such utter transformation does not seem tangible. When you board and clamber to the top deck to tower over much of the surrounding city, or make a beeline to one of the comfy passenger lounges or restaurant areas, it still does not really sink in. But you are bound for a very far-flung place.

It is only after the first few hours, with the placid mainland coast just a horizon smudge, and when this giant four-deck ferry starts to toss and turn – and the might of one of the world's most turbulent sea

NORSE HERITAGE

Until 1472, the Orkney and Shetland Islands were owned by Norway, following a Viking takeover during the preceding centuries. Many elements of Scandinavian culture remain, from the islands' dialect to the place names to buildings such as Orkney's St Magnus Cathedral, constructed to symbolise the might of Norse influence on these isles.

crossings, the Pentland Firth, is felt in every fibre of the vessel – that the sense of otherworldliness smacks into you. Now, during this most tempestuous leg of the voyage, it is easier to understand how the islands you are heading for, hemmed in by a sea like this, stayed cut off for so long.

To port, South Ronaldsay and Burray slide by, the first of the Orkney Islands, marking the eastern edge of one of the world's great harbours, Scapa Flow. It was chosen as a strategic point to control the entrances to the North Sea during WWI; it was also here, in 1919, that Rear Admiral Ludwig von Reuter decided to scuttle all 74 vessels of the interned German High Seas Fleet to prevent them from falling into British hands. As a result, Scapa Flow is now one of Europe's most fascinating dive sites.

You touch land soon after at Kirkwall, chief port of the Orkney Islands. The town was once chosen by the Norse as the capital of their powerful earldom,

which at its zenith included northern Scotland, all of the Orkneys and the Shetlands. The huge cathedral of St Magnus, raised in the 12th century and still dominating the Kirkwall skyline, is the most impressive surviving evidence of the Norse legacy. These islands are also known for having the highest concentration of Neolithic sites anywhere in Europe, and on the Orkneys and the Shetlands both, a vast array of stone circles and burial cairns stand, many barely visited, like sentinels to a mystery-steeped era.

The pale green Orkney hills fade into the murk as evening approaches, and the next part of the voyage takes place in darkness for most of the year. Early in the morning the route cuts past Fair Isle, known for its knitwear and for being Britain's remotest populated island. Next in view are the more jagged silhouettes of the Shetland Islands, intimating that your final destination is near. First, Mousa Island, home to one of Europe's best-preserved prehistoric monuments, Mousa

 Marvel at Aberdeen's mesmerising Maritime Museum.

 Take a leisurely pre-departure late lunch at one of Aberdeen's upmarket restaurants.

 Start the voyage by sampling an award-winning Orkney Brewery ale as the sandy shores of Aberdeenshire fade behind you.

FROM LEFT: Lerwick's Town Hall on Shetland Island; a shaggy Shetland pony on Unst. **PREVIOUS PAGE:** Sea stacks in the Pentland Firth at Duncansby Head.

© MOOREFAM / GETTY IMAGES

Broch, slews by to port. Finally you are embraced by the olive-green promontories, bays, hills and skerries that surround Lerwick. This surprisingly bustling port, which grew on the herring, whaling and oil trades, is the de facto capital of the Shetlands by virtue of the fact that there is no other town around, nor another heading north, before you hit the North Pole.

❷ LIFE ON BOARD

Two large vehicle ferries are in operation on this route, MV *Hrossey* and MV *Hjaltland*. Both are comfortable and spacious, with shops, restaurants, a bar and viewing decks. This route is an overnight crossing, and there are several levels of accommodation. Most basic are the padded reclining seats (staff provide blankets), while some premium cabins have satellite TV, coffee-making facilities and complimentary shortbread.

❸ OTHER ROUTES

Northlink Ferries offers an alternative, far-shorter route to the Orkneys: crossing from Scrabster on Scotland's north coast to Stromness. Run time is merely an hour and the scenery is spectacular, with the sheer rock stack of the Old Man of Hoy rearing to starboard near the conclusion and arrival into Stromness's quaint hill-backed harbour.

❹ MAKE IT HAPPEN

There is a sailing daily each evening from Aberdeen to Lerwick, Shetland. Book tickets via Northlink Ferries (Jamieson's Quay, www.northlinkferries.co.uk). Overnight sleeping options range from reclining seats to two- and four-person cabins. Travel via Kirkwall on the way out and stop off there; then return direct from Lerwick to Aberdeen. **LW**

 Travel in summer to see almost 24-hour daylight ethereally illuminating Scotland's northerly mainland coast and islands.

 Alight at photogenic Kirkwall, with its charming waterfront and poignant Norse history.

 Visit the Boat Hall of Lerwick's spellbinding Shetland Museum; examples of the islands' distinctive boats are suspended in mid-air.

Hurtigruten Fjords

NORWAY

START **BERGEN**

END **KIRKENES**

DISTANCE **1464 MILES (2358KM)**

DURATION **7 DAYS**

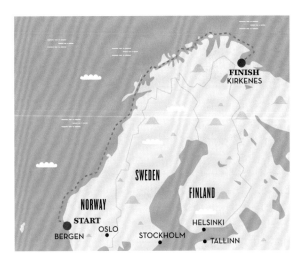

FINISH
KIRKENES

SWEDEN

FINLAND

NORWAY

START

OSLO

HELSINKI

BERGEN

STOCKHOLM

TALLINN

Since 1894 the historic Hurtigruten ships have been shuttling up and down Norway's fjord-crinkled coastline, providing a non-stop ferry service between Bergen and Kirkenes, and a vital lifeline for the nation's far-flung coastal communities. Climbing aboard allows you to experience one of the world's landmark ferry journeys, not to mention some of the finest views Norway has to offer, including soaring fjords, craggy coastal peninsulas, remote fishing stations and wild, isolated islands. And if you're really lucky, Mother Nature might even decide to put on some fireworks just for you in the form of a spectacular aurora display.

❶ RIDING THE WAVES

Picture it. It's a bitter winter's night, slightly north of the Arctic Circle, and you're standing on the deck of a ferry somewhere in the dark expanses of the Norwegian Sea. In the distance you can see the faint outline of Norway's west coast; otherwise all is blackness. There's no sound except the splash of the sea and the thrum of the ferry's engines. You're wrapped up in three layers of polar clothing, but you're still chilled to the marrow. By now, saner passengers have retreated into the coddling warmth of the ship's cabins, but there's a compelling reason you

can't bring yourself to head inside. Because overhead, the sky is on fire – a kaleidoscope of greens, pinks, purples and reds, crackling and flickering in patterns across the blackness of space. For the opportunity to watch nature's greatest light show, chilly fingers are really a small price to pay.

No one ever forgets the first time they see the aurora borealis, but on the Hurtigruten, it's par for the course. In fact, the Hurtigruten is so confident that you'll see the Northern Lights on its 12-day winter journeys that if you don't, you're guaranteed another week's cruise free of charge.

Seeing the aurora borealis is just one reason to ride this most fabled of ferries. For more than 120 years, the Hurtigruten has been an integral part of Norwegian life, linking the prosperous southern port of Bergen, the far-northern town of Kirkenes, and 30-odd ports in between. It's the only ferry that regularly crosses the Arctic Circle, and its fleet of 11 ships ensure a non-stop, year-round service.

The journey begins in handsome Bergen, once the centre of the Hanseatic League, a network of trading ports that once stretched across the northern Atlantic. After a wander around the colourful wooden buildings of Bryggen, followed perhaps by a lobster roll and an eye-wateringly expensive beer at the city's fish market, passengers head for the harbour to begin their trip into Norway's far north.

Before the advent of the Hurtigruten, the journey along Norway's coast was long, arduous and – especially in winter – fraught with danger. Shipwrecks were common, and even for the fastest ships, the route took weeks to complete. When the Norwegian government proposed a regular ferry service, an ambitious young sea captain by the name of Richard With took up the challenge. In 1893, his steamer, DS *Vesteraalen*, completed the journey in just seven days, and he named the new service Hurtigruten – the 'fast route'.

These days the Hurtigruten is as popular with tourists as locals. With comfortable cabins, on-board restaurants and nightly lectures, the ferries make it possible to cruise the coast in style. The Hurtigruten's trump card, though, is the perspective it provides on Norway's epic scenery – the towering, waterfall-lined walls of Geirangerfjord, the elegant towns of Ålesund and Trondheim, the serene inlet of Hjørundfjord and the spiky, snow-dusted summits of the Lofoten Islands.

Beyond the Arctic Circle, in Norway's far, far north, the trip really kicks into gear. This is the land of the Midnight Sun and the Polar Night, where, depending on the time of year, the sun either never sets or never rises. As you glide past Tromsø and Hammerfest (stopping, perhaps, to meet Sami reindeer herders, steer a snowmobile across the snow or try your hand at dogsledding), the magic of the Arctic takes over, and you enter a world of isolated fishing communities, uncharted mountains, wild fjords and Norwegian nature at its rawest. With luck it's also where you're most likely to spy the Northern Lights.

After about 1273 nautical miles (2358km), the ferry calls at its final port: Kirkenes, 644 miles (400km) north of the Arctic Circle and 26 miles (16km) from the Russian border. Here the Hurtigruten unloads, restocks, refuels and welcomes new passengers on board before heading south for Bergen – where, seven days later, whatever the season, whatever the weather, it will turn around and begin its northbound journey once again. Come rain or shine, winter or summer, every day of every week of every year, there's guaranteed to be at least one Hurtigruten plying the icy-cold waters of the Norwegian Sea. This is more than simply a boat trip; it's a journey into Norway's heart and soul.

❷ LIFE ON BOARD

There are four types of cabins on the Hurtigruten ships: Polar Inside, Polar Outside, Arctic Superior

 Wander round the wooden, Unesco-listed buildings of Bryggen in Bergen.

 Cruise up Geirangerfjord, one of Norway's mightiest and most dramatic fjords.

 Sail past the serrated peaks of the Lofoten Islands.

THE HURTIGRUTEN FLEET

The Hurtigruten fleet currently includes 11 vessels, the oldest of which is MS *Lofoten*, built in 1964. The fleet is supplemented by four custom-built expedition ships, specially designed to cope with polar conditions during cruises to the Arctic and Antarctic. Two are named after famous Norwegian explorers: the *Fridtjof Nansen* and *Roald Amundsen*.

ABOVE: Aurora borealis on Hardangerfjord.
PREVIOUS PAGE: Bergen lit at night. **FIRST PAGE:** Passing through Geiranger fjord.

and Expedition Suite. Tickets are priced according to availability and comfort level. Activities and lectures are available on board, and onshore excursions can be arranged at many ports. Food is a strong point: ships have an à la carte restaurant and buffet-style cafe, offering dishes like Lofoten cod, Finnmark reindeer, Geiranger lamb and Arctic char (there's even a vegan-friendly menu).

❸ OTHER ROUTES

The standard north–south, Bergen–Kirkenes route takes seven days, or 12 days including the return journey. You can also extend the journey to the Arctic island of Svalbard, or south to Germany and the Netherlands.

❹ BUDGET ALTERNATIVE

While cabins aren't compulsory, they make the journey a lot more pleasurable. For the cheapest deals, book early, opt for less popular interior cabins, and travel during the shoulder season, March and October.

❺ MAKE IT HAPPEN

Boats depart from Bergen most days of the year, but if you want to travel on a particular boat, you'll need to time your trip according to its schedule. Bookings can be made directly through the Hurtigruten website. There are three classes (Basic, Select and Platinum), offering perks such as early-bird discounts, shore excursions, captain's dining and free wi-fi.

The quickest, most convenient way to do the trip is to travel one-way from Bergen to Kirkenes, then fly direct back to Oslo. **OB**

 Look out for the Northern Lights as you sail past the Arctic town of Tromsø.

 Explore the serene and little-known Hjørundfjord, where few other vessels venture.

 Round the Nordkapp, mainland Norway's most northerly point at 71° north.

Paris on the Seine

FRANCE ⬤

Paris holds its river in an intimate embrace. The city grew outwards from the Seine, and its 2000 years of history adorn the banks like jewels. This is no nostalgic love affair, but a daily-renewed passion: Parisians use the banks of their river to meet, to pass the time, to marvel, as tourists do, at the grandeur and beauty of the city that surrounds them. The Seine is a living, flowing historical monument, and to float through its Parisian heart is to experience the centuries drift by. For romantics, a sunset cruise shows off the City of Light at its shimmering best.

❶ RIDING THE WAVES

If you board at Quai de Montebello, you're facing Notre-Dame Cathedral, one of the most outstanding examples of French Gothic architecture, still resplendent despite the loss of its spire. It reigns over Île de la Cité, the larger of two islands in the middle of the Seine, once the home of a Gallic tribe called the Parisii. Paris started here around 250 BC and grew outwards.

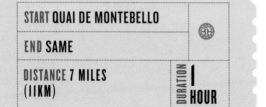

START **QUAI DE MONTEBELLO**

END **SAME**

DISTANCE **7 MILES (11KM)**

DURATION **1 HOUR**

You'll head upstream, towards Île St-Louis, the smaller island, a calm haven of elegant 17th- and 18th-century apartment buildings. Rounding its eastern edge, you'll skirt the newly pedestrianised Right Bank, alive with strollers, joggers and skateboarders. In summer there are plentiful pop-up bars and cafes, deckchairs and umbrellas, with overheated Parisians enjoying the poplar trees' shade.

Above the riverbank sits the impossibly grand Hôtel de Ville, the city hall of Paris. On your left, with its heavy, round towers, is the Conciergerie. In medieval times it was a royal palace; it eventually became a prison, taking a grisly starring role in the bloodiest period of the French Revolution, when it was the

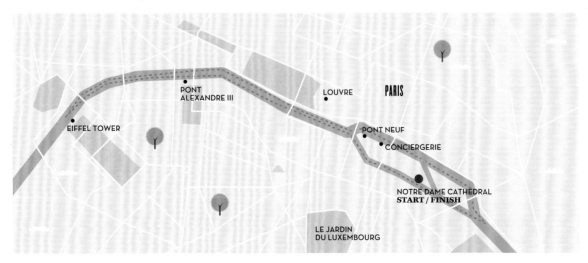

PARIS

PONT ALEXANDRE III

LOUVRE

EIFFEL TOWER

PONT NEUF

CONCIERGERIE

NOTRE DAME CATHEDRAL
START / FINISH

LE JARDIN DU LUXEMBOURG

final stop for hundreds of prisoners before they were guillotined.

The imposing Pont Neuf, or New Bridge (actually the city's oldest bridge, finished in 1606), now stands resolutely before you. Once you've passed under it, you're at the Louvre. A royal palace in the Middle Ages, the Louvre is now the world's largest art gallery; the unbroken stretch of elaborate wall as you sail by will demonstrate its scale. The Tuileries, its extensive gardens, are marked by a long row of perfectly pruned foliage. You'll catch a glimpse of the Luxor Obelisk's golden tip, marking the enormous Place de la Concorde. During the French Revolution, this was where public executions took place; King Louis XVI and Marie Antoinette were among those who lost their heads here.

Now comes the most spectacular vista of the cruise, as Pont Alexandre III and the Eiffel Tower emerge in full panorama. With its quartet of golden statues, fancy lamp posts and graceful arch, the Beaux-Arts bridge is the city's most ornate. The cruise takes you almost to the very foot of the Tower; the river aspect of the 'Dame de Fer' (Iron Lady) is one of her most impressive.

From here, the boat turns and retraces its way. Turn your attention to the Left Bank, where you'll spot the Assemblée Nationale, the lower house of the French government, with its classical colonnaded facade. A little further on is the Musée d'Orsay, the former train station that now houses the world's largest collection of impressionist masterpieces. The bijou (jewel) with the golden cupola sitting at the end of the Pont des Arts pedestrian bridge is home to the Académie Française.

Close to where the cruise reaches its end, among a handful of residential péniches (barges), you can spy the péniche of the aquatic brigade of sapeurs pompiers – Paris's firefighters, emergency responders and all-round superheroes: a glimpse of modern-day river life in this timeless city.

CRUISE THE CANALS

Already cruised the Seine? Discover the lesser-known waterways of Paris on a canal cruise. Departing from Port de l'Arsenal near Bastille, the barge traverses an underground tunnel to emerge at Canal St-Martin, the heart of hipster Paris. Pass through double locks and swing bridges, and see a different side of the city, ending at Bassin de la Villette in the 19th arrondisement.

 Look back to see the famous flying buttresses of Notre-Dame Cathedral, added in the 14th century (the cathedral was built 1160–1260).

 Observe the imposing Conciergerie, the main palace of the medieval kings of France from the 10th to 14th centuries.

 Enjoy the gallery of grotesque faces as you pass under the Pont Neuf's stone gargoyles.

LEFT AND BELOW: The immense Palais du Louvre; Pont d'Iena leading to the Eiffel Tower. **PREVIOUS PAGE:** A view of the Seine as it cuts through Paris.

LEFT: © ADRIENNE PITTS / LONELY PLANET; RIGHT: © MATT MUNRO / LONELY PLANET

❷ LIFE ON BOARD

Boat design varies among companies; all boats, however, have large open-seating decks on top. This is where you'll get the best view, weather permitting. Boats generally have a small snack stand, and at most of the departure docks you'll find a restaurant or bar, in case you need a pre-cruise glass of champagne.

❸ MAKE IT HAPPEN

A number of companies run exactly the same cruise for very similar prices. There are differences in boat size and design and in commentary method (live versus audio guide). Your main factor for choosing will be location, as the boats depart from different points along the river; all cruises end back at their departure point.

Bateaux Mouches is the largest company (with the largest boats), departing from the Right Bank of Pont d'Alma. Boats from Bateaux Parisiens depart from the Eiffel Tower (as do the boats of Vedettes de Paris), and from Quai de Montebello on the Left Bank. Vedettes du Pont Neuf depart from Pont Neuf on Ile de la Cité.

Boats make frequent (often every half hour) departures all day, every day. Book online to be assured of a place on your boat of choice, especially in high season. The cost is typically €12 to €15. **JE**

 Pass by the Louvre; when the first fortress was built on this site in 1190, it was on the walled city's outskirts.

 Note the nymphs decorating the Pont Alexandre III, celebrating the French-Russian alliance.

 Be thankful the photogenic Eiffel Tower wasn't pulled down as planned 20 years after its erection for the 1889 World's Fair.

Baltic Sea Crossing

FINLAND TO SWEDEN

When visiting the Nordic countries, why not go as the Vikings did – by the high seas? As the Arctic tern flies, Helsinki and Stockholm are only 247 miles (398km) apart, but a drive is a 21-hour slog that nearly skirts the barren Arctic Circle. Alternatively, you can fly from Helsinki to Stockholm in under an hour – 55 minutes on a good day. After you've taken off, strapped into a cramped seat and breathing in the recycled air, you might glance down briefly at the islands below and think, 'Wow, that looks pretty down there.' Or you could be down there yourself, taking to the seas on an overnight mini cruise through the stunning Stockholm archipelago and past the picturesque Åland Islands.

❶ RIDING THE WAVES

Scandinavia and the Nordic countries have been home to seafarers for centuries, and while modern ferries have upgraded a few amenities since Viking days, the carousing on board is still legendary. The trip from Helsinki to Stockholm is a 16- to 17-hour ferry ride on a 3000-passenger, 400-car ship that wends its way

© JEPPE WIKSTROM / GETTY IMAGES

START HELSINKI, FINLAND	
END STOCKHOLM, SWEDEN	
DISTANCE 247 MILES (398KM)	DURATION 17 HOURS

from Helsinki to Mariehamn in the Åland Islands, sails through the Stockholm archipelago just outside Sweden's capital and finishes in Stockholm itself (or vice versa). Nordic locals have long known this particular ferry journey as a cheap mini cruise, and tourists have discovered it's cheaper than a single flight or a hotel night in either city and faster than a car or train. It also takes in a surprisingly beautiful setting that spans the region between the Gulf of Bothnia and the Baltic Sea. The ferry terminal in Helsinki is practically walking distance from the centre of town, and Stockholm's ferry terminal is just a quick bus or taxi away from Gamla Stan, the Old Town centre of Stockholm dating back to the 13th century. (One note

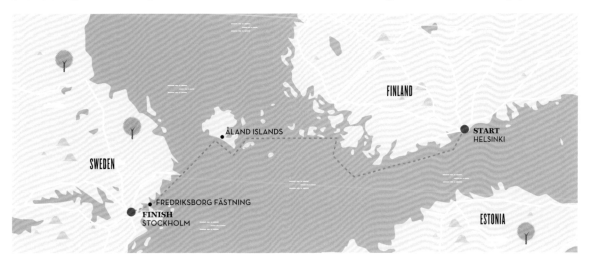

while you're here: Scandinavia is Sweden, Norway and Denmark; the Nordic countries also include Finland and Iceland. Now you know.)

Each mini cruise is an adventure. Ferries crossing the Baltic Sea have a reputation for being booze cruises, and especially on Friday nights, they can be. Every ferry stops in the VAT-exempt Åland Islands in the middle of the night so stores can sell duty-free alcohol. If you stay away from the discos on weekends, though, the ferry ride can be downright family-friendly. Little is as charming as watching karaoke battles between heavy-drinking adults and eight-year-old children. Every voyage features on-board casinos, nightclubs, an entire shopping complex filled with duty-free shops, a day spa and the requisite Finnish saunas. A half-dozen on-board restaurants serve everything from fine dining to a Swedish smorgasbord-type buffet. Think gravlax, potato salad, Swedish meatballs – everything you'd want on a Nordic sea voyage. Because ferries make their money from gambling, boozing, shopping and dining, the passage itself can be unbelievably inexpensive. To create a more serene cruise, book a cabin on a quieter (meaning, not the cheapest) level. Or party it up all night. Both options are yours for the choosing.

On all but the foggiest, darkest days (of which there are admittedly many in the depths of winter), you'll most likely see archipelagic scenery and forest-covered islands picturesque enough to rival the most beautiful tropical seas. And, once in a while, you might see the occasional Finnish rockabilly club, complete with tail-finned American hot rods and bouffant hairdos. It's an unforgettable way to explore the Baltic.

❷ LIFE ON BOARD

Two main ferry companies, Viking and Tallink Silja, run similar voyages on nearly identical vessels. Viking Line

SWEDISH FINNS

Did you know that about 5% of the population of Finland is Swedish-speaking? The Åland Islands are a majority Swedish-speaking region with a semi-autonomous status; Sweden ceded them to Russia in 1809, which brought them into the semi-autonomous Grand Duchy of Finland. It's the smallest region of Finland, with .49% of the country's land area and .50% of its population.

Browse the waterfront stalls and Finnish market of Hakaniemi in Helsinki's city centre.

Picnic on the hills surrounding Helsinki harbour's Suomenlinna, an 18th-century fortress island.

Island-peep while docking in the middle of the night at Mariehamn in the Åland Islands.

LEFT AND BELOW: Old Town pier in Helsinki; a traditional flat-bottomed boat sailing near Norröra Island in Sweden.
PREVIOUS PAGE: Cottages in the Stockholm archipelago.

doesn't require passengers to book a cabin, so many passengers, especially young people, stay awake all night. These are state-of-the-art ships with reasonable cabins and more amenities than passengers might expect for a ferry service.

❸ OTHER ROUTES

A dozen ferry companies traverse routes in the Baltic Sea, including to and from Estonia, Latvia, Lithuania, Germany and Poland, all reasonably enough priced to create an inexpensive, do-it-yourself cruise. Estonia's capital, Tallinn, has one of the most beautiful medieval city centres in all of Europe.

❹ MAKE IT HAPPEN

Ferries cross between Helsinki and Stockholm usually twice daily each way. They leave around 4pm or 5pm and arrive by 9am or 10am. The two main ferry companies are Tallink Silja (www.tallinksilja. com) and Viking Line (www.vikingline.com); you can also compare prices and times (www.directferries. com). Book ahead in summer, around holidays or on popular weekends. Sailing one-way is plenty to see the sights, but return ferry tickets are usually cheaper. No additional paperwork or visas are needed beyond what's necessary for Sweden or Finland.

For a near–midnight sun, travel close to midsummer (around June 21). To avoid the loudest neighbours, upgrade a cabin class or two, or travel Monday through Wednesday. **AL**

 In summer, enjoy the Baltic Sea's midnight sun, while winter brings a chance of the Northern Lights (the ships are undeterred by icy waters).

 Daydream about life in the enchanted Stockholm archipelago, home to Fredriksborg Hotel, a 1724 castle-turned-hotel.

 Window-shop and dine in Old Town, Stockholm's bustling harbourside.

OCEANIA

AMAZING BOAT JOURNEYS

The Marquesas Islands

FRENCH POLYNESIA

START **PAPE'ETE, TAHITI**

END **SAME**

DISTANCE **2361 MILES (3800KM)**

DURATION **14 DAYS**

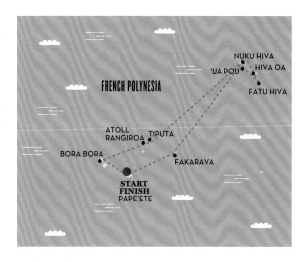

If you've ever dreamed of exploring remote South Pacific isles on a freight ship, this voyage is for you. The wildly rugged Marquesas Islands are linked to the rest of French Polynesia by only a few small aircraft and supply boats. The Aranui 5, the largest of these vessels, also happens to be a comfortable hybrid cruise liner/freight ship. Watch as all manner of cargo is unloaded to the docks, visit ancient stone tiki (images of human figures), hike tropical mountains and feast on Marquesan cuisine. You'll even get to visit some white sand beaches in the Tuamotu atolls and Bora Bora along the way.

❶ RIDING THE WAVES

Drums boom through the jungle as a high-pitched wail resonates off ancient, moss-covered stones. Just ahead, at the base of a four-storey-tall banyan tree, a troupe of dancers clad in leaf skirts are slapping their thighs in time to the traditional pahu drums as they begin singing in warrior-like tones. It feels like you've stepped back in time and that these crumbled Polynesian temples are alive. This isn't a touristic-feeling performance, even if it's being performed for you and your shipmates. This performance feels like what it is: a dramatic, cultural welcome filled with power and warmth.

This is the magic of a voyage on the *Aranui*. Yes, you're on a cruise ship, but it's also a cargo ship that's the lifeline of the Marquesas Islands. The dances you see, the feasts prepared and the smiles from the locals are more a part of the islanders' traditions than something they are paid to do. These arts are breathing and evolving. By coming here, you're not giving these performances a reason to be – they have that on their own – but you are helping them flourish.

The journey begins in Pape'ete, the flower-filled and car-exhaust-choked capital of French Polynesia. But by day two you're far, far away already, to low-slung, white-sandy Fakarava in the Tuamotu Archipelago; the island's brilliant blue lagoon is a Unesco Biosphere Reserve for its uncommon biodiversity. This is your first chance to see cranes unloading cargo onto smaller launches that head to island docks. Seemingly half the population waits to pick up their boxes of food, building supplies and maybe a motorbike or two. Then you're off again. After a day at sea you'll arrive to high and chiseled Nuku Hiva, the largest of the Marquesas Islands. You'll stop at the three largest villages here, again with all the inhabitants coming out to welcome your ship and receive their supplies. You'll also have the chance to visit artisans, hike to vistas over endless and wild dark-blue seas, visit archaeological sites and hear about Herman Melville's experiences in Taipivai village, the basis of his book *Typee* (1846).

The next day you'll arrive at small 'Ua Pou with its famous silhouette of surreal-looking basalt spires. Here you'll dine on Marquesan specialties like goat and coconut milk stew, then be awed by the island's bird dance, which has lots of clapping, singing and hip swaying. Next it's on to Hiva Oa, the final home and burial place of French post-impressionist Paul Gauguin – and later in history, Belgian singer Jacques Brel. Here you'll get to visit a recreation of Gauguin's home, see Jacques Brel's beloved Beechcraft airplane Jojo and have the chance to visit both men's graves. With four port stops over two days on Hiva Oa, you'll have plenty of chances to explore eerie and remote archaeological sites including Tiki Takaii, the largest ancient tiki in French Polynesia (9ft/2.67m), at the Iipona site.

You're now a week into your voyage as you come to port at the most remote island on the itinerary, Fatu Hiva. This island is only accessible by boat, and yet the majestic Bay of Virgins, with its otherworldly rock formations and knife-chiseled ridges, is so striking that it's famous in photographs. Thor Heyerdahl, who came up with the theory that Polynesians came from South America, not Southeast Asia (which was later disproved by genetic research), lived here for a year and a half in the 1930s looking to find an untouched paradise; he later wrote his book *Fatu-Hiva: Back to Nature* about the experience. You'll visit the two villages here and see some giant petroglyphs.

The next stop is another small island, 'Ua Huka, known for its wood carvings. Here you'll get to feast

© HEMIS / ALAMY STOCK PHOTO

GAUGUIN IN THE MARQUESAS

Post-impressionist French painter Paul Gauguin sailed to the Marquesas in 1901 after six years on Tahiti. Dying of syphilis and gravely alcoholic, he had become disenchanted with the modernity of Tahiti - though for moderns, it's his own behaviour which is disenchanting. Gauguin spent his final years painting what he considered his masterpieces of primitivism on Hiva Oa.

 Snorkel with reef sharks, colourful fish and thriving corals in the Fakarava lagoon.

 Wander past towering stone tiki and crumbling Polynesian temples at Puama'u on Hiva Oa, the second largest island in the Marquesas.

 Pay homage to painter Paul Gauguin and admire the sculpture on his gravestone, Oviri.

© DAVE G. HOUSER / ALAMY STOCK PHOTO

ABOVE, FROM LEFT: A dolphin in Hanavave, the Bay of Virgins in Fatu Hiva island; an *Aranui* tender heads ashore. **PREVIOUS PAGE:** Sunset at a Fakarava jetty. **NEXT PAGE:** Fakarava lagoon.

at a large ceremonial site and visit a woodcarving and historical museum and the island's extensive arboretum. Watching artisans create fantastic tiki out of local wood is a definite highlight. Bowls, drums and other useful and beautiful items are for sale at very reasonable prices.

Backtracking to the Tuamotu atolls, you'll arrive at Rangiroa, the second-largest atoll in the world. After the Marquesas, sleepy Rangiroa will feel downright lively. Besides finding resorts and restaurants, you'll have the chance to visit a pearl farm. Don't miss watching the dolphins leap through Avatoru Pass at sunset, snorkelling, or diving with sharks in the pass.

The last stop is Bora Bora, the lap of French Polynesian luxury. The famous square-topped peaked island is surrounded by an exquisitely blue lagoon dotted with outlandishly decadent over-the-water bungalow resorts. Here you'll have lots of activity choices, from helicopter tours to shark and ray feeding in the lagoon. Then it's back to Pape'ete to unload supplies from the more remote isles and to be reminded that the rest of the world still exists.

The itinerary here is changeable depending on the day of the week the ship leaves Pape'ete, along with sea and weather conditions.

❷ LIFE ON BOARD

While the hulls are packed with supplies and a giant crane traverses the front deck, the *Aranui 5* also has a handful of comfortable passenger decks, a restaurant, four bars, an outdoor pool, a massage room and a gym.

 Be awed by chiselled basalt cliffs at the remote Bay of Virgins in Fatu Hiva.

 Enjoy Marquesan dishes and a lively local dance performance on 'Ua Huka.

 Get fancy in magnificent Bora Bora, the aquamarine playground of honeymooning jet-setters.

© MAFELIPE / GETTY IMAGES

Guest lectures (speakers might include an archaeologist or cultural specialist) and grand dance performances are held on deck. You'll mingle with foreign passengers as well as island locals heading home and the friendly deckhands who load and unload the freight.

The ship accommodates 254 passengers. Sleeping options range from dorm beds to small double staterooms and a variety of suites with their own terraces.

❸ OTHER ROUTES

The *Aranui 5* made its first trip through the Gambier, Austral and Pitcairn island groups in 2019; Pitcairn Island is known for being home to the Bounty mutineers, romanticised in the book and film *Mutiny on the Bounty*. These are among the most remote inhabited places on the planet, many reachable only by boat or cargo ship.

❹ MAKE IT HAPPEN

The *Aranui 5* makes around 20 voyages per year. Reserve through a travel agent or by email with the *Aranui 5* itself (details are found on https://aranui. com). You'll want to book around a year in advance for special or themed voyages and at least six months in advance for those in high season (July, August and around Christmas holidays). You may be able to get lower-season bookings at the last minute. **CB**

© MLENNY PHOTOGRAPHY / GETTY IMAGES

Sydney's Manly Ferry

AUSTRALIA

START	CIRCULAR QUAY
END	MANLY WHARF
DISTANCE	8 MILES (13KM)
DURATION	30 MINUTES

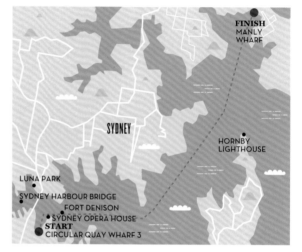

FINISH
MANLY WHARF

SYDNEY

HORNBY
LIGHTHOUSE

LUNA PARK

SYDNEY HARBOUR BRIDGE

FORT DENISON

SYDNEY OPERA HOUSE

START
CIRCULAR QUAY WHARF 3

The Manly Ferry is Australia's best-known and most-loved boat ride for good reason. With a backdrop of Sydney's Harbour Bridge, Opera House, Luna Park and the glossy skyscraper skyline, this trip is big on impressive photo

opportunities. It's also an excellent way to tick off some major sights in a short period of time at little cost. In 30 minutes you can be in Manly for a dose of Aussie beach culture before soaking up stunning sunset views on the return trip.

❶ RIDING THE WAVES

Sydney's Circular Quay is a busy hub of five double-sided wharves, but don't worry: you'll head straight for wharf 3, the dedicated departure point for traditional Manly services. A little higher than the other wharves, it was rebuilt in the 1980s to accommodate the Freshwater class ferries' on-board gangways. Which of the four green-and-gold ferries will you board today: *Collaroy, Freshwater, Narrabeen* or *Queenscliff*? As seagulls squawk and quayside buskers sing, the clanking of the gangway on the mezzanine level for disembarking passengers is your first prompt that it's almost time to board.

Deciding where to sit will be the most difficult decision you'll make for the next half hour. Since the ferry service is deservedly popular and there's no set seating, it's best not to get too attached to a particular spot. The big sights appear early, as you depart Circular Quay: with Sydney Harbour Bridge on one side and Sydney Opera House on the other, it's not unusual for people to rush from one side of the ferry to the other. Here are prime photo opportunities; the forward or rear decks are the best for the slow, tantalising pull out of Sydney Harbour.

Don't miss Luna Park, with the gigantic smiling clown-face entrance to its amusement park on Sydney's northern shore, spotted briefly underneath Sydney Harbour Bridge. Oh, and what are those things on top of the bridge apart from the flags of Australia? They're people doing the BridgeClimb! Once the Harbour Bridge versus Opera House battle is out of the way, it's the remarkable Sydney skyline that competes for attention, with the distinctive Centrepoint Tower rising above the shiny skyscrapers.

After that, it becomes a gentler trip of admiring the elaborate mansions adorning the shores and waving at other sea-goers, whether they're on luxury yachts, windsurfers, canoes or dinghies. The diversity of the Sydney landscape is striking, but remember to look in the water around the cliffs and national parks lining the harbour, where you may spot dolphins, whales and seals.

"The fun isn't over once you hit Manly Wharf; it's only a very short stroll to an excellent swimming beach and the Corso."

Now's a good time to get a coffee, a snack or even a beer before you pass some of the historical sites, such as Mrs Macquarie's Chair, a sandstone-carved chair made by convicts for Governor Macquarie's wife, or Fort Denison, a stark reminder of Australia's penal colony days. Before things get a little choppy at South Head, you'll also see the red-and-white-striped Hornby Lighthouse.

The fun isn't over once you hit Manly Wharf; it's only a very short stroll to an excellent swimming beach and the Corso, buzzing with restaurants and pubs.

❷ LIFE ON BOARD

Depending on the time of day and season, this trip could be the most pleasant, relaxing half hour of your life (the maximum speed is 15 knots, about 17mph or 28km/h), or you could be trampled by obnoxious selfie-takers, screaming children, argumentative families and surly teenage surfers. Despite appearances sometimes, it's not a tourist vessel but a working ferry for commuters too. Don't be surprised if you're sipping coffee next to a suited businesswoman much more interested in the *Australian Financial Review* on her tablet than the views.

The boat journey itself is generally a smooth one, if conditions are good, though it usually gets a little bouncy as the ferry crosses the heads at the start of Sydney Harbour. Be prepared for some choppiness and a bit of spray for a dramatic interlude. Anyone of a nervous disposition might want to sit inside at this point.

Since early 2018, Sydney's 4 Pines Brewing Company has a dedicated bar selling its beer on board during late afternoon and evening services. It's the first Freshwater-class bar service since 2012, with consumption on the

© SHUTTERSTOCK / TARAS VYSHNYA

 Enjoy uninterrupted views of Sydney Harbour Bridge during the chug out of Circular Quay.

 Peer beneath the bridge towards Luna Park's vibrant entrance: the huge, grinning clown face.

 Sail right by the distinctive Sydney Opera House for an exclusive photo vantage point.

SURF'S UP

Manly is considered the birthplace of Australian surfing, and Manly-Freshwater is now recognised as a World Surfing Reserve. Swell here averages 1.5m and can reach several metres. In a country filled to the brim with world-class breaks and surf enthusiasts, the surf culture of the Northern Beaches still manages to stand out from the crowd. Try out a lesson during your visit.

LEFT: Manly Beach is backed by distinctive Norfolk Island pines.
PREVIOUS PAGE: The Manly ferry sets out across Sydney Harbour.

forward upper deck only. Healthy food options for breakfast trips include granola with Greek yogurt, seasonal fruit coulis and fresh fruit; there are toasted sandwiches or wraps for lunch, as well as muffins, brownies and smoothies. Be sure to pack your bathing suit to take advantage of Manly Beach.

❸ MAKE IT HAPPEN

Ferries depart daily, depending on weather conditions – expect delays or cancellations in fog. The most efficient way to pay for the ferry or any public transport in Sydney is by purchasing an Opal Card (www.opal.com.au), which can be ordered online or purchased at over 2100 retailers bearing the Opal symbol. Otherwise, Opal single-trip tickets are available from machines at the ferry wharves.

You can start your journey from either direction, but most tourists focus on Manly as their destination for a day trip, departing from Circular Quay and returning at the end of the day. For maximum scenic beauty, try to time your trip to catch the sunset over Sydney Harbour.

Be sure to wear sunscreen (Australia's UV levels are mostly fierce throughout the year, including cloudy days) and a hat. **KN**

 Glimpse Mrs Macquarie's Chair, an exposed sandstone bench hand-carved by convicts in 1810.

 Pass historic Fort Denison, a small island where convicts were confined in colonial times.

 At South Head, spot the candy-cane-striped Hornby Lighthouse (1858), the third oldest in New South Wales.

Cargo Freighter to Pitcairn

PITCAIRN ISLANDS

START **MANGAREVA, FRENCH POLYNESIA**

END **PITCAIRN ISLAND**

DISTANCE **336 MILES (541KM)**

DURATION **2 DAYS**

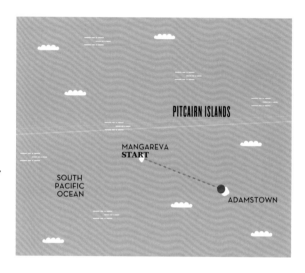

🚢 *Pitcairn, one of the most remote and sparsely inhabited places on earth, would give Robinson Crusoe's island a run for its money. Long considered a figment of a tired captain's imagination, this island in the South Pacific was only spoken about as gossip among 18th-century sailors, until Fletcher Christian and his band of mutineers set sail in search of the mythical destination while trying to escape treason charges from the British Crown. In January 1790 they landed ashore, burned the HMS* Bounty *in the harbour and lived as castaways with their Tahitian brides until the end of their days. Fifty citizens – the direct descendants of the mutineers – make up the island's population today, all living in a scattering of houses collectively known as Adamstown. The trip to this tiny British Overseas Territory aboard a rusty cargo freighter remains one of the most adventurous water journeys on the planet.*

❶ RIDING THE WAVES

If you want to get to Pitcairn, be ready to work for it. When Enric Sala, an explorer-in-residence at National Geographic, led a small oceanographic team to the pristine waters around the island, exploring vast coral gardens and cavorting with

hundreds of sharks, it took him over five days to reach the tropical isle from Washington, DC, with two days aboard a cargo-carrying vessel as the big finish. The final leg begins in Tahiti when travellers hop on a prop plane at the crack of dawn, bound for even more remote recesses of French Polynesia. After a stop to let passengers off on an atoll in the Tuamotu archipelago, you'll reach Mangareva. This is one of the larger islands in the Gambier belt, a collection of volcanic crags secreted away in the most easterly corner of the South Pacific. While no one thinks of Tahiti as bustling or densely populated, its almost 190,000 inhabitants put Mangareva's mere 1200 residents to shame. It's an indicator of what's to come on even more remote and lonely Pitcairn.

From the runway on Mangareva – embanked over a beach of crushed shells – it's an hour's boat ride across the iridescent lagoon to Mangareva's capital (using that term lightly here), Rikitea. The rusting MV *Claymore II,* isolated Pitcairn's lifeline, looms over the village,

PITCAIRN CASTAWAYS

Long presumed dead, the remaining mutineers of the HMS *Bounty* were discovered in 1808, 18 years after their self-exile on tiny Pitcairn, by the *Topaz*, an American whaling vessel helmed by Captain Mayhew Folger. Imagine Folger's surprise when the 'native' they found spoke perfect English! Polynesians lived on the island centuries ago, but were long gone by the time the mutineers arrived.

 Explore the convent ruins in Rikitea village, erected by draconian Catholic missionaries.

 Hike over the ridge of Mangareva to find a quiet, swooshing bay, home to a scattering of quaint pensions.

 Take in the ribbons of low-lying clouds in the middle of the Pacific, without a speck of land in sight.

seemingly as large as the double spires of the nearby stone-hewn Catholic church, which is the biggest in the region. You'll have plenty of time to explore as the crew of the *Claymore* prep for the passage across the vastness of the Pacific.

Before reaching Mangareva, the *Claymore* has already spent two weeks at sea lugging goods from New Zealand. The last two days of its journey, from Mangareva to Pitcairn, give 12 passengers the opportunity to gain access to the faraway island, unreachable by aircraft due to its limited amount of flat ground.

The *Claymore's* passenger cabins, each with three beds, are on a windowless submarine deck below the portholed crew quarters. A lounge with a TV and plenty of DVDs is one floor above sea level, as is the mess: two picnic tables pushed together in a humid room encased in a see-through tarp. It's possible to visit the bridge and hang out with the officers as they chart their course; a breezy back deck is also open for sunset snaps or a casual cigarette with the rest of the crew.

Your eyes start to play tricks on you when the ship putters away from Mangareva and the stony isles disappear along the horizon. The clouds start to look like cities, easily anthropomorphized when there's nothing else to look at besides the endlessness of the sea.

After 40-some hours of travel, landfall on Pitcairn at sunrise feels desperately pleasant, as a wooden longboat steers out to meet the freighter still bobbing in the deep blue. The immigration process is completed on the picnic tables of the mess; then

luggage and passengers are duly hoisted overboard and into the rounded keel of the shuttle.

Hugs are feverishly exchanged between Pitcairners and their returning relatives; even strangers arriving for the first time get subsumed in the joy of the *Claymore's* return. Meanwhile, the freighter lies waiting in the deep, visible from practically every lookout on the island. It's a constant reminder that you'll have to do the whole thing over again in due time to get back to civilisation. Never has the travel cliche 'it's not the destination but the journey' been more true than of the passage to Pitcairn Island.

❷ LIFE ON BOARD

On a vessel with practically as many passengers as crew members, travellers are put on a limited meal schedule with fixed meal times throughout the day. Berths are basic but clean; expect shared toilet and shower facilities, and plenty of hot water.

❸ MAKE IT HAPPEN

The freighter delivers cargo from New Zealand to Pitcairn on four separate journeys throughout the year, stopping in Mangareva, French Polynesia, along the way to pick up passengers for the final two days of the trip. During each haul, the ship zippers back and forth between Pitcairn and Mangareva a couple of extra times, shuttling locals to Tahiti for medical care; there are about 12 total opportunities for travellers to reach Pitcairn each year. The weather is fairly constant for a tropical isle, so it's more a matter of securing one of the limited berths on the freighter than it is about being strategic about seasons. Pack both savoury and sweet snacks for the trip, and bringing saltines is a must for anyone prone to seasickness. **BP**

LEFT, TOP TO BOTTOM: The freighter approaches; hermit crab residents outnumber human ones. **PREVIOUS PAGE:** The Pitcairn cliffs.

 Follow your guide 'down rope' to see ancient petroglyphs along Pitcairn's only sandy beach.

 Cool off in the crystalline waters of the natural tidal pool at St Paul, a volcanic escarpment on Pitcairn.

 Avid birders will be able to add several new species to their life lists on a Pitcairn birding walk.

Cook Strait Ferry

NEW ZEALAND

A ferry journey from New Zealand's compact harbour capital across Cook Strait is a unique way to experience the country's North and South Islands. Absorb the culinary and cultural energy of Wellington before heading south through the spectacular Marlborough Sounds to the sleepy port town of Picton. Join holidaying Kiwi families as the ferry negotiates a careful path past forested islands and concealed coves. Once in Picton, embark on boat trips to remote beaches and lodges, or conquer the Queen Charlotte Track by foot or mountain bike.

❶ RIDING THE WAVES

Proud locals in New Zealand's national capital are quick to claim you can't beat Wellington on a good day, and when the sun is shining and the air is infused with a brisk southern hemisphere freshness, the city harbour is indeed a fine place to be. Colourful wooden houses tumble down the city's hills like a mini San Francisco, while Wellington's compact downtown features streets and laneways concealing a great eating and drinking

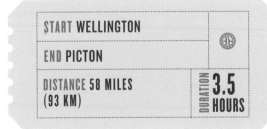

START WELLINGTON	
END PICTON	
DISTANCE 58 MILES (93 KM)	DURATION **3.5 HOURS**

© IMAGE BROKER / ALAMY STOCK PHOTO

scene. Excellent craft beer, coffee and authentic ethnic flavours from New Zealand's increasingly diverse population fuel a hip, younger crew working in the tech and film industries.

The harbour itself is framed by two of Wellington's most iconic buildings. The Museum of New Zealand Te Papa Tongarewa (known informally as Te Papa or 'Our Place') is an architecturally stunning showcase of the country's natural history, culture and society. At the harbour's northern end, close to where ferries depart to link New Zealand's North and South Islands, the circular structure of Westpac Stadium is dubbed 'the Cake Tin' by waggish locals. Time a journey well, and before travellers depart on a ferry they might catch an

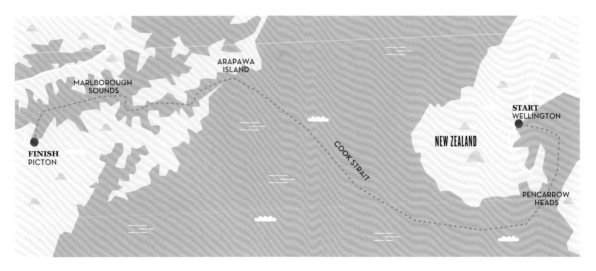

international rugby match featuring the All Blacks, New Zealand's world-champion rugby team.

Leaving Wellington's Aotea Quay, ferries headed to Cook Strait are at first cocooned within Wellington Harbour. On the ferry's port side, tiny Matiu/Somes Island drifts by, reputedly a landing place for the legendary Polynesian navigator Kupe. Formerly a quarantine station, it is now a wildlife reserve in close proximity to the nation's capital city. With cafes and beaches, nearby Days Bay and Eastbourne are popular weekend escapes for Wellingtonians, and the final harbour exit into Cook Strait is marked by the dual lighthouses of Pencarrow Head.

Named after the legendary British naval explorer Captain James Cook – himself prevented by a turning tide from entering Wellington Harbour in 1773 – and spanning the Tasman Sea and the South Pacific Ocean, this stretch of water is just 14 miles (23km) wide at its narrowest point. The strait can sometimes be capricious, but the sturdy ferries are well equipped to handle any rougher waters, and time spent in more open seas is only around 90 minutes. Once the ferry squeezes past Arapawa Island to enter the sheltered Marlborough Sounds, the final and most interesting hour of the journey begins, and the importance of booking a daytime crossing becomes immediately obvious. Especially spectacular is how the eastern and western sides of the entrance to Tory Channel resemble a continuous stretch of land from the boat's deck, and the way through for vessels is revealed only at the last moment. Dwarfed by a labyrinth of soaring, forested coastline and islands, the ferry feels at times as if it were actually traversing an inland river. In fact the Marlborough Sounds are most correctly referred to as rias, or drowned river valleys. From Queen Charlotte Sound, ferries then turn into narrow Grove Arm for the final 10-minute stretch into Picton. It's not uncommon

© MATTEO COLOMBO / GETTY IMAGES

© IMAGE BROKER / ALAMY STOCK PHOTO

 Escape the compact arc of Wellington Harbour past Matiu/Somes Island.

 Enter Cook Strait with views of the two lighthouses of Pencarrow Head.

 See South Island approaching as the boat crosses Cook Strait.

for dolphins and New Zealand fur seals to be seen feeding nearby.

Garlanded by a palm-tree–lined esplanade and pretty English-style foreshore gardens, Picton is a relaxed place to begin or end a journey across Cook Strait. Dotted with a few luxury lodges and other more rustic accommodation, the area is best explored on two legs or two mountain-bike wheels on the popular Queen Charlotte Track. Count on covering the 43-mile (70km) trail in around four days for this iconic New Zealand outdoor adventure. Picton's harbourfront cafes do a roaring trade in good coffee, cold beer and hearty meals, recharging 'trampers' (Kiwi parlance for hikers) starting or finishing the Queen Charlotte Track. A flotilla of smaller boats whisk travellers off to enjoy isolated greenery-clad lodges or embark on more discovery of the Sounds' diverse wildlife.

A popular way to continue independent exploration of the area is to rent a car and negotiate the sinuous and beautiful coastal road to Havelock, home of New Zealand's famous green-lipped mussels, or to travel the scenic route on New Zealand's SH1 south to the Marlborough wine region around Blenheim. Adjacent to the sun-kissed vineyards that produce New Zealand's zingy sauvignon blanc wines, relaxed but sophisticated restaurants like Arbour and Rock Ferry are the perfect place to toast completing one of the world's most spectacular ferry journeys. For fans of New Zealand's equally distinctive hops, the beers crafted by Blenheim's Renaissance or Moa Brewing are equally effective in creating a celebratory vibe.

SWIMMING THE STRAIT

There is a history of long-distance swimmers crossing 22.5-km Cook Strait, a southern hemisphere version of conquering the English Channel. Taking 11 hours and 13 minutes, the first successful swimmer was Barrie Devenport in 1962. The record of four hours and 37 minutes was set by 21-year-old Casey Glover in 2008. In 2017 the youngest swimmer yet made the crossing, age 12.

 Be surprised as you pass Arapawa Island to enter the Tory Channel.

 Cruise through the blue-and-green-forested labyrinth of the Marlborough Sounds.

 Celebrate with a harbourside drink in Picton after the final sail down Grove Arm.

"The final harbour exit into Cook Strait is marked by the dual lighthouses of Pencarrow Head. "

❷ LIFE ON BOARD

There's no shortage of scenic distractions on the journey across Cook Strait, but New Zealand's modern ferries also pack in plenty of diversions. Special areas incorporate scenic windows and atriums to maximise viewing opportunities, and for travelling families there are children's play areas, a cinema and entertainment including clowns and magicians during the school holidays. As the journey is less than four hours, there are no private cabins, but adult travellers can take refuge in bars serving a wide variety of Wellington's excellent craft beers. Anything from Garage Project, ParrotDog or Tuatara is bound to be a good bet. Popular sporting events are screened in the bars on board, and there are also occasional live bands to help pass the time. A cafe and restaurants are open throughout the journey, selling both snacks and light meals. For a frozen treat try a FruJu or a Jelly Tip, both much-loved New Zealand ice blocks (ice lollies or popsicles).

❸ MAKE IT HAPPEN

Ferries operated by Great Journeys of New Zealand (www.greatjourneysofnz.co.nz) and Bluebridge (www. bluebridge.co.nz) run daily, including day and night crossings. There is only one passenger class, but travellers 18 years and older have the option of paid access into private lounges. One-way travel is more common, and it is usually cheaper to leave rental cars in Wellington and pick up a different car in Picton. Booking ahead online is highly recommended, especially for the busy Easter and Christmas/New Year's periods. The ferries also get very busy during New Zealand school holidays. **BA**

Kimberley Coast Cruise

AUSTRALIA

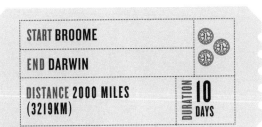

START BROOME	
END DARWIN	
DISTANCE 2000 MILES (3219KM)	DURATION 10 DAYS

Look at a map of Australia's remote Kimberley region and one thing becomes apparent: for all its vast length, not a single road reaches the coast. The only way to see this extraordinary coastline is by ship, and even then it requires effort. Exploration comes in hours and days aboard Zodiacs, skimming along bays and estuaries under the watch of crocodiles and past rust-red cliffs, tumultuous waterfalls, some of Australia's most striking Aboriginal rock-art sites and a reef the size of Barbados that emerges only at low tide. Afterwards, guests return to the welcome luxury of butler service, a ship sommelier and poolside cocktails lit by luminous tropical sunsets.

❶ RIDING THE WAVES

At the end of each wet season, the Kimberley wrings itself dry. Waterfalls pour off the red cliffs that mark the edge of one of Australia's greatest natural frontiers, and boab trees stand fat and full of water. Unlike large cruise ships, the small Silversea expedition vessels that run this itinerary can edge into bays and close to shore, anchoring as tawny nurse sharks and reef sharks swim lazy circles around the ship.

By day the *Silver Discoverer* functions like a mother ship, dispatching Zodiacs to the shores and estuaries

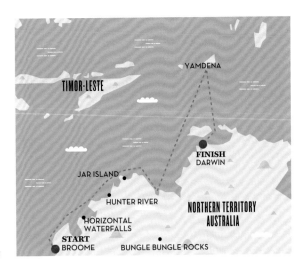

and into the channels that run like veins through the remarkable Montgomery Reef. Described by Sir David Attenborough as 'one of the greatest natural wonders of the world,' this 154-sq-mile (400sq km) reef has an ephemeral existence, surfacing from the Indian Ocean at low tide and disappearing like Atlantis with each incoming tide. Turtles and sharks feed at its edges as nutrients spill off the reef with the disappearing ocean.

The tides dictate more than the reef's presence on this expedition cruise. The Kimberley has one of the highest tidal ranges in the world – up to 39ft (12m) in places – so that activity schedules on Kimberley cruises are set by the tides rather than by clocks.

North of Broome the ship meets up with a sleek 900-horsepower fast boat, which propels passengers through an explosion of spray and white water in the Horizontal Waterfalls. Up to 264,200 gallons of water (about one million litres) pours through two narrow sea canyons every second as the tide inhales and exhales.

On the ocean each dawn arrives like the beginning

of time itself, with placid seas and glowing horizons that are matched by the glowing cliffs of the Kimberley coastline. Passengers gravitate to the decks as crew members circulate with coffee – aboard the *Silver Discoverer* or *Silver Explorer*, the crew to passenger ratio is almost one-to-one.

In such peaceful moments lethargy is a constant temptation, but even the lure of the pool deck and the endless sunshine can't entice quite like the Kimberley's shores, where the only visible evidence of tens of thousands of years of human existence is the Aboriginal rock art. Zodiacs glide onto the beaches, boab trees balloon above the sands, and large estuarine crocodiles swim territorial laps less than 33ft (10m) offshore, their eyes rolling past like sinister yellow balls.

The grandest moment of all on the trip comes as you near Wyndham, at the Kimberley's eastern end. Here the King George River leaps off the Kimberley plateau as a pair of 328-foot-high (100m) waterfalls split by a wedge-like promontory of rock.

At the end of abundant wet seasons, the waterfalls churn like thunderstorms, and the Zodiacs edge towards them through clouds of water spray. A break in the cliffs opens up a faint walking trail to the top of the falls, where one of the world's great natural infinity pools is balanced at the edge of a continent, staring down a gorge lined with rock almost half the age of the Earth itself. No ship's pool deck will ever compare to this.

❷ LIFE ON BOARD

The Silversea expedition vessels carry just 116 passengers. Suites have a personal butler, and the indoor dining room is supplemented by a pool-deck Grill, serving open-air dinners. Each evening expedition crew and guest lecturers assemble in the large lounge to give talks about the Kimberley, from its geology to the local Aboriginal art.

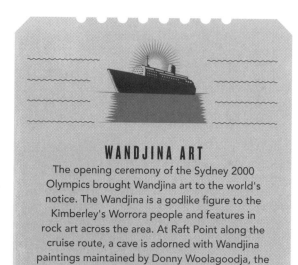

WANDJINA ART
The opening ceremony of the Sydney 2000 Olympics brought Wandjina art to the world's notice. The Wandjina is a godlike figure to the Kimberley's Worrora people and features in rock art across the area. At Raft Point along the cruise route, a cave is adorned with Wandjina paintings maintained by Donny Woolagoodja, the Worrora man who created the Olympic figures.

❸ OTHER ROUTES

Outside of its Kimberley season (July–August), the Silversea expedition vessels ply a variety of routes, including Bali to Phuket, Cairns to Darwin, Colombo to Mahé and Zanzibar to Durban.

❹ MAKE IT HAPPEN

Silversea typically cruises the Kimberley coast through July and August. Sailings are one-way, with departures alternating between Broome and Darwin. Trips may include a detour to Saumlaki on Indonesia's Maluku Islands. Booking details are available through the Silversea website, and companies like Coral Expeditions and Kimberley Cruises offer the route as well. All visitors to Australia, except New Zealanders, need a visa, best arranged at www.homeaffairs.gov.au. **AB**

© RONNYBAS / ALAMY STOCK PHOTO

 Sprint through the tidal Horizontal Waterfalls in a fast boat.

 Watch Montgomery Reef seem to rise from the Indian Ocean at low tide.

 Eyeball crocodiles at their own level in a Zodiac on the Hunter River.

ABOVE: Spa Pool, Hamersley Gorge, in Karijini National Park.
PREVIOUS PAGE: Zodiacs approach the famous Horizontal Waterfalls of Talbot Bay.

 Walk across Jar Island to see the elaborate figures of the Gwion Gwion rock-art sites.

 Climb to the top of the thunderous King George Falls for a swim in a gorgeous natural pool.

 Fly in a light aircraft over the curious, beehive-like Bungle Bungle Range.

Sailing Ningaloo Reef

AUSTRALIA

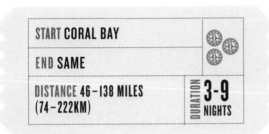

START CORAL BAY	
END SAME	
DISTANCE 46–138 MILES (74–222KM)	DURATION **3-9** NIGHTS

For sure you've heard of Australia's Great Barrier Reef, but the Ningaloo Reef in Western Australia is every bit as astonishing and far less visited. This off-the-radar Unesco World Heritage–listed marine park is the go-to reef for encounters with humpbacks, manta rays, dugongs, turtles, goofy whale sharks: you name it. One of the longest near-shore reefs on earth, it's pristine thanks to the eco initiatives that keep it that way. While you can easily visit on a day's excursion, super-stylish liveaboard catamaran Shore Thing gets you properly out on the reef and under the water to experience all its hidden nooks and crannies.

❶ RIDING THE WAVES

As snorkellers glide along in wide-eyed wonder in the translucent turquoise water, cobalt damselfish descend like a tropical storm cloud, pouty sweetlips poke their heads out of rocky enclaves, iridescent parrotfish gnaw away at blooms of plate coral, and Nemo-like clownfish play peek-a-boo in sea anemone tentacles. A blissed-out turtle beats time with the ocean as it glides effortlessly over a forest of blue-tipped staghorn coral. Shoals of neon-coloured fish flash past like strobe lights. Manta rays – the flying carpets of the deep – begin a strange watery

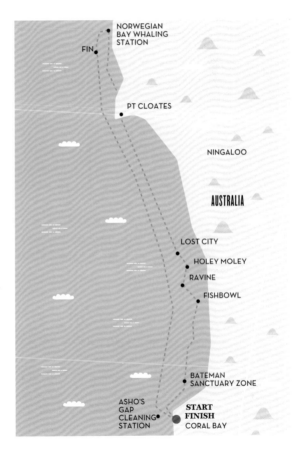

dance, their 23ft (7m) wingspans and graceful moves eliciting wonder. Meanwhile, over at Asho's Gap, grey reef sharks in need of a parasite polish queue at a cleaning station for their fish-nibbling spa treatment.

This is just another day in the sub-aquatic paradise that is the Ningaloo Reef. One of the world's largest and most accessible fringing coral reefs, it spreads some 1931 sq miles (5000sq km) off the mid-west coast of Western Australia. Here more than

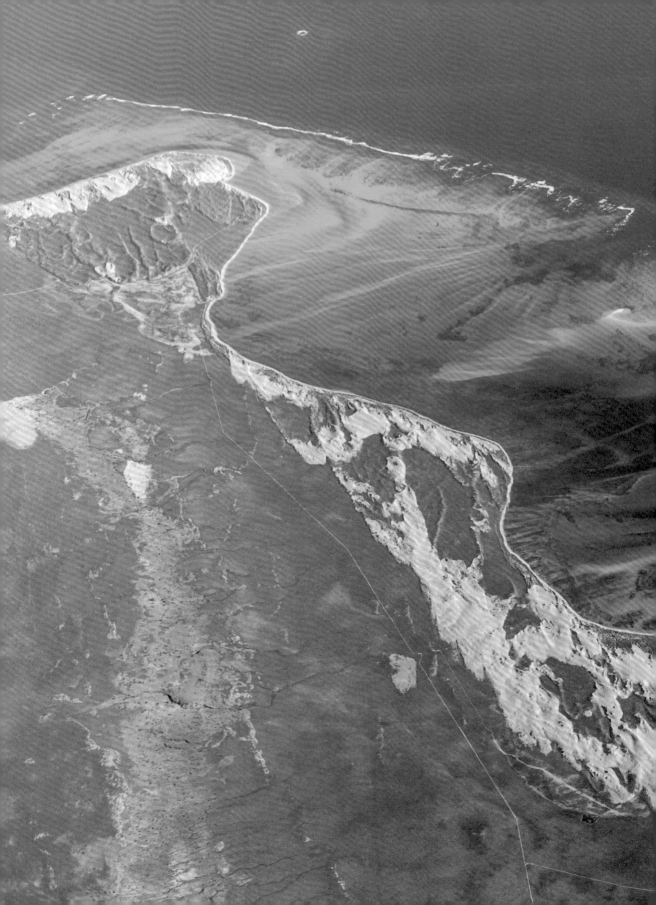

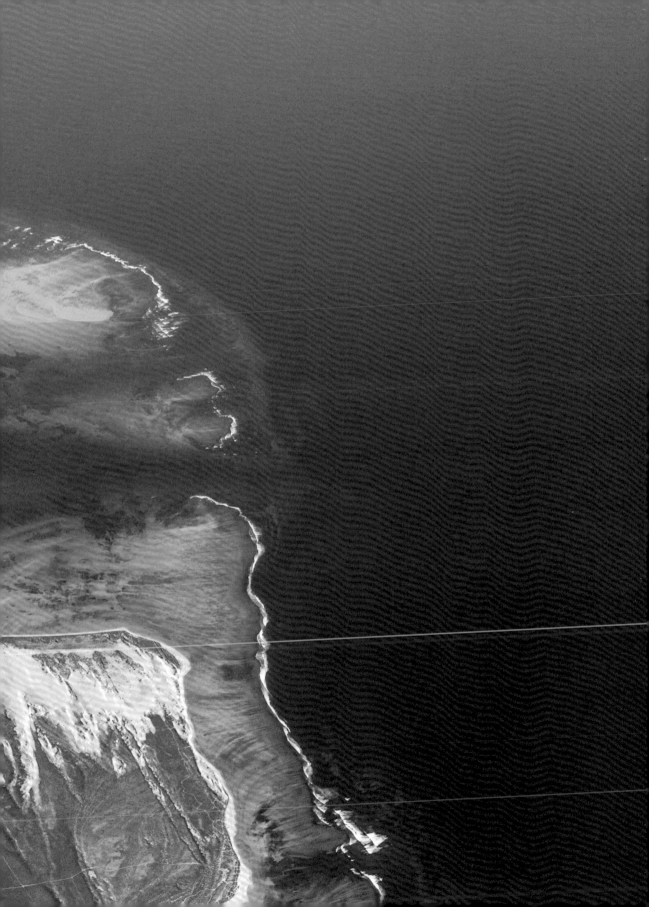

500 species of fish, as well as turtles (hawksbill, loggerhead and green), manta rays, dugongs, whales, whale sharks and dolphins splash around in the calm, shallow, clear-as-glass Indian Ocean.

Unlike the Great Barrier Reef, the real beauty of Ningaloo is that you pretty much have it to yourself, especially on liveaboard catamaran *Shore Thing* from Sail Ningaloo, which sets sail from Coral Bay with a maximum of 10 guests. Besides showing their guests the 'sights', skipper Luke and his friendly crew go about the important business of gathering data on marine life and ensuring that their tours have impeccable eco credentials. On their three-, five- and nine-day marine tours, the days blend mellowly into one and time ceases to have meaning. Life on the reef is more intuitive, ruled by the coming and going of tides, the migration seasons of marine life and the underwater discoveries each new day brings. Wetsuits quickly become second skins for the daily guided snorkels in the shallow reef lagoons and dives in deeper waters.

Back on the boat, the vibe is low-key and intimate. The chipper crew offer plenty of insight into the marine life, and they offer beautifully cooked meals (think tandoori chicken with mango salsa, Moroccan-spiced lamb and home-baked berry cheesecake) and sunset drinks on deck. After dark, it's all about the sensationally starry nights – providing the skies are clear – as zero light pollution boosts your chances of sighting the Southern Cross.

Seasonal highlights for sea-life spotters include migratory humpback whales from July to October; whales use the reef as a giant nursery and can often be seen playing with their calves. Every bit as special is the chance to swim alongside the world's biggest fish – the whale shark – from mid-March to July, when these humongous filter feeders flock here to feast on krill during coral spawning season.

Whale sharks are distributed in a band 35° south and 30° north of the equator, but nowhere are they found in such abundance as at Ningaloo. Powering through the ocean as if on autopilot, these monster-sized fish, with yard-wide (metre-wide) mouths held cartoonishly agape, hoover up the plankton, krill and crustaceans in their path. Here, coming eye-to-eye with one of these 22-ton (20-metric-tonne) giants is as simple as slipping on a snorkel and diving in.

❷ LIFE ON BOARD

The luxe catamaran *Shore Thing* has bright, appealingly designed cabins ranging from deluxe doubles with shared facilities to the air-conditioned king stateroom with en-suite toilet and shower. One triple is also available. Some cabins feature skylights for bedtime stargazing. All are very comfortable.

 Swim alongside twirling manta rays in the Bateman Sanctuary Zone.

 Discover remote snorkel and dive sites around 'Holey Moley' like the Lost City and the Fishbowl.

 Sip a cool drink on the sand dunes of Point Cloates as the sun dips into the Indian Ocean.

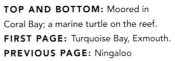

TOP AND BOTTOM: Moored in Coral Bay; a marine turtle on the reef.
FIRST PAGE: Turquoise Bay, Exmouth.
PREVIOUS PAGE: Ningaloo Reef from above.

❸ OTHER ROUTES

The classic Sail Ningaloo tours are the three- to five-night snorkel and dive breaks, but depending on the season you can also book specialist tours including a seven-night humpback whale safari or whale shark tour, or the nine-night Ultimate Ningaloo tour.

❹ MAKE IT HAPPEN

The boat departs twice weekly on scheduled tours from March to December – see www.sailningaloo.com.au for exact dates. Rates include gourmet meals and snacks, unlimited soft drinks, sun cream, and all snorkelling, diving, kayaking and fishing equipment. The nearest regional airport to Coral Bay is Learmonth, with connecting flights to Perth International. Airport transfers can be arranged on request. Advance tour bookings are highly recommended – secure your place at least several months ahead. **KW**

GOING DEEPER

While the snorkelling at the Ningaloo Reef is out of this world, those keen to go deeper might want to try scuba diving. Besides all the equipment, Sail Ningaloo offers dedicated three-night liveaboard dive trips (from $1800) as well as PADI Open Water dive courses ($550) and PADI Advanced Open Water courses ($450). It's a uniquely special place to learn.

© MIGRATION MEDIA - UNDERWATER IMA / GETTY IMAGES

 Tour the remains of an old whaling station at Norwegian Bay and snorkel the wreck of a whaler at the 'Fin'.

 Watch harmless reef sharks getting a good scrub at Asho's Gap cleaning station.

 Bathe on the sands of Paradise Beach back in Coral Bay.

North Island's Hauraki Gulf

NEW ZEALAND

START **AUCKLAND**	
END **AOTEA / GREAT BARRIER**	
DISTANCE **56 MILES (90KM)**	DURATION **4 1/2 HOURS**

Wild and raw Kiwi nature is the centrepiece of this enthralling ferry trip from New Zealand's 'City of Sails' across the fertile waters of Hauraki Gulf Marine Park to the off-grid wilderness paradise of Aotea/Great Barrier Island. Keep your binoculars handy for whales, dolphins, little penguins and a variety of seabirds as you leave downtown Auckland and head out into the gulf, sailing past numerous islands, rocky outcrops, nature reserves and even an active volcano. Hold on to your breakfast as you lurch across the infamous Colville Channel, open to Pacific Ocean swells, before reaching sanctuary in idyllic Tryphena Harbour.

❶ RIDING THE WAVES

At 8am sharp, Sealink's *Island Navigator*, a modest, open-deck car ferry, shudders slowly away from Auckland's Wynyard Wharf into the glassy waters of Waitematā Harbour. Depending on the weather, grab a seat outside or on an inside bench opposite the big sightseeing windows. Soon the green mound of dormant Mt Victoria slides past and the grassy knoll of North Head marks the edge of Auckland's northern suburbs.

The conical Rangitoto, New Zealand's youngest volcano, stands aloof, cloaked in dense pohutukawa

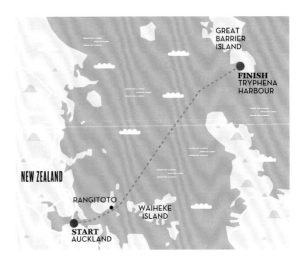

forest, connected to neighbouring Motutapu Island by a boardwalk. Both islands are nature reserves, and their easy trails are a popular day out for many Aucklanders. Seabird rookeries dot their coastlines, seals bask lazily on outcrops and little penguins inhabit the surrounding waters.

On the other side of the channel lies tiny Motukorea Island, home to oystercatchers, dotterels and several photogenic green lumps. Students of vulcanology will delight in the remnant *scoria* (cinder) cone and ancient lava flows. Opposite Motutapu, the anvil-shaped cliffs of Pare Torotika herald Motuihe Island, in previous times a Māori settlement, quarantine station, WWI internment camp and naval base. These days it's home to rare plants and wildlife, with a restoration project replanting native flora and resettling threatened birds and reptiles, including New Zealand's iconic tuatara, the reptile and so-called 'living fossil' that's a large, scaly throwback to the age of dinosaurs.

It might be time to grab a cuppa and sammie and check out your fellow travellers at the on-board cafe. In summer expect a mixture of holidaying families, romantic couples, foreign backpackers and groups of university students. Aotea/Great Barrier locals will be the ones sitting inside with a beer and pie, intently watching an old rugby game on the TV. In winter you'll be outside on your own, with a handful of locals, truck drivers and public servants inside propping up the bar.

"There's a good chance of spotting resident Bryde's whales."

Next up, you'll pass several bays at Waiheke Island off to starboard. If your idea of roughing it is no quince on the cheese plate, then you're on the wrong ferry. Weekend gourmets flock to Waiheke for its wineries, restaurants and luxury boutique accommodations, all within reassuring view of the chrome-and-glass towers of the CBD (Central Business District). It's also a good alternative for nervous sailors less keen to take on the open waters of Hauraki Gulf.

Speaking of which, as you leave the Motuihe Channel, the sheltering islands dwindle, with just bite-sized Rakino (pop 20) and its train of rocky, overfished outcrops, known as The Noises, off to port. You might be tempted to head back inside, but bundle up and stay put because as you enter the full gulf, there's a good chance of spotting resident Bryde's whales and pods of both common and bottlenose dolphins, with orca, minke and humpback whales also regular visitors.

In clear weather you should be able to see the tip of the Coromandel Peninsula. You'll certainly know once you've rounded Cape Colville; the engine note changes as the swell gets rougher in the unprotected Colville Channel. Whether you find it exciting or arduous depends on the strength of your stomach.

ISLAND OF RENOWN

Before Captain Cook christened the island with his ingoa Pākehā (foreign name), Great Barrier was, and still is, known to the Ngāti Rehua hapū (clan) as Aotea whakahirahira – 'The Island of Renown'. Ngāti Rehua have continuously occupied Aotea as their whenua (ancestral land) since the 1600s. Since 1987, the Māori Language Act has helped to reinstate the native names alongside later English monikers.

 Watch Auckland CBD slowly recede as you enter Waitematā Harbour.

 Slide past smoking Rangitoto, New Zealand's youngest volcano, covered in pohutukawa forest.

 Look for little penguins and seals off Motutapu Island.

LEFT: Aerial view of Putaki Bay.
PREVIOUS PAGE: The Auckland harbour skyline at sunrise.

rugby. In good weather you'll want to be outside spotting wildlife and enjoying the scenery. Bring a waterproof jacket for that stiff nor'wester when things get funky crossing Colville Channel.

❸ OTHER ROUTES

Once a week (in summer), the *Island Navigator* sails to Port Fitzroy, location of Aotea/Great Barrier's walking trailhead. Tracking west of Rangitoto, the northerly transit passes south of Tiritiri Matangi, skirts Flat Island near the entrance to Man of War Passage and then reaches Port Fitzroy in the lee of Kaikoura Island.

❹ LUXURY ALTERNATIVE

If you'd prefer less boat time or wish to avoid the swell from Colville Channel, or just want a location with more luxuries (wineries, anyone?), try Waiheke Island, only 80 minutes from downtown Auckland.

❺ MAKE IT HAPPEN

Services run daily in summer and three times weekly in winter. Book tickets from www.sealink.co.nz as early as possible for peak holiday periods, and keep in mind that December–January is the busiest period. Either direction is stunning; you can also sail one-way and fly the other. Hikers should consider sailing into Port Fitzroy and returning from Tryphena.

The trip is fantastic in all seasons, though the crossing is more enjoyable in good weather. Island stores stock basic staples, but bring anything fancy with you. The Tryphena ferry port is actually in Shoal Bay, 3 miles (4.5km) from the settlement. **SW**

For some, the tranquil waters of Tryphena cannot come quickly enough.

While infrastructure is largely non-existent on Aotea/Great Barrier – there is no public power, water or sewerage – the island is blessed with pristine beaches, unrivalled surf, tall kauri forests, hot springs, low-key coastal campgrounds and an abundance of native birdlife. Most visitors aim to climb Hirakimata/Mt Hobson (2057ft/627m), the island's highest point, offering exceptional 360-degree views of Hauraki Gulf and the Pacific Ocean. Although the ferry returns to Auckland the same day, stay a week to really 'unplug'.

❷ LIFE ON BOARD

The twin-hulled ferry's enclosed passenger deck contains a small cafe and bar, no-frills seats, large viewing windows and a TV screen most likely showing

 Identify rare seabirds near Motuihe Island.

Search for dolphins and Bryde's whales in Hauraki Gulf.

 Spot Cape Colville, the tip of the Coromandel Peninsula.

© DENIZUNLUSU / GETTY IMAGES

Coastal New Guinea

PAPUA NEW GUINEA

| START BRISBANE, AUSTRALIA |
| END SAME |
| DISTANCE 3331 MILES (5363KM) | DURATION **10** NIGHTS |

With pristine beaches, traditional tribal villages and untouched ports that have only recently opened to cruise tourism, Papua New Guinea is becoming a must-do for travellers seeking a unique cruise experience. One of the great joys of cruising in Papua New Guinea is that it remains largely undiscovered, offering passengers the chance to rekindle their spirit of adventure by exploring the culture and beauty of an immensely diverse country. If you've always dreamed of cruising the Pacific but crave something more meaningful than palm trees and colourful cocktails, this fascinating place could be just what you're looking for.

❶ RIDING THE WAVES

Cruising in Papua New Guinea is a notable exception from cruise norms for many reasons, not the least of which is that no formal cruise-ship shore excursions are available at many ports. This proves a delight rather than a disappointment. At the tiny island of Kitava, located just off the larger Trobriand Island of Kiriwiña, bare-chested islanders of both sexes greet passengers with flower leis and shy smiles. Rows of elaborately decorated bamboo rafts line the shore, ready to take snorkellers to a sandy atoll that looks

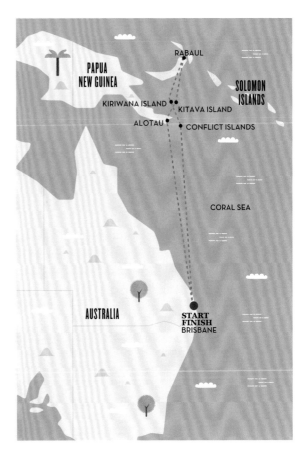

so idyllic it resembles a picture postcard.

Passengers cheer as their crew grin and paddle even harder, determined to beat the rival raft from another village. Each victory is heralded with a conch shell fanfare from the captain of the winning ship. Passengers spend the day snorkelling over pristine coral and admiring the untouched beauty of their surroundings, interrupted only by a midday tender ride back to the ship for lunch, as there is

"Woven mats form a marketplace selling exquisite wood carvings inlaid with mother-of-pearl."

little available to eat onshore.

Rabaul, on the island of New Britain, offers just two excursions, with the most popular involving a climb up a volcano to Tovanumbatir, one of eight active vents in the Rabaul caldera (fortunately this is easier than it sounds). Here a volcanological observatory monitors 14 active and 23 dormant volcanoes through the Global Volcanism Program.

Kiriwina Island, the largest island in the Trobriands, is home to over 10,000 islanders yet remains largely undeveloped. When passengers awake to find the ship anchored close to shore, in a deep natural harbor created by rock walls plunging into the sea, the rugged shoreline, coral reef, beaches and secluded coves seem close enough to touch. Local kids get the day off from school when a cruise ship comes to visit, and they perform traditional ceremonial dances, wearing elaborate handwoven lap-laps (loincloths). It is impossible not to be moved by their joyful enthusiasm at performing to the centuries-old music.

Older children cruise alongside swimmers in dugout canoes, handling their craft with the skill of seasoned sailors as they offer rides to the fringing reef. Back on the shore, woven mats form a marketplace selling exquisite wood carvings inlaid with mother-of-pearl. Kiriwina is famous for its carving, and many passengers return to the ship with beautiful souvenirs that have little in common with the 'Made in China' trinkets commonly found elsewhere in the Pacific.

Alotau, the capital of Milne Bay Province in south-

SKIP THE SHELLS

While you'll probably see beautiful nautilus and conch shells for sale, harvesting these damages local reefs. Don't perpetuate the problem by purchasing marine souvenirs. Support the locals by buying the high-quality wooden carvings for which the islands are famous. The craftsmanship is superb and the environment will thank you.

 Join a WWII military history tour in Alotau.

 Take a rollicking raft ride to a top snorkelling spot on Kitava Island.

 Climb up an active volcano to a volcanological observatory in Rabaul.

© MARTIN HRISTOV / GETTY IMAGES

LEFT: School of striped sweetlips at a coral reef. **PREVIOUS PAGE:** View of Tavurvur volcano from Rabaul, New Britain Island.

cruise-ship fun such as trivia to theatre productions, comedy shows and delicious dining venues (most of which are included in the fare). There is also the P&O Edge Adventure Park, an outdoor activities area on the top deck with over a dozen options, such as walk the plank, ropes courses and rappelling/ abseiling.

❸ ADVENTUROUS ALTERNATIVE

Small ship expeditions to some of Papua New Guinea's more remote island locations are offered several times a year by Coral Expeditions. These journeys focus on the region's WWII history and include myriad opportunities for in-depth cultural immersion at traditional villages.

❹ MAKE IT HAPPEN

Round-trip 10-night cruises to Papua New Guinea are available throughout the year, and operate once or twice per month from Brisbane, and once a year from Sydney. Sydney cruises are one night longer but don't include the port of Rabaul. Bookings can be made via the P&O Cruises Australia website (www.pocruises.com. au). Cheaper fares are available outside the Australian school holidays, when the trip is popular with families. While a balcony is always nice to have in a cabin, the port-intensive itinerary and extensive on-board entertainment options make it far from essential if you want to save a few dollars. Visas are issued for all guests on arrival in Papua New Guinea and are charged to your on-board cruise account. **TT**

eastern Papua New Guinea, is the exception when it comes to organised tours, with numerous shore excursions on offer. This area played a pivotal role in the Battle of Milne Bay, which took place in 1942, and war history tours are deservedly popular. It is not unusual for cruisers to have connections to someone who served here, and passengers often share fascinating family stories during these tours, adding another layer to the experience.

❷ LIFE ON BOARD

While most of the locations on the itinerary are remote, this is a mainstream cruise experience, with a number of P&O Cruises' ships plying the same route. All are virtually identical aside from a slight difference in size. P&O Cruises appeal to all ages and offer plenty of entertainment, from classic

 Play a quirky game of Trobriand cricket with the locals on Kiriwina Island.

 Find your own piece of paradise on the untouched Conflict Islands.

 Explore one of the world's most biodiverse reef systems at the Conflict Islands atoll.

ENDS OF THE EARTH

OF THE

AMAZING BOAT JOURNEYS

Marine Mammals Expedition

ANTARCTICA

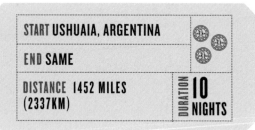

START	USHUAIA, ARGENTINA
END	SAME
DISTANCE	1452 MILES (2337KM)

DURATION **10** NIGHTS

An expedition voyage to Antarctica is a journey to the end of the world as we know it. Here nature has its finest moment, and people are just passing through. This isn't random bucket-list stuff: once you've set foot on the White Continent, you'll never view the planet in quite the same way again. Its power and singular beauty linger long after you've left its frozen expanses behind. Board an icebreaker in Ushuaia bound for up-close encounters with marine mammals. With breaching whales as your morning wake-up call and penguins porpoising past icebergs as big as castles, Antarctica enthralls and stays with you forever.

🛈 RIDING THE WAVES

While getting to Antarctica now might seem a piece of cake compared to those treacherous, ice-thwarted journeys of the early explorers, this is still probably one of the most remote and intrepid journeys you'll ever make. The dread Drake Passage is its literal rite of passage, including on the One Ocean Expedition Marine Mammals cruise. Leaving Ushuaia in Argentina and sailing out of the Beagle Channel, you slam into the wave-tossed open waters of the 600-mile-wide (966km) passage, where the South Atlantic and the Pacific collide. This is the roughest

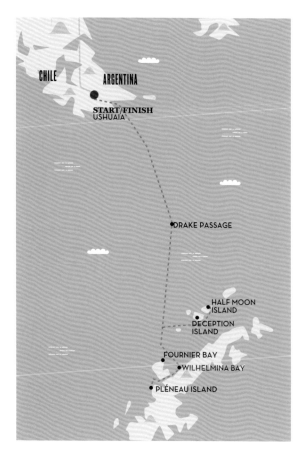

CHILE / ARGENTINA

START/FINISH
USHUAIA

• DRAKE PASSAGE

• HALF MOON ISLAND
• DECEPTION ISLAND

• FOURNIER BAY
• WILHELMINA BAY
• PLÉNEAU ISLAND

stretch of ocean in the world. If you're lucky, you'll get the calm 'Drake Lake', but for most travellers the two-day crossing involves the 'Drake Shake', where the ship tilts giddily from side to side in a relentless, gut-churning swaying that sends everything that isn't nailed down flying and leaves you staggering around your cabin like a raging drunk. When the rocking subsides, heading up on deck reveals endless ocean and stiff winds, with storm petrels and wandering albatrosses gliding overhead in lonely skies.

Just when you think you'll never glimpse land again, Antarctica emerges like a Dorothy arriving in Oz moment. No matter how many documentaries you've seen, nothing can brace you for the heart-quickening sensations you feel when you see it for real. Pulling back the blinds in Fournier Bay on a spring day as clear as cut crystal is like seeing the world for the very first time: pure light bounces off rippling, pearl-white mountains, brash ice chinks in still waters, and colossal icebergs glimmer in shades of ethereal blue. In the distance there is the thunder of a calving glacier or the mighty 'pffft' of a humpback blowing. Getting out on a smaller Zodiac boat for a spin of the bay gets you even closer to the action in the form of frolicking penguins and their biggest enemies, hefty leopard seals, weighing in at up to 660lb (300kg) and chilling on bergy bits.

On steep-sided, ice-capped Cuverville Island, it's possible to step ashore to hang out with the resident colony of 15,000 gentoo penguins, one of four penguin species living in Antarctica. While strict guidelines are in place regarding how close you can get, these honking birds seem to have missed the memo and often come waddling right up to you, as curious and comical as can be. Gentoos may be slick and as fast as bullets in the water, picking up speeds of up to 22mph (35km/h), but they are downright clumsy on land and watching them waddle, slide and sled headfirst down the icy slopes is comedy gold.

One of the unsung joys of being aboard an eco-friendly One Ocean expedition cruise is the chance to get acquainted with the team of on-board researchers and scientists, who give regular lectures shedding light on everything from whale tagging to monitoring behaviour to the idiosyncrasies of penguins. Perhaps the highlight, however, is the chance to visit Palmer

© PETE SEAWARD / LONELY PLANET

ANTARCTICA BY KAYAK

Zodiacs do a good job of getting you within close range of marine mammals, but sea kayaking is arguably better and less intrusive. Many of the voyages offer the chance to sign up for a kayaking programme, with frequent guided tours taking small groups out through the brash ice. Some kayaking experience is advisable.

 Rock and roll on the wave-tossed Drake Passage, your entry ticket to Antarctica.

 Hang out with a colony of 15,000 honking gentoo penguins on Cuverville Island.

 Gawp at the frozen wonders of the 'Iceberg Graveyard' at Pléneau Island.

ABOVE AND BELOW: A kelp gull peers out on Half Moon Island; **PREVIOUS PAGE:** A humpback whale dives into the Antarctic's rich waters. **NEXT PAGE:** Zodiacs ahoy.

Station on Anvers Island, the smallest of three US Antarctic research stations, to see some science in action. Here scientists study the marine ecosystem, from sea-ice habitats to nesting sites.

Many people come to Antarctica for the marine mammals and return for the ice. The reason becomes apparent when you sail through the narrow Lemaire Channel, nicknamed 'Kodak Gap'. It's a place of unfathomable beauty, with huge, dark, fang-like mountains jutting above glassy waters, where penguins glide by and seals bask on icebergs, seemingly oblivious to the boat's presence. Nearby, passengers board Zodiacs to view the 'Iceberg

Graveyard' around Pléneau Island, where icebergs have run aground and are slowly melting. Some are little bergy bits and growlers, while others are enormous. Backlit in the fading light of a pastel sunset, they resemble the ruins of an epic fantasy fortress.

If ever an experience is deserving of the once-in-a-lifetime tag, setting foot on the Antarctic continent proper in Neko Harbour is it. When its glaciers calve with an echoing boom, they bring waves that send the resident gentoo penguins toppling along the beach like bowling pins. On a still, crisp morning Andvord Bay is in sharp relief. Ascending the rise to a lookout opens up the view of the horseshoe-shaped bay – it's breathtaking in every sense of the word.

Just when you think Antarctica can't get any more spectacular, it surprises you, for instance at Wilhelmina Bay, nicknamed 'Whalhelmina' for reasons that swiftly become apparent. On blue-skied days the waters here are looking-glass clear, beautifully reflecting the glacier-encrusted mountains rearing above them. Humpback whales, crabeater seals, fur seals and minke whales flock to the bay to feast on krill at different times of year and in incredibly high numbers. At any given moment you might find humpbacks blowing, breaching, lobtailing and bubble-net feeding within a hair's breadth of the Zodiacs.

Responsible tourism is the watchword in Antarctica today, with conservation-minded expedition voyages following strict environmental guidelines. It wasn't always that way, however. At Whalers Bay on Deception Island in the South Shetlands, commercial whaling decimated the whale population from 1906 to 1930. Getting there involves sailing through a narrow channel called Neptune's Bellows and into the caldera of an active volcano. On the desolate, ashen beach, nothing remains of the whalers but the rusting remains of oil tanks and ramshackle huts. Wildlife has returned to the island, with fur seals

 Set foot on the Antarctic continent proper in glacier-rimmed Neko Harbour.

 Sail into the caldera of an active volcano at Whalers Bay on Deception Island.

 Take a Zodiac to Half Moon Island and be amazed by the colony of cavorting chinstrap penguins.

and penguins loafing around the eerie remains.

The final Zodiac trip of the expedition heads across to Half Moon Island, where a large colony of chinstrap penguins show off their rock-climbing skills. As the setting sun paints the sky in pastels and silhouettes the ice formations, passengers board the boat for the return journey to civilisation. It's as tough as goodbyes get, and you'll savour every last moment.

❷ LIFE ON BOARD

One Ocean's ice-strengthened, small-ship expedition boats are very comfortable, with observation decks, libraries, lecture theatres and 'mud rooms' for kitting up for off-ship excursions. The open-bridge policy means you can spot seabirds and whales with the navigating crew. Substantial meals are included. Cabins range from simple triple shares with bunks to private twins and more spacious, luxurious suites.

❸ OTHER ROUTES

One Ocean offers longer itineraries too, from the 12-night, adventure-driven Antarctica Off the Beaten Track trip, including hiking, snowshoeing, overnight sea kayaking and ski touring, to the 17- or 18-night Falkland Islands, South Georgia, Antarctica trip and the 21-night Epic Antarctica expedition.

❹ MAKE IT HAPPEN

Expedition voyages to Antarctica run from late October to early April. There are two departures for the Marine Mammals voyage in March, peak season for wildlife. Bookings can be made online at www. oneoceanexpeditions.com, and it's highly advisable to book at least several months in advance. The cheapest way to travel is in a triple cabin. Many people travel solo, and to avoid paying a single supplement you can ask to be matched with a fellow guest of the same gender. All routes include offshore excursions in Zodiac boats. An expedition gear package is included in rates, including waterproof, windproof clothing and rubber boots suited for the frigid polar climate. **KW**

The World Cruise

GLOBAL

START SAN FRANCISCO, USA	
END LONDON, UK	
DISTANCE 2019 INCLUDES 5 CONTINENTS, 31 COUNTRIES, 52 PORTS	DURATION 130-140 DAYS

The first word to describe a four-month-long world cruise is luxury. You spend days seeing, doing, and learning, then return to wine over dinner and a bed with high thread count sheets. The second word is friendship. Unlike on a short cruise where you only socialise with your own party, the length of the journey makes the ship into a floating village filled with like-minded people from all over the world. Lifelong friendships are formed. World cruises are especially good for solo travellers, offering both safety and companionship.

❶ RIDING THE WAVES

Few are able to take a round the world cruise, but for those who do, the experience is unforgettable. The world cruise starts with a cost-included business class flight to the cruise embarkation point. Your luggage has been sent ahead, so you travel with just a carry-on. The first night is a gala welcome dinner where there is a lot of squealing and hugging as friends see each other again. Because the itinerary is different for each world cruise, many people go every year and think of themselves as 'Worlders'. After a night at a five-star hotel, passengers are driven to the ship, where they are greeted by butlers holding trays with flutes of champagne. As might be expected from such an over-the-top, months-long adventure (with a daunting price), there are no holds barred here.

The cabins are ready, with suitcases waiting inside. The suites are all lavishly furnished; most have balconies, and they range in size from 287 sq ft

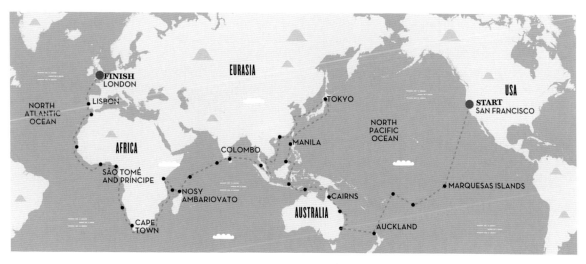

SOCIALISING ON THE SEAS

One of the best things about the Silversea world cruise is that the same staff and crew return year after year. Seeing Gilbert, Fernando, Erich, Jon and Tracy, and all the others each year, is a big part of the deep friendships formed on the trip. You aren't travelling with strangers; you are at home. Just as much as the destinations spread across the globe, it's the appeal of the relationships waiting to be built that makes this cruise special.

(27sqm) to the huge Owner's Suites. All the suites have the same amenities: free laundry and expert ironing, TV with the latest movies, 24-hour internet. All of them have marble bathrooms and walk-in closets too. With four months on the ship, the details of your accommodation loom large. The butlers will fill your fridge, as all food and drink, including alcoholic beverages, are included in the price – no signing tabs, ever. Want a cold martini at 6pm? How about a plate of exotic cheeses to go with that? Your butler will serve them.

Sea days make up a major part of the journey, and everyone loves them. There are many things to do on board: lectures, bridge games, art, photography, dance lessons, gym classes, cooking demos, pool volleyball. There's even an aqua aerobics class that gets crew and passengers dancing. Best of all, there's getting to know your fellow cruisers.

Fresh, delicious food seems to be everywhere.

Four restaurants range from white-cloth elegant to poolside casual, and there are no seating assignments. Afternoon tea is a lavish service with tiny sandwiches and cakes. Sit down anywhere and you'll be asked if you want something to eat or drink, while room service is 24/7.

Because the *Silver Whisper* is a small ship (382 guests; 302 crew members) it can dock places large ships can't. The welcome at these ports often includes local shows, and the locations are a photographer's delight. A small ship means no waiting in line for anything, either. At each port – about 50 of them – there are excursions ranging from easy and short to all-day jaunts with a lovely local lunch. Activities for all interests, energetic or sedentary, are plentiful: crafts, history, music, animals, boating, beaches, wine tastings. Excursions are purchased but Worlders are allotted US$4000 per cabin to spend. Fully guided land tours can be purchased as well. Leave the ship to fly to Bhutan, Beijing, Myanmar; go see the Great Wall or the Taj Mahal. Stay in a tent on safari and wake to hippos snuffling outside. Wherever you go, on your return to the ship you are greeted with a cool towel and champagne. It's an opulent style of travel.

Segments of the cruise can be booked on their own, but full Worlders get special events. Lavish local shows, private exhibits, and places opened just for the Worlders are presented often.

Leaving the ship is often tearful; no one wants to go. There are lots of hugs and exchanges of home information, with promises to meet on another cruise to come. Cruising this way is an addictive habit.

❷ LIFE ON BOARD

The atmosphere on board is friendly and hospitable as the staff soon learn your name and your preferences. The public rooms offer something for everyone. Some

 Go up to deck 10 to watch the sunrise, especially over Sydney Harbour.

 Don't miss the ancient Muscat souk in Oman.

 Visit the Bedouin camps and ride a camel through the desert.

are filled with chatter and socialising, some are quiet respites. It's your choice as to what you want to do.

You need three types of clothes for a world cruise. First, take cotton or linen for excursions. Roll-up-sleeve shirts work well to block out the sun, and hats are a must. Second, pack nice clothes to wear around the ship. Shorts and tops are okay, but leave the car-washing clothes at home. Third, don't forget dressy outfits for the evenings. Lots of sparkles are fine. On formal nights, men wear tuxedos and women go all out, or you can stay in and order room service from the dinner menu. Most people carry a light backpack or a tote bag with them on excursions. You need some rain gear and a jacket for chilly days.

❸ LUXURY ALTERNATIVE

Many land tours are offered by the ship, but it's possible to organise your own. Abercrombie & Kent arranges many of the tours for Silversea, and the company can book independent trips. Your travel agent can coordinate these. For a fee, the ship offers private cars at each port. A driver/guide will take you

ABOVE: Cádiz in Andalucia.
PREVIOUS PAGE, CLOCKWISE FROM LEFT: Taipei's Chiang Kai Shek memorial; Osaka's busy Dotonbori district; safari in Africa; Bora Bora.

wherever you want to go. Many places even offer scenic helicopter rides. The excursion staff on board is extraordinarily good, and can find whatever you need.

❹ MAKE IT HAPPEN

You can book directly through Silversea – preferably months in advance – but a specialised cruise travel agent can give you excellent deals or perks like shipboard credits and days with a car and driver. If the agent is affiliated with organizations like Virtuoso or Signature, there are exclusive, private tours. Ask an agent what they offer. Once you book, Silversea's website will tell you what visas you need. The forms for China, Russia and India are lengthy, and the visas can take months to get. These hurdles passed, the rest of the planning is out of your hands. **JD**

 Walk up Nathan Road in Hong Kong and wander the busy, fascinating streets near the Ladies' Market.

 Take a land tour to Punjab in India; the food is among the best in the world.

 Buy soft, warm wool and possum sweaters in New Zealand.

Index

BA A travel and food writer based in Auckland, New Zealand, **Brett Atkinson**'s favourite waterborne memories include island-hopping along Croatia's Adriatic Coast and crossing from Europe to Asia in Istanbul.

AB Andrew Bain is an Australian writer who specialises in the outdoors and adventures. He's the author of *A Year of Adventures* and *Headwinds*, the story of his 20,000km bike ride in Australia.

RB Ray Bartlett has written numerous guidebooks for Lonely Planet. He is the author of novels *Sunsets of Tulum* (a Midwest Book Review selection), and *The Vasemaker's Daughter*.

LB Loren Bell writes features, articles, and essays as well as the occasional travel guide. His work has appeared in Mongabay.com, *The Guardian*, and Lonely Planet among others.

GB Greg Benchwick has been exploring by water since he was a little boy. Since then, Greg's written dozens of Lonely Planet books and interviewed heads-of-state and Grammy-award winners.

OB Oliver Berry is a writer, photographer and filmmaker, specialising in travel, nature and the great outdoors. He has travelled to sixty-nine countries and five continents. See his latest work at www.oliverberry.com.

JB Joe Bindloss has been writing travel books for more than a decade, roaming across India, Nepal, Southeast Asia, Africa, Europe and Australasia. As well as writing guidebooks for Lonely Planet, Time Out and more, Joe writes for numerous newspapers, magazines and websites, including *The Guardian* and *The Independent*.

CB Celeste Brash has contributed to over 75 Lonely Planet titles and splits her home time between French Polynesia and the Pacific Northwest, covering remote and island destinations that get her on hiking trails or underwater.

LC Lucy Corne is a freelance writer, Lonely Planet author and passionate traveller currently calling Cape Town home. She writes on travel, beer and food.

AC A regular contributor for *National Geographic Travel*, *The New York Times*, and *Lonely Planet*, **Alex Crevar** has written about destinations in North America, South America, Asia, Africa, and Europe.

JD Jude Deveraux is the author of forty-three *New York Times* bestsellers, including *For All Time*, *Moonlight in the Morning*, and *A Knight in Shining Armour*. She received a Romantic Times Pioneer Award in 2013, and there are more than sixty-million copies of her books in print. She has been on five world cruises and counting.

JE Janine Eberle is a Paris-based freelance writer specialising in travel, gastronomy and culture. She's written for LP titles including *Food Trails*, *Global Beer Tour* and *Amazing Train Journeys*. Find her at janineeberle.com.

EF Emilie Filou is a journalist specialising in business and development issues, with a particular interest in French-speaking Africa. She is on twitter as @EmilieFilou and is online at www.emiliefilou.com.

MG Michael Grosberg has worked on over 55 Lonely Planet guidebooks. He also worked in development on Rota in the Pacific and investigated political violence in South Africa. He has a Masters in Comparative Literature and taught as an adjunct professor.

AJ Alicia Johnson is Lonely Planet's destination editor for the Caribbean and Central America. Previously, she was the sports editor for the *Wilkes-Barre Times Leader* and covered sports at the *Glens Falls Post-Star*.

AK Anna Kaminski is a freelance travel writer who has contributed to Lonely Planet guidebooks to over 30 destinations, as well as to *The Independent*, *BBC Travel* and other publications and travel websites.

JL Jessica Lee swapped a career as an adventure-tour leader for travel writing; her travels for Lonely Planet have taken her across Africa, the Middle East and Asia. She lives in the Middle East and tweets @jessofarabia.

JL John Lee is a Vancouver-based travel and feature writer who has contributed to dozens of Lonely Planet books as well as more than 150 different global magazine and newspaper publications.

AL Alex Leviton is a long-time Lonely Planet writer (*Italy; Happy; The Caribbean*) who grew up on a peninsula, spent four months at sea, and travels by water whenever she can.

CM Craig McLachlan is a freelance adventurer, tour leader, writer, photographer, interpreter, media co-ordinator, 'tourism consultant' and Marriage & Civil Union Celebrant.

EM Emily Matchar is a writer based in Hong Kong and Pittsboro, North Carolina. She writes about travel, culture, science, social issues and more, and has contributed to dozens of Lonely Planet books.

AMM AnneMarie McCarthy is Lonely Planet's Social News Coordinator and has lived in Dublin for the last two years.

CM Carolyn McCarthy's work has appeared in *BBC Magazine, National Geographic, Outside, Boston Globe*, and other publications. She is a former Fulbright fellow and Banff Mountain Grant recipient.

SM Sophie McGrath is a London-based travel writer who has written for many UK publications and was named 2017 AITO Young Travel Writer of the Year.

KM Kate Morgan is based in Victoria, Australia when not travelling the world. She has been a Lonely Planet writer and editor for over 10 years, working on more than 30 books.

KN Karyn Noble is a senior editor at Lonely Planet's London office and freelance writer, specialising in gourmet food, health and luxury travel among other topics.

ZO Zora O'Neill is the author of the Lowell Thomas Award-winning *All Strangers Are Kin: Adventures in Arabic and the Arab World* (HMH, 2016). She has written more than a dozen travel guides (for Rough Guides, Lonely Planet and Moon).

MP A Vancouverite who has called London home for the past 14 years, **Matt Phillips** is currently Lonely Planet's Destination Editor for sub-Saharan Africa.

BP Brandon Presser has an apartment in NYC that collects a lot of dust while he's out on assignment for *Bloomberg, Travel + Leisure*, and his American television show, *Tour Group*.

NR Nick Ray is the author of several Lonely Planet guides including Cambodia and Vietnam. He lives in the Mekong region, writing and working as a Location Scout, Location Manager and Film Producer for films and tv.

BS Brendan Sainsbury has been travelling, researching and writing for Lonely Planet since 2005. He has co-authored three books about Alaska, a region he loves.

SS Sarah Stocking is the California and Mexico destination editor at Lonely Planet. Prior to landing her dream job at LP she helped people plan trips to polar regions.

PT Phillip Tang writes about travel from his two loves, Asia and Latin America. He contributes to Lonely Planet's Peru, Mexico, China, Japan, Korea, Vietnam and Canada. Follow him at hellophillip.com and on Instagram as @mrtangtangtang.

TT Dr. Tiana Templeman is a Brisbane-based travel author, award-winning freelance journalist, radio presenter and media industry academic who writes for Australian and international newspapers, magazines and websites.

KW Kerry Walker is an award-winning travel writer and photographer. Based in Wales, she has authored/co-authored more than a dozen Lonely Planet titles. Kerry's wanderlust has taken her to all seven continents.

SW When not at his desk in Lonely Planet's Melbourne office, **Steve Waters** can usually be found in a remote Kimberley gorge or thigh-deep in Tasmanian bog.

LW Luke Waterson is a novelist and travel writer based in Wales. A four-time winner of the Bridport Prize for his short stories, he also wrote the novels *Roebuck* and *Song Castle*.

Amazing Boat Journeys
October 2019
Published by Lonely Planet Global Limited
CRN 554153
www.lonelyplanet.com
10 9 8 7 6 5 4 3 2 1

Printed in China
ISBN 978 17886 8130 8
© Lonely Planet 2019
© photographers as indicated 2019

Managing Director, Publishing Piers Pickard
Associate Publisher Robin Barton
Art Director Katharine Van Itallie
Maps Daniel Di Paolo
Illustrations Jon Dicus
Editor Nora Rawn
Print Production Nigel Longuet

Lonely Planet Offices

Australia
The Malt Store, Level 3,
551 Swanston St, Carlton, Victoria 3053
T: 03 8379 8000

USA
124 Linden St, Oakland,
CA 94607
T: 510 250 6400

Ireland
Digital Depot, Roe Lane (Off Thomas Street)
The Digital Hub,
Dublin 8, D08 TCV4

Europe
240 Blackfriars Rd,
London SE1 8NW
T: 020 3771 5100

STAY IN TOUCH lonelyplanet.com/contact

Front cover photo © Matt Munro / Lonely Planet   Back cover photos, clockwise from top left © Matt Munro / Lonely Planet, Matt Munro / Lonely Planet, Matt Munro / Lonely Planet, f11photo / Shutterstock, Mark Read / Lonely Planet, Andrew Montgomery / Lonely Planet, Matt Munro / Lonely Planet, Drop of Light / Shutterstock

Paper in this book is certified against the Forest Stewardship Council™ standards. FSC™ promotes environmentally responsible, socially beneficial and economically viable management of the world's forests.